Urban Political Economy

Urban Political Economy

Edited by Kenneth Newton

St. Martin's Press, New York

All rights reserved. For information, write:
St. Martin's Press, Inc., 175 Fifth Avenue, New York, New York 10010
Printed in Great Britain
First published in the United States of America in 1981

Library of Congress Cataloging in Publication Data

Library of Congress Card Catalog Number 81-1708
ISBN 0-312-83457-8

CONTENTS

Preface

The study of urban political economy needs no justification, for cities are the heart (and arguably the soul) of our civilisation, and their political and economic conditions are the linchpins of its existence. The question is not whether to study urban political economy, but how to do so. The 10 essays in this volume deal with different nations — Belgium, Denmark, France, Norway, the U.K. and the U.S.A. — and with different problems — expenditure patterns, service provision, economic development, fiscal strain, budgetary cuts, and borrowing systems — but they all agree on two fundamental points about the study of their subject matter.

First, the urban economy cannot be understood outside its political context, just as urban politics cannot be understood without its economic background. The essays by Sharpe, Skovsgaard and Kuhnle make it plain that the urban patterns they analyse are generated by such a complex tangle of political and economic circumstances, that the terms political and economic must be treated as abstractions not as 'real' entities. Similarly Glassberg demonstrates that different political interpretations of fiscal crisis in London and New York produce economic outcomes which are surprisingly different from those normally expected of unitary and federal systems. And Sbragia shows how local borrowing systems in Britain, France, and the U.S.A. are created by a fusion of political and economic forces, and how the system so created then sustains and reinforces broader political patterns in these countries.

In his original and creative approach to the much discussed question of why urban authorities differ in their service expenditure patterns, Hansen takes the matter of political economy further. He concludes that: "Rather than treating political variables as additive, marginal effects in determining public expenditure, this approach suggests that political factors determine *the effects* that socio-economic variables have on expenditures. Thus, socio-economic variables are regarded as decision-making criteria rather than causal factors, and the relationship between political and socio-economic factors in determining expenditures is conceived as one of *interaction*". In other words, in order to understand urban expenditure patterns it is not enough to add political socio-economic variables together; rather socio-economic conditions must be understood in terms of how they are interpreted, evaluated, and acted upon by political actors and decision-makers. In other words, Hansen sees that the impact of social and economic factors is dependent upon the way in which they fuse with political considerations, and he therefore develops an approach to urban political economy which transcends the political and the economic as separate considerations.

The same idea of fusion of factors lies behind the second theme of the essays, namely the extent to which the local and the national are knitted together so closely and so tightly that it is necessary to think of them as forming a single system. The essays do more than simply stress the links between local and national conditions; they demonstrate the extent to which they react upon one another, like chemicals heated in a crucible, to form an amalgam of both. Sbragia uses the term 'local borrowing system' to denote the full complexity of local-national-political-economic constraints on local authority borrowing; Clark and Crowley Ferguson examine the interplay of local and national factors in generating fiscal strain in American cities; and Sharpe, Hansen, Skovsgaard and Kuhnle explore the ways in which national parties and national government interpenetrate in different ways with local parties and local government to generate local variations in urban policy and service expenditures.

It is not just that cities are caught up in a national system and a national set of economic circumstances, a point made often in the past, but that they themselves form a national urban system consisting of an integrated and hierarchically organised set of urban places in which each unit plays a particular economic role. The role and position of any given city in the system appears to have a strong influence over its internal social, political and economic features. Thus, Aiken and Depre conclude on the basis of their Belgian study that the extent to which a city is the centre of production and consumption for a surrounding area, goes a long way toward explaining this pattern of service provision and expenditure. The same conclusion applies to the cities of England and Wales insofar as rank in the urban hierarchy is closely related to service expenditures. These two studies suggest that work on city-systems may have a great deal to offer to future urban research.

The preparation of this volume would not have been completed without the invaluable help of Doris Tindall whose great efficiency and capacity as a secretary kept this enterprise, and its editor, on course. Thanks are also due to Mrs Betty Bowman for typing some of the chapters and for carrying out many of the other tasks necessary to put the manuscript together.

K. Newton

1 DOES POLITICS MATTER? AN INTERIM SUMMARY WITH FINDINGS*

L.J. SHARPE

I Introduction

The aim of this paper is to discuss the 'state of play' in the study of the political determinants of policy outputs primarily at the local-government level and with special reference to Britain. The results of an analysis of the determinants of outputs in English local authorities will also be given.

Economists have taken an interest in the determinants of the level of public expenditure for a very long time, especially in explanations for its inexorable growth in aggregate terms.[1] In the post-war period, although public sector expenditure growth studies continued,[2] the adoption of multiple regression techniques and the advent of the computer made it possible to examine the causes of expenditure levels in a systematic fashion applying a range of independent variables to the dependent dis-aggregated expenditure variables over time for large categories of political jurisdictions including nation states, sub-national units of federal systems and units of local government.[3] It is important to note that only rarely were these studies, which at this early stage were almost wholly under-taken by economists, concerned with examining the possible influence of factors that might be regarded as political: occasionally, political factors were examined but were not usually recognised as such. So, the fact that these studies failed to show that political factors had any bearing on expenditure levels could hardly be said to demonstrate, as some claim,[4] that political factors are relatively unimportant as compared with economic factors. Later output studies by economists did look at political factors. A notable example is that by Wilensky who examined the effects of the ideology of ruling parties in twenty-two countries on social-security expenditure.[5] Also, it must be recognised that other cross-national studies by economists, such as that by Pryor for example, implicitly study the effect of political variables on policy outputs, since they compare countries with very different political systems.

Political scientists, or rather American political scientists, started to take an interest in output studies somewhat later than their economist

* This paper forms part of a research project on local government outputs in Britain made possible by a grant from the Centre for Environmental Studies. The author would like to thank Clive Payne and Terence Karran for assistance with computing.

colleagues[6] and, as might be expected, the omissions of their predecessors regarding political variables was to some extent repaired. As a result, over a relatively short period a sizeable body of literature emerged on the determinants of service expenditures at both the state and at the local level in the United States.[7] Although these studies gave political attributes as much attention as the economists had given economic and social factors, however, broadly speaking the same results obtained: economic and social characteristics such as urbanization, population density and above all per capita income, were more strongly associated with expenditure levels than any other factors.

It is important to note that the political factors that were tested were derived from an earlier phase in the literature of American State Government notably the work of V.O. Key, Duane Lockard, and others.[8] In this literature it was claimed that the key factors affecting the kind of policies pursued were characteristic of the state political system such as the degree of party competition, the level of turnout and malapportionment. It was assumed that where there was party competition, where turnout was high, and where seats were evenly divided among the electorate, there would be higher levels of state expenditure. We will return to this model of the representative process later; at this stage we may note that one of its implications is that what governments do is a direct reflection of the popular will. What is crucial to the effective working of the system is the transmission process. If it is defective because citizens fail to exercise their right to vote, or are prevented from doing so, then their interests will not be met by government. Especially vulnerable in this model are the poor who will be ignored by the parties in power if they fail to, or are prevented from, exercising their vote or participating generally, since there will be no incentive to cater for their interests in order to keep or attract their votes.

No one would wish to deny that it is highly likely that if the bulk of the poor opt out (or are kept out) of a system, the level of redistributive policies is likely to be less than in a system where they constitute the same proportion of the electorate but *do* participate. This participation model is too crude however; representative government is not merely a transmission process from voter to government. Governments do and must have autonomy in representative systems[9] and there is little room in the transmission model for any conception of parties which may, when in power, act autonomously of the socio-economic structure of the jurisdiction they govern. That is to say, majority parties instigate expenditure patterns according to party ideology, and only modify their policies in order to attract enough votes to win. For such a party the level of participation of any group, including the poor, is unlikely to have any necessary bearing on government outputs. In other words, one political variable that may be considered as being crucial in other Western countries — party colour — was largely missing from the research. Curiously enough, as Godwin and Shepard have pointed out, despite the strong assumption in this research that outputs are the direct result of a transmission process from electorate to government (this is what they call a linkage model), these same studies in their pursuit of the effects of independent political variables assume a *non*-linkage model.[10]

Slowly but surely the various techniques used in the American output studies have been applied to European conditions, and party colour was, as might be expected, a central feature of many of these analyses. In Britain there have been at least half a dozen of such studies of local-government outputs[11] and in terms of how far they reveal a party effect, results have been mixed but with a clear bias towards party colour appearing to have an effect. This result neatly reflected the extent to which the more traditional literature has been divided between those who have claimed, usually writing in very general terms, that party has little or no effect on policy[12] and those who, as a result of particular case studies, have found that it has.[13]

If, however, the British research tended to suggest a party effect, many of the other non-American output studies had found little or no relationship between the party variable, or indeed any other political variables, and expenditure patterns. Robert Fried has summarized the findings of almost four dozen of such studies covering twelve countries in the following way:

> Political variables have relatively less direct and independent impact than socio-economic variables. In many, probably most cases, some socio-economic variable has been found more useful in explaining the variance in outputs than any political variable. Somehow, the nature of the socio-economic environment seems more important than the nature of community politics in shaping community policies.[14]

If politics is as unimportant as Fried's summary suggests, an enormous question mark is of course placed against not just a great deal of political science, but also some of the most cherished assumptions of representative democratic theory. Nevertheless, before European democrats or political scientists surrender to the 'near panic' that Dye claims seized some American political scientists,[15] it may be a useful exercise to explore some of the reasons why these research findings, important as they undoubtedly are in empirical terms for improving our understanding of how political systems work, ought not to be treated as definitive.

The findings of output studies despite their number are, in short, the beginning rather than the end of the potential capacity of the technique to tell us what are the determinants of policy.[16] We must be particularly careful not to jump to the dramatic conclusions, or overstate the case. Fried seems to have succumbed to precisely such a temptation: 'the weakness of party differences even in apparently more polarised urban systems seems to suggest that all urban systems are, in effect, non-partisan systems'.[17]

No, the watchword must be first, caution and secondly a frank recognition of the more obvious weaknesses of the existing research in telling us anything definitive; a discussion of some of these weaknesses will be the main burden of the next section of this paper.

II

The first weakness to note, which is shared by all output studies, even the very best of them, is that they have had perforce to employ some rudimentary data. The dependent variables suffer, as do those of most later studies including the one from which this essay is derived, from the general deficiency that they are usually financial statistics, substituting for policy, with all the well known problems that this entails.[18] At the present state in the evolution of techniques for comparing outputs this is largely unavoidable. What is, perhaps, less avoidable is that many of the studies Fried was summarizing were comparing total expenditures. In other words, what was being tested was whether one party when in power spent more in aggregate than another. Now it is possible that total expenditure is a slightly better guide to party effect at the local level than at the central level because local, unlike national, expenditure is more closely tied to what it was intended would be spent. This is because local authorities do not indulge in deficit financing as a deliberate act of policy, and therefore only raise what they plan to spend, net of transfers and other estimated receipts. But this difference is only marginal; the crudity of taking total expenditure as a policy substitute remains. Moreover, there is some evidence that the apparent imperviousness of total expenditure to party, like the incrementalist claim covering the imperviousness of budgets to anything but the accepted marginal increase from one year to the next, may be largely a function of the degree of aggregation.[19] The higher the degree of aggregation the lower the likelihood of variation, precisely because of the greater impact that such change has on total expenditure and hence tax levels. Since local government systems throughout the West have, in the post-war period, been required to provide an ever rising range and quality of services, without in most cases having a commensurate expansion of their tax base, sensitivity to the tax effect of increasing expenditure has been sharpened.[20] It follows that for sub-sector expenditures and low-spending whole sectors, such tax effect constraints will be weaker, and so the possibility of parties raising spending levels correspondingly increases.

Sectoral expenditure totals are in one sense accounting abstractions: they may have little *operational* meaning for either politicians or bureaucrats except at budget making and perhaps none at all for those elements of the general public who count, namely the various 'policy communities'.

In order to get to grips with the operational reality of a given service, we need to disaggregate to what may be called the agency level.[21] These are, in British terms, the sub-departments responsible for the sub-functions around which the possible sources of change emanating from decision makers are likely to focus.

It is possible that at this politically relevant sub-functional level it will become apparent that many of the key policy changes have no expenditure effects in any case, and this may be partly because of the constraints on expenditure just noted. Because of such constraints the bulk of political effort may be steered into policy change that has least expenditure impact. But such party-derived policy change will not reveal itself in conventional output studies. We will have more to say on policy change that has little or no expenditure effects in a moment.

One of the most favoured measures of party impact that has been employed in output studies outside the US is the strength of the left-wing parties: Labour, Social Democrat or Communist. The reason why this particular measure has been specially favoured is partly, no doubt, its availability — parties of the Left almost always identify themselves as such — and partly because it is assumed that parties of the Left, much more than those of the Right, seek to diminish inequality in society by pursuing redistributive policies in government. Like political factors generally, however, it has been found wanting as a significant determinant factor of outputs. As Fried again has it,

> It is certainly not clear that the presence of Communist, Social Democratic, or Labourite party majorities in a city make as much difference as might be expected. A direct, independent and strong impact on urban policymaking owing to leftish party control is quite exceptional, though the aggregate (rather than distributional) performance measures that have been used may mask the true extent of interparty differences and of party control impact.[22]

As we have just seen, Fried notes one exception to this general trend and this is British Local Government, and it is to a closer and more detailed examination of the British case and possible reasons why it is deviant that we now turn.

III

In their work on the financial behaviour of English county boroughs, Oliver and Stanyer conclude that 'there is no evidence that political attitudes have any effect on current expenditure or on rate receipts'.[23] As King pointed out, however, they may have underestimated the importance of the relationship they discover between Labour strength and per capita expenditure, even though the relationship is not statistically significant. He argues that, insofar as central-government grants are supposed to equalize the financial resources of local authorities, any positive relationship between Labour strength and per capita expenditure, may represent a real tendency for Labour areas to spend more.[24] This argument is strengthened by the finding that central-government grants do not, in fact, equalize financial resources, the purchasing power of a given tax rate in areas such as Merthyr, Burton-on-Trent, and Rotherham being considerably lower than that in Brighton, Westminster or Kensington, even after central-government grants are taken into account.[25]

Alt's figures for the 1958–68 period show that the usual relationship between rate levels and Labour Party strength was temporarily disturbed by the 1963 revaluation, the situation returning to its normal state of affairs after one or two years.[26] As it happens, Oliver and Stanyer chose the financial year 1964–5 for their work and consequently their figures, though accurate for their time, may not be typical. In this respect, Boaden's study of 1965–6 and Davies's study of 1965–7 may prove a more reliable guide. Also, as both Alt and Oliver and Stanyer argue, total revenue expenditure figures may conceal party variations in expenditure on particular services. There are certainly good grounds for this claim since Alt himself, together with Boaden and Davies, do find highly significant differences in the service spending patterns of Labour and Conservative councils. Even if the disaggregation argument has no validity, Oliver and Stanyer's findings have to be set against those of Alt, Boaden, Davies, Danziger and Ashford, which do find marked differences associated with party control.

The other British study which finds no evidence of significant political effect on expenditure patterns is that of Nicolson and Topham.[27] It must be emphasized, however, that they deal with capital and not revenue expenditure. This is an important distinction because capital expenditure is more dependent on central-government control and therefore may be less susceptible to local-party control. Moreover, in order to overcome the problem of the 'lumpiness' of capital expenditure Nicolson and Topham averaged out their expenditure figures over a ten-year period, which may have rendered them much less sensitive to revealing variations that are related to changes in party control.

Size of Labour majority is the most favoured variable used in British studies for measuring party effect, yet it is doubtful whether this is very helpful since Labour parties with a small plurality may be in just as secure a position for pushing through policies as those with 90 per cent of the seats. The Labour Party, moreover, almost invariably will take full control of the council with the barest majority and in the technical sense sometimes even without a majority.[28] All that can be said with any confidence is that a very small majority may be more constraining than a comfortable one. One possible way of refining the scale problem is to use the logarithm of the Labour majority, or perhaps, more simply, whether the Labour Party is or is not in control. What is almost certainly more important than size of majority is the length of the Labour Party's tenure in office. Most major policy change takes time and only when sufficient time has elapsed can we expect any change of course to reveal itself.

The general hypothesis that is usually being tested in relation to the party effect, as we noted earlier, is that left-wing controlled councils will spend more than anti-left-wing controlled councils, but it must be emphasized that, whatever the broad accuracy of the high spending socialist hypothesis for aggregate expenditure, it is a somewhat crude measure since we may presume that a socialist party's tendency to spend more is unlikely to operate across the board for all services. Indeed, some studies have suggested that such discrimination takes place.[29] It seems likely, for example, that Labour will tend to spend more on those services that are, or are thought to be,[30] overtly redistributive and socially ameliorative, such as primary and secondary education, housing and the welfare, personal health and children's services, rather than highways, police and the environmental health services. Even this assumption however, has been questioned by some on the grounds that whereas socialist parties may in general favour redistribution, where such parties are dominated by working-class members they may take a hostile attitude towards certain classes of adult recipients of the redistributed expenditure and, therefore, curtail it.[31]

The association of left-wing control with high aggregate expenditure may be misleading on other grounds. Where high levels of expenditure are seen as being essential to maintaining the overall prosperity of the town — in a seaside resort or tourist centre for example — anti-socialist parties, as parties broadly speaking representing the interests of local capital holders, may be enthusiastic big spenders.[32] It is also possible that since a more middle-class population is likely to make more demands on local government for some services than a predominantly working-class population, and it is in these areas that bourgeois parties tend to flourish, it follows that this provides another example of high spending reflecting bourgeois rather than socialist dominance. Both Aiken and Martinotti for Italy, and Hansen and Kuhnle for Norway have detected this phenomena operating.[33] There is also the boosterism of some distinctly non-left-wing city councils who spend in order to attract industry and promote growth. Given the greater mobility of some factors of production, this may be a more likely phenomenon in the US however.[34]

Also, as we noted earlier, the application of some ideological differences between the Right and Left may not have very big, or any, expenditure effects for certain services. As Irwin suggested in relation to Dutch Local Government, 'many of the desires of the socialist programme cannot be described in monetary terms. Democratization and influence are not matters requiring more money to be spent but on the reorganization of social and political life'.[35]

Where the Left has come relatively recently to power it will, like all 'new brooms', be searching for policies, the effects of which will be felt reasonably quickly. In competitive politics there is nothing to be gained from changing policy that will bear fruit when you are no longer in power. But, since large items of expenditure are difficult to alter rapidly, the tendency again will be to seek out policies with high visibility, especially to its own supporters, but with small expenditure effects. It follows that such time considerations also have a close bearing on the assumption that the party effect can be isolated by conventional output studies, for if major policy change does take a long time in electoral terms to take effect, parties have to be in power long enough if we are to relate outputs to party majorities. Where local authorities have changed hands, moreover, we may need to know the colour of the preceding regime in order to determine the party effect.[36] For some policy issues, however, the Left may favour expenditure cuts in one service so as to ensure higher expenditure on another, on straight redistributional grounds. The net effect of Left policies in such cases for all the different services may not involve any increase in expenditure overall.

One of the prime examples of such relatively non-financial ideological policy change can occur in planning where a majority of the Left could make substantial changes in the discretionary powers in exercising development control on ideological grounds. Similarly, the expansion of comprehensive schools — a policy objective dear to some European socialist parties — could be achieved in some cases with minimal expenditure increases by re-allocating resources.

Examples of important policy change that has little or no expenditure effects; policy change that has high visibility, low cost and can be implemented fairly quickly; and finally, change which is disguised in aggregate by changing priorities between services are well illustrated in the Annexe to this paper which sets out in very broad terms the expenditure consequences of policy change for the major services introduced by the Labour Party after it had won a majority for the first time ever on an English city council.

It was not possible to put precise monetary values on each of the fifteen new policies introduced by the party in its first two years in office, but despite the fact that the majority of them had positive expenditure effects, the net long-term result in expenditure terms was undoubtedly negative and not positive, as a great deal of past research has assumed. This was because of the considerable saving made by cancelling the urban motorway. There may be grounds for arguing that the British Labour Party is more ideological — that is to say, more left-wing — than its counterparts in other countries, but that is not a subject that can be pursued here.

IV

There remain two further aspects of the impact of political factors on outputs that will be discussed. The first concerns cross-national output studies and the second concerns the impact on outputs of party competition. Our foray into cross-national research will be brief.

Bearing in mind that it is fraught with even more difficulties than intra-state output analyses, cross-national output studies carried out with the express intention of seeing how far political variables (i.e. the party effect) are associated with outputs have also tended to suggest that party is of more importance than had been evident in the earlier studies by economists discussed at the beginning of the paper.[37]

For example Christopher Hewitt examined the relationship between socialist party dominance in twenty-five democracies and a series of welfare and egalitarian measures, and found a clear, positive relationship.[38] Cameron has also found over the period 1960–75 a strong relationship between the growth of the public sector in eighteen Western democracies and left-wing support for the government,[39] and other comparative studies have found a relationship between political variables and redistributive policies,[40] while more specialized comparative studies conclude that parties influence outputs. Headey for example, in his study of housing in Sweden, Britain, and USA claims that 'parties appear to have made a vast difference to housing programmes'.[41] Similarly Castles and McKinlay have shown, in a sample of nineteen democracies, that high levels of transfer payments and educational expenditures tend to be associated with left-wing party dominance, or rather, the absence of a strong and united party of the Right.

The Castles and McKinlay reformulation is interesting because its assumption that measuring party effect by using the Right rather than the Left party dominance is persuasive. For it may be hypothesized that the task of the party of the Right is easier than that of the Left, since it may be argued that maintaining the status quo is easier than changing it. It follows that the existence of a strong and united party of the Right may provide better conditions for measuring the party effect than a party of the Left.[42]

So much for the party effect at the cross-national level. We must now turn to another aspect of the impact of politics on outputs in British Local Government — the impact of the interrelationship between competing parties. The most commonly used measure of this type is the competitiveness of the party system. This is employed by Alt for the British county boroughs, but British studies generally have not paid the same attention to it as has the American literature. The assumption in this literature, as we noted earlier, is derived from V.O. Key and others who postulated that the smaller the majority, and therefore the closer the competition, the more likely the incumbents are to increase spending. Behind this assumption lies a species of Downsian model[43] whereby the competing parties when in power increase welfare policies in order to retain and increase their support because the poor are more numerous than the rich.[44] Although he used a slightly different measure, Alt found no evidence that more intense party competition did lead to higher expenditures, and impressionistic knowledge of British Local Government would suggest that the reverse may be true. That is to say, parties with small majorities tend to pursue budgetary caution because of the impact of increased expenditure on the rates. This type of response also seems to be apparent among parties in Norwegian cities.[45] But even if closer competition did not produce caution, it is not at all clear that incumbent parties are skilful enough to manipulate welfare outputs with the necessary precision.[46]

The difficulties involved in manipulating services so as to achieve the desired redistributive effect in order to attract votes raised of course a very much larger and considerably more fundamental problem, namely that a great deal of what is often regarded as redistributive, and which for this reason figures in many output studies, is not redistributive. For example, it does not follow that an increase in welfare expenditure is redistributive unless both the tax system itself is progressive and the income distribution structure is, in fact, pyramidal.[47] Similarly, it seems likely that education expenditure and especially post-secondary education expenditure[48] is not redistributive despite its almost hallowed place as a measure of egalitarianism in a large swathe of the literature on comparative welfare that extends well beyond output studies.[49] These considerations raise very large questions, the further explanation of which lie outside the ambit of this paper, but they will have to be explored if output studies are to develop their fullest potential.

To return to party competition, different types of party could also affect the extent to which closeness of competition between them affects expenditure. Closeness of competition between two parties may reflect no more than a division of allegiance within an homogeneous electorate. Alternatively, it may reflect a division of the electorate into two socially distinct sub-communities. In the former case, increased expenditure may induce more support for the government party since a change of allegiance signifies no more than a change in tastes. In the latter case by contrast, increased government welfare may evoke no response from minority party supporters since a change in voting choice may signify disloyalty to the voters group.[50] In other words, we are back to the problem noted at the outset, namely that the party competition explanation for output variation assumes both non-ideological parties and highly volatile voters. While the assumption may hold, broadly speaking, for USA and possibly Canada, it is inadequate for European party systems. It is of some interest that research undertaken since Alt's does suggest that in British Local Government, at least, a competitive system with parties alternating in power rather than the smallness of their majorities affects spending levels,[51] and there would seem to be considerable scope for deriving additional variables from the party system itself.

One potentially important one is the distinction between competitive and one-party systems, and competitive and weak or non-party systems. The party system effect may be another reason why the impact of the party of the Left on outputs has been obscured in past research, since party competition may lead to policy convergence, i.e. the reverse of the V.O. Key hypothesis. In other words, in a competitive party system the impact of party cannot be measured solely by the extent of party policy differences at any point in time. We can only get a true measure of the party effect if we know what the majority parties would have done had they not had competitors. We have already noted this possibility in relation to overall expenditure patterns, and it is possible to postulate some of the forms of policy convergence generated by the party system. The tendency to policy convergence in the British party system has been long recognized and at one stage led to the formulation of Hatscheks law on the inevitability of one party's decline and the others' resurgence.[52] But by convergence is meant first, the moderation effect, that is to say the tendency for a newly-elected party to preserve the main features of its predecessor's policy, while changing some of the details.[53] This may have a greater relevance where Conservatives come to power than for Labour, since the latter (for the reasons just discussed) may be more inclined, other things being equal, to introduce new policies. On these grounds, one would expect the spending patterns of Conservative majorities which supplant Labour majorities to be closer to Labour spending patterns than are those of long-established Conservative majorities, and especially those where the Labour Party has never achieved power.

The second form of policy convergence is what may be called the secular leftward movement. This is the tendency for the party of the Left to shift the parameters of acceptable public policy and the proper scope of government leftward along the Left–Right continuum.[54] This tendency is akin to what Duverger has called the 'contagion from the Left' whereby the emergence of parties of the Left forces the Right to form a party in order to retain its influence.[55] This phenomenon has been clearly apparent in British Local Government[56] and it brings us back again to the apparent failure of the party of the Left effect to show itself in output research to the extent that might have been expected. If left-wing parties do influence policy in this way, they will, paradoxically, obscure that party impact as it is conventionally formulated. It may be that the secular leftward movement can arise even where the socialists do not actually achieve power.[57] All these effects are likely to render the expenditure patterns of authorities operating under a full-blown party system different from non-party or one-party systems.

Since the magnitude of correlation coefficients depends on the range of variability of dependent and independent variables, the absence of party-system variables among county boroughs, which tend to be dominated by a two-party system, may explain the relatively weak association between straight party strength and expenditure patterns. The conclusion is that output research in Britain should be historical, and should analyse both county borough and county councils, for it is only among the latter that we find a sizeable group of non-party systems.

The inclusion of county councils, incidentally, also makes possible the introduction of a larger range of other non-political variables that could have a bearing on expenditure, such as population density, territorial size, and the agricultural–industrial employment ratio. In any case, as Stanyer has pointed out, counties are important political entities in their own right, and because they have been ignored in much of the general academic literature on local government, they therefore warrant special attention.[58]

Another set of political variables that could repay further investigation are those derived from the interplay of party at local *and* national level, both in a reinforcing and cross-pressuring sense. A set of hypotheses in relation to the possible impact of party congruence at the central and local level on local expenditure levels is set out in Fig. 1.1.

		CENTRAL GOVERNMENT	
		Labour	Conservative
LOCAL GOVERN-MENT	Labour	Left-wing local expenditure patterns — high redistributive spending	Mixed local expenditures
	Conservative	Mixed local expenditures	Right-wing local expenditure patterns — low distributive spending

Fig. 1.1

Having laid special emphasis on developing new political variables, no claim is being made that they will somehow explain all, or indeed that they can all be operationalized. It must also be stressed that whatever view is taken of some of the earlier research in relation to the mis-specification, or non-specification, of political variables there can be no gainsaying that political variables are often likely to be closely connected with economic and social variables.[59] So, no matter what the explanatory power of new political variables may be, there will remain the statistically insoluble problem of sorting out the independent effects of factors which co-vary. Hansen's conception of socio-economic variables (see Chapter 2) as forming part of the *criteria* from which decision makers select before acting, the selection process being 'determined by the political values of decision makers',[60] offers a potentially very fruitful avenue for resolving some of the co-variation problem. Hansen's formulation also gives priority to the political variables, and in formal terms this must be the right way to view the relationship between the two types of variable. We can all agree that the dependent variables being compared are the product of some kind of political process; they do not usually emerge spontaneously from the socio-economic structure. Therefore, whatever the degree of association between the output and socio-economic variables we cannot say the former were determined by the latter unless we can demonstrate that the given output would have occurred if there was no political mechanism at all, for example by the market. If that cannot be demonstrated then at the very least all unexplained variations can be assumed in a formal sense to be a product of the political process.

V

So far we have been discussing research into the impact of political variables on outputs in a general way. It now remains in this final section of the paper to move from the general to the particular, from the critical to the constructive, and set out some of the interim results on the impact of political variables on services derived from a research project into the determinants of local government outputs in England and Wales over the period 1959-73.

At this stage in the research not all the precepts and suggestions discussed in the earlier part of the paper have been applied and it is hoped that any such omissions will be made good at a later stage in the project. There are, however, three key recommendations that emerged from the general discussion in Parts I-IV of the paper that have been employed in this phase of the research which deserve mention. The first is that four of the political variables are time series, so that they constitute a more acceptable measure of political control than is often employed. Secondly, not only is aggregate expenditure compared, but it is also disaggregated to main service heads thus making it possible to see to what extent parties discriminate between different services. Thirdly, the research is historical in that the service expenditures are analysed at three points over a 13-year period. The possibility of aberrant relationships emerging is thereby minimized. Finally, both the urban and the rural authorities have been examined, thus ensuring a wider range of party systems than would have been possible if only urban authorities were covered.

The analysis presented here is for the financial years: 1960-1, 1968-9, and 1972-3. They cover the two types of main local authorities at the time: the larger cities and towns (county boroughs), and the rest of the country, i.e. mixed suburban, small towns and rural (counties). The analysis covers 14 per capita service expenditures, 2 per pupil/child expenditures and total expenditure. A set of independent political variables that lend themselves relatively easily to regression analysis were devised, as follows:

County Boroughs	County Councils
Turnout	Turnout
Uncontested seats %	Uncontested seats %
Conservative seats %	Conservative seats %
Labour seats %	Labour seats %
Liberal seats %	Liberal seats %
Independent seats %	Independent and Conservative seats %
Other seats %	Other Independents %
Years Conservative control	Other %
Years Independent control	Seats of controlling party %
Years Conservative and Independent control	
Years other control	
No party control	

The county and the county-borough list varies slightly because of the difficulty of obtaining some data for the counties, and because of the different nature of their councils and parties. Two matrices (one each for counties and one for county boroughs) showing the correlations between political variables were then drawn up, and inspected for strongly associated variables. When two or more variables measuring similar or complementary characteristics are correlated at ±.70, then the one with the weaker association with expenditure variables was dropped from the analysis. Variables which had either very weak or insignificant correlations with expenditures were also dropped. In this way, the analysis included variables which were relatively strongly correlated with the independent variables and relatively weakly correlated with each other. These political variables were then correlated with the expenditure variables, and the results are shown in Tables 1.1 and 1.3.

Taking the county boroughs first, Table 1.1 sets out the significant simple correlations between the six most powerful political variables and the seventeen service expenditures. As is usual in such correlations the outcome is decidedly patchy and both turnout and uncontested seats emerge as poor predictors of any of the service expenditures. Despite the possibility discussed earlier that Conservative (i.e. party of the Right) control and duration of Conservative control may be a better party colour variable than control of the Left, the two Labour control variables reveal themselves to be the best predictors. Also, despite the earlier discussion to the contrary, total expenditure is revealed as being unmistakably susceptible to which party is in power.

Contrary to the earliest output research and thus to Fried's conclusions

Table 1.1 *Zero-order correlation coefficients between selected political variables and service expenditures, county boroughs 1960/1, 1968/9 and 1972/3*

Expenditure per capita	Year	Turnout	Uncontested seats	Conservative seats (%)	Labour seats (%)	Years Con. control	Years Lab. control
Education	a			-0.39***	0.51***	-0.50***	0.43***
	b			-0.28**	0.35***	-0.48***	0.49***
	c			-0.34**	0.36***	-0.26*	
Libraries	a						
	b						
	c						
Sewerage	a						
	b		0.23*		0.24*		
	c						
Refuse	a						
	b	-0.41**					
	c						
Parks/Baths	a						
	b						
	c						
Public Health	a						
	b						
	c			0.23*			
Local Health	a				0.34**	-0.28*	0.28*
	b						
	c						
Children	a	-0.22*			0.31**	-0.34**	0.26*
	b				0.22*		
	c						
Welfare	a		0.23*				
	b						
	c						
Housing	a	-0.22*		-0.49***	0.61***	-0.51***	0.59***
	b	-0.24*		-0.45***	0.59***	-0.43***	0.58***
	c			-0.36***	0.38***	-0.32**	0.29**
Planning	a						
	b						
	c						
Highways	a			0.24*	-0.43***		-0.31**
	b	0.37***					
	c			-0.26*	0.23*		
Fire	a						
	b						
	c						
Police	a			0.23*			
	b						
	c						
Children (per child)	a						
	b						
	c						
Education (per child)	a						
	b						
	c						
Total expenditure	a			-0.34**	0.50**	-0.41***	0.38***
	b			-0.31**	0.39***	-0.37***	0.42***
	c			-0.31**	0.34**	-0.23*	0.23*

Notes

1. a = 1960/1
    b = 1968/9
    c. = 1972/3
    N = 83 for all three years
2. Turnout is defined as the % of the electorate voting in contesting areas.
3. The table includes only those figures significant at the 5% level, using a two-tailed test.

* significant at 0.05
** significant at 0.01
*** significant at 0.001

quoted earlier, but in line with other research on British Local Government, party colour reveals itself as being relatively strongly associated with expenditure variation, especially for the redistributive (or what are conventionally assumed to be redistributive) and socially ameliorative services. Interestingly too, party seems to have an impact on highway expenditure with Labour control exerting a clear negative effect. As might be expected, the two services most affected by party colour are education and housing, which are also politically sensitive services over which most of party dog-fighting has occurred over the post-war period. Education is also the largest item on the rate-fund account, while the Housing Revenue Account is also extremely large in gross, if not net, terms.

These findings, however, take no account of the possible impact of the social and economic circumstances of the county boroughs. Consequently a list of relatively powerful social and economic variables was drawn up in much the same way as the political variables. That is to say, a correlation matrix based upon a list of fifty-five social and economic indicators was inspected, and where two or more variables indicating essentially the same or complementary characteristics correlated at ±0.70 or more, then the variable which was least strongly related to expenditures was dropped. Variables which were weakly or insignificantly correlated with expenditures were also removed. The fourteen social and economic variables left in the analysis at the end of this weeding out process were: overcrowding, housing quality, mortality rates, manual workers, proportion of council tenants, retail turnover per capita, population density, rateable values, domestic rateable values, offices and industry as a percentage of rateable value, retired population, inflow of population into the local authority for work, school-age population, and population size. In other words, there is good reason to believe that a range of the most powerful social and economic indicators were entered into the regressions, this being the most conservative and stringent test of the strength of political variables.

Finally, the six political and fourteen social and economic variables were entered into a stepwise regression equation, and the standardized regression coefficients (beta weights) for political variables which are significant at the 0.05 level or more are reported in Table 1.2. It should be noted that since this analysis is concerned only with testing the 'Does politics matter?' hypothesis, Table 1.2 reports only the most significant political variables which emerged from the regression analysis. It is not concerned with the significant social and economic variables, and nor does it report the amount of the expenditure variance explained by the regression equations. The table also includes only those political variables which repeatedly emerged as significant in the regressions. It does not include more isolated cases.

The first feature of Table 1.2 to be noted is rather surprising for turnout emerges as being the strongest of the political variables. So, despite our strictures earlier on the V.O. Key transmission model, there

Table 1.2   Multiple regression of selected political characteristics on service expenditure, county boroughs, 1960/1, 1968/9 and 1972/3

Expenditure per capita	Year	Turnout	Labour seats (%)	Years Con. control	Years Lab. control
Education	a	0.22*	0.36*		
	b				
	c	0.27*		-0.26*	
Libraries	a	0.22*	0.36*		
	b				
	c	0.27*			
Sewerage	a				
	b	-0.24*			
	c				
Refuse	a				
	b	-0.46***			
	c		-0.49*		
Parks/Baths	a		0.33*		
	b				
	c				0.66**
Public Health	a		0.81***		-0.37*
	b				
	c				
Local Health	a				
	b				
	c				
Children	a				
	b				
	e				
Welfare	a	0.24*			
	b				
	c				
Housing	a				0.37**
	b				0.41***
	c			-0.32***	
Planning	a				
	b	0.41***			
	c				
Highways	a			0.30*	
	b	0.35***			-0.32**
	c				
Fire	a				
	b				
	c				
Police	a				
	b				
	c				
Children (per child)	a				
	b				
	c				
Education (per pupil)	a		0.51**	-0.32*	-0.34*
	b		-0.27*		
	c				
Total expenditure	a		0.55**		
	b				
	c				

Notes
1. a = 1960/1
   b = 1968/9
   c = 1972/3
   N = 83 for all three years

* significant at 0.05
** significant at 0.01
*** significant at 0.001

2. Turnout is defined as the % of the electorate voting in contested areas.
3. The table shows the standardized regression coefficients (beta coefficients) which are significant at the 5% level using a two-tailed test.

does appear to be some statistical relationship between public participation and outputs. Again the party of the Left effect emerges clearly and decidedly more strongly than the party of the Right effect. The expenditure most strongly associated with political variables are education (per pupil and per capita, but especially the latter), public health, with libraries, parks and baths, welfare, housing and highways. Again, aggregate expenditure is also apparently related to the party of the Left effect. As in Table 1.1, this list includes some of the redistributive and socially ameliorative services but it does not include them all. There is no correlation with child care and local health for example. The list includes services that are not usually associated with welfare, moreover, such as libraries, parks and baths. As in Table 1.1, highways emerge as having a negative relationship with Labour control. Summarizing the results as set out in Table 1.2, we may say that political variables do appear to have a significant effect on a fairly wide range of services expenditures and especially the big spending, highly politicized, and redistributive services. These political variables seem to be no less powerful than as a whole battery of social and economic variables, even when the effect of these variables is taken into account in the multiple regression analysis.[61]

We now come to the analysis of county expenditure. The first analysis is set out in Table 1.3. Apart from a slightly different range of functions and a similarly adjusted range of political variables, it is derived in the same way as Table 1.1. That is to say, it shows the statistically significant simple correlations between the most powerful political variables and service expenditures in the counties. Table 1.3 reveals that in the counties the political variables have a stronger relationship with service expenditures than in the county boroughs, and in this sense it amply justifies the case for including the counties in the analysis.

The political variable with the strongest association with expenditure is, surprisingly, turnout; which is even stronger than for the county boroughs. Before drawing any dramatic conclusion from this result it must be emphasized that, over the period, many of the seats in the county councils between 40 and 50 per cent are not contested and in some of the more rural counties the percentage of uncontested seats rises to 70 per cent.[62] This means that the turnout level is unlikely to be representative of any county as a whole except in the highly politicized counties where the majority of seats are contested. Another feature of Table 1.3 is that the percentage of Conservative seats is generally more strongly associated with service expenditures than the percentage of Labour seats, and it is generally associated in the direction expected, i.e. negatively.

We now come to the second analysis of the counties, and this is set out in Table 1.4. The table is derived in precisely the same way as Table 1.2. It shows that the percentage of Labour seats has a particularly significant, positive relationship with spending on education and health, fire and libraries, and again on total expenditure. The association, however, with

Table 1.3   Zero-order correlation coefficients between selected political variables and service expenditures, county boroughs, 1960/1, 1968/9 and 1972/3

Expenditure per capita	Year	Turnout	Uncontested seats	Conservative seats (%)	Labour seats (%)	Con. and Ind. seats (%)	Other Ind. seats (%)
Education: milk and meals	a	0.57***	0.33**	-0.31*			0.39**
	b						
	c						
Education other	a	0.74***	0.26*	-0.30*		-0.26*	0.26*
	b						
	c						
Total education	a	0.76***	0.29*	-0.32*		-0.26*	0.29*
	b	0.65***					
	c	0.70***		-0.35***			
Education per pupil	a	0.64***	0.29*	-0.28*	-0.26*		0.39**
	b	0.66***	0.27*	-0.29*			0.36**
	c	0.71***	0.35**	-0.31*		0.36**	0.36**
Local health	a	0.49***				-0.38**	
	b	0.81***	0.41**	-0.45***			
	c		0.42***				0.48***
Public health	a	0.45***	0.36**	-0.32*	-0.39**		0.43**
	b						
	c						
Welfare	a	0.48***	0.35**				
	b	0.55***	0.39**	-0.41***			0.33**
	c						
Children	a	-0.33*			0.26*		
	b		-0.40**	0.41***			-0.44***
	c						
Children (per child)	a	-0.32*					
	b		-0.34**	0.38**			-0.36**
	c						
Highways	a	0.73***	0.55***	-0.45***	-0.49***		0.64***
	b	0.71***	0.53***	-0.49***	-0.34***	0.30*	0.62***
	c	0.81***	0.50***	-0.47***	-0.26**	0.27*	0.58***
Fire	a	0.31*				0.30*	
	b	0.37***					
	c	0.29*					
Police	a						
	b	0.34*					
	c	0.58***	0.38**	-0.44***			0.37**
Libraries	a		-0.44***		0.31*		
	b						
	c	0.43***					
Total expenditure	a	0.82***	0.54***	-0.48***	-0.27*	-0.26*	0.56***
	b		-0.47***	0.60***			-0.45***
	c	0.85***	0.41***	-0.52***			0.47***

Notes

* significant at 0.05
** significant at 0.01
*** significant at 0.001

1. a = 1960/1   N = 61
   b = 1968/9   N = 58
   c = 1972/3   N = 58
2. Turnout is defined as the percentage of the electorate voting in contested areas.
3. The table includes only those figures significant at the 5 per cent level using a two-tailed test.

Table 1.4 Multiple regression of selected political characteristics on service expenditure, Counties England and Wales, 1960/1, 1968/9 and 1972/3

Expenditure per capita	Year	Turnout	Labour seats (%)	Other Independent seats (%)
Education: milk and meals	a	0.55**		
	b			
	c			
Education: other	a	0.20*	0.37***	-0.21*
	b			-0.53***
	c	0.47***	0.19*	
Total education	a		0.46***	
	b			-0.53***
	c	0.47***	0.19*	
Education per pupil	a		0.61***	
	b			-0.50**
	c	0.46**	0.42**	
Local health	a		0.56**	
	b	0.37*		
	c			
Public health	a	0.37*		
	b			
	c			
Welfare	a	0.54**		
	b		0.35*	
	c			
Children	a			
	b			
	c			
Children (per child)	a			
	b			
	c			
Highways	a			
	b			
	c	0.35**		
Fire	a		0.52*	
	b			
	c			
Police	a			
	b		0.49**	
	c		1.03*	
Libraries	a		0.53+*	
	b			-0.58**
	c			-1.55*
Total expenditure	a		0.19*	
	b		0.27**	
	c		0.62*	

Notes
1. a = 1960/1
   b = 1968/9
   c = 1972/3

* significant at 0.05
** significant at 0.01
*** significant at 0.001

2. Turnout is defined as the percentage of the electorate voting in contested areas.
3. The table includes only those figures significant at the 5 per cent level using a two-tailed test.

total expenditure is much less strong than for some of the other expenditure items. As in the earlier tables not all the services that are strongly
associated with Labour control can be defined as socially ameliorative or
redistributive, and it must remain something of a puzzle why Labour
control should be so strongly associated with high expenditure on the
library and fire services. Again turnout appears to have had a strong
association with some services, but, as we have already noted, this is
likely to be misleading because so many seats were on average uncontested
among the counties, so that the turnout variable is not in any way representative of the majority of counties.

To summarize very breifly the findings of the preliminary analyses of
the data for the English and Welsh county boroughs and counties for the
period 1959-73 as set out in Tables 1.1-1.4, some of the suggestions for
improving output studies made in earlier sections of the paper do not, at
this stage in the analysis, appear to be as potentially fruitful as was expected.
Notable among such is the apparent failure of right-wing dominance to be
a better predictor than left-wing dominance of service expenditures.
Equally too, total expenditure does appear to be quite strongly affected
by party colour despite suggestions to the contrary in the earlier discussion.
Finally, turnout at least in the counties, seemed to have a much more
significant bearing on some service expenditures than was anticipated,
but this is likely to be a spurious correlation.

It may be claimed, however, that over-riding these unexpected results
is the confirmation of one of the central claims of the earlier discussion,
namely the undoubtedly strong association that is shown between the
political variables and expenditure as compared with the socio-economic
variables. Secondly, the results also show that the left-wing dominance
variables emerge as having a strong association with some of the redistributive and socially ameliorative services. In short, politics does seem to
matter.

Notes

1. One of the earliest students of the causes of state expenditure growth is Adolph
   Wagner who propounded the co-called 'Wagner's Law'. See Richard M. Bird,
   'Wagner's "Law" of Expanding State Activity', *Public Finance*, XXVII (1971).
   For a discussion of those economists who developed and adapted Wagner's
   thesis see Daniel Tarschy's, 'The Growth of Public Expenditures: Nine Modes
   of Explanation', *Scandinavian Political Studies*, 10 (1975), 9–31.
2. For example, Solomon Fabricant, *The Trend of Government Activity in the
   United States Since 1900* (New York, National Bureau of Economic Research,
   1952) and Alan T. Peacock and Jack Wiseman, *The Growth of Public Expenditure in the United Kingdom* (London: Allen and Unwin, 1967), 2nd edition.
3. In 1968 Pryor listed fourteen 'recent' public expenditure studies using long time
   series for national expenditure levels and fifty-two studies of the determinants
   of service expenditures for state and local government. Not all the latter were
   by economists however. Frederic L. Pryor, *Public Expenditures in Communist*

and Capitalist Nations (London, Allen and Unwin, 1968), Appendix E-4.
4.   Thomas R. Dye, *Policy Analysis* (Alabama, University of Alabama Press, 1976), p. 29. One study by economists which did look at the effect of political variables and recognize them as such is Peacock and Wiseman, op. cit.
5.   Harold L. Wilensky, *The Welfare State and Equality* (Berkeley, University of California Press, 1975), Ch. 2. Also R. Jackman, *Politics and Social Equality: A Comparative Analysis* (New York, Wiley, 1975).
6.   There were earlier studies by political scientists on state politics that linked party competition with their economic characteristics. See for example Austin Ranney and Wilmore Kendall 'The American Party System', *American Political Science Review*, 48 (1954), 477-85.
7.   One of the most notable of these early studies was Richard E. Dawson and James E. Robinson, 'Inter-Party Competition, Economic Variables, and Welfare Policies in American States', *Journal of Politics*, 2 (1963), 265-89. There followed Richard I. Hofferbert, 'The Relation Between Public Policy and Some Structural and Environmental Variables in the American States', *American Political Science Review*, 60 (1966), 73-82; Thomas R. Dye, *Politics, Economics and the Public* (Chicago, Rand McNally, 1966), and 'Governmental Structure, Urban Environment and Educational Policy', *Midwest Journal of Political Science*, 11 (1967), 353-80; Ira Sharkansky, 'Economic and Political Correlates of State Government Expenditure', *Midwest Journal of Political Science*, 11 (1967), 173-92. For an assessment of this work see Herbert Jacob and Michael Lipsky, 'Outputs, Structure and Power: An Assessment of Changes in the Study of State and Local Politics', *Journal of Politics*, 30 (1968), 510-38. Later work which finds political variables to be more important includes Charles F. Cnudde and Donald J. McCrone, 'Party Competition and Welfare Policies in the American States', *American Political Science Review*, 63 (1969), 858-66; Ira Sharkansky and Richard I. Hofferbert, 'Dimensions of State Politics, Economics and Public Policy', *American Political Science Review*, 63 (1969), 857-79; Brian R. Fry and Richard F. Winters, 'The Politics of Redistribution', *American Political Science Review*, 64 (1970), 508-22; Robert L. Lineberry and Edmund P. Fowler, 'Reformism and Public Policies in American Cities', *American Political Science Review*, 61 (1967), 701-16; James W. Clarke 'Environment, Process and Policy: A Reconsideration', *American Political Science Review*, 63 (1969), 1172-82. Also see R. Kenneth Godwin and W. Bruce Shepard, 'Political Processes and Public Expenditures: A Re-examination Based on Theories of Representative Government' *American Political Science Review*, 70 (1976), 1127-36 and Michael S. Lewis-Beck 'The Relative Importance of Socioeconomic and Political Variables for Public Policy', *American Political Science Review*, 71 (1977), 559-67.
8.   V.O. Key, *American State Politics* (New York, Knopf, 1956); Duane Lockard *The Politics of State and Local Government* (New York, Macmillan, 1963).
9.   See L.J. Sharpe 'American Democracy Re-considered: Part 2, *British Journal of Political Science*, 3 (1973), 137-44 for a discussion of the necessity for governmental autonomy in a democratic system.
10. Godwin and Shepard op. cit., p. 1131.
11. The most important results are reported in J. Alt, 'Some Social and Political Correlates of County Borough Expenditures', *British Journal of Political Science*, 1 (1971), 49-62; Douglas Ashford, 'Resources, Spending and Party Politics in British Local Government', *Administration and Society*, 7 (1975); Noel T. Boaden, *Urban Policy-Making* (Cambridge, Cambridge University Press, 1971); Noel T. Boaden and Robert Alford, 'Sources of Diversity in English Local Government Decisions', *Public Administration*, 47 (1969), 203-23; B.P. Davies *et al.*, *Variation in Services for the Aged* (London, Bell, 1971), pp. 133-4; Noel T. Boaden 'Innovation and Change in English Local Government', *Political*

Studies, 29 (1971), 416–29; F. Oliver and J. Stanyer, 'Some Aspects of the Financial Behaviour of County Boroughs', *Public Administration*, 47 (1969), 203–23; James N. Danziger *Making Budgets: Public Resource Allocation* (Beverly Hills, Sage, 1978). K. Newton, 'Community Performance in Britain', *Current Sociology*, 26 (1976), 49–86 summarizes the British research.

12. British writers who have argued the relative unimportance of local politics in policy making include Peggy Crane, *Enterprise in Local Government: A Study of the Way in which Local Authorites Exercise their Permissive Powers* (London, Fabian Society Research Series, No. 156), pp. 32–3; William A. Robson, 'The Central Domination of Local Government', *Political Quarterly*, 4 (1933), 85–104, and *Local Government in Crisis* (London, Allen & Unwin, 1964) especially pp. 51–75; L. P. Green, *Provincial Metropolis* (London, Allen and Unwin, 1959), p. 156; R. M. Jackson, *The Machinery of Local Government* (London, Macmillan, 1965), p. 275; J. G. Bulpitt, *Party Politics in English Local Government* (London, Longmans, 1967), pp. 10–19. For commentaries on this literature see John Dearlove, *The Politics of Policy in Local Government* (Cambridge, Cambridge University Press, 1973), pp. 11–21; Boaden, op. cit. 'Central Departments and Local Authorities: The Relationship Examined', *Political Studies*, 18 (1970), 175–86.

13. See, for example, Kenneth Newton, *Second City Politics* (Oxford, Clarendon, 1976); D. Peschek and J. Brand, *Policies, Politics in Secondary Education* (London, LSE, 1966); R. Batley *et al.*, *Going Comprehensive* (London, Routledge, 1970).

14. Robert C. Fried, 'Comparative Urban Peformance', in F. Greenstein and N. Polsby (eds.). *The Handbook of Political Science* (Reading, Addison-Wesley, 1975), vol. 6, p. 71.

15. Dye (1976), op. cit., p. 30.

16. Studies of parties of even quite recent vintage, still ignore the output literature. See, for example, Richard Rose, *The Problem of Party Government* (Harmondsworth, Penguin, 1974); G. Sartori, *Parties and Party Systems*, (London, Cambridge University Press, 1976) vol. 1; W. E. Paterson and A. H. Thomas (eds.), *Social Democratic Parties in Western Europe* (London, Croom Helm, 1977). M. Kolinsky and W. E. Paterson (eds.), *Social and Political Movements in Western Europe* (London, Croom Helm, 1976); S. Henig, *Political Parties in the European Community* (London, Allen and Unwin, 1979).

17. Fried op. cit., p. 345. Also see Dye, (1976), op. cit., Ch. 2, who also tends to invest existing output research findings with the definitive accolade somewhat prematurely.

18. See Kenneth Newton and L. J. Sharpe, 'Local Outputs Research: Some Reflections and Proposals', *Policy and Politics*, 5 (1977), p. 63.

19. See, for example, Danziger, op. cit., Ch. 5.

20. For a discussion of local finance in a selection of Western states see L. J. Sharpe (ed.), *The Local Fiscal Crisis in Western Europe' Myths and Realities* (London, Sage, 1981) and Kenneth Newton *et al.*, *Balancing the Books: The Financial Problems of Local Government in Western Europe* (London, Sage, 1980).

21. For a fruitful study of budgeting in a large city that adopts the agency disaggregated model see Andrew Cowart, Karl-Erik Brofoss, and Tore Hansen, 'Budgetary Strategies and Success at Multiple Decision Levels in the Norwegian Urban Setting'. *American Political Science Review, 69* (1975), 543-58.

22. Fried, op. cit., p. 74.

23. Oliver and Stanyer, op. cit., p. 183.

24. David N. King, 'Why do Local Authorities Rate Poundages Differ?', *Public Administration*, 51 (1973), 165–73.

25. See Julian Le Grand, 'Fiscal Equity and Central Government Grants to Local Authorities', *The Economic Journal*, 85 (1975), p. 546.

26. Alt, op. cit., pp. 54-5.
27. R. J. Nicholson and N. Topham, 'The Determinants of Investment in Housing by Local Authorities: An Econometric Approach', *Journal of the Royal Statistical Society*, Series A, 134, No. 3 (1971), pp. 273-303, and 'Investment Decisions and the Size of Local Authorities', *Policy and Politics*, 1 (1972), 23-44.
28. G. W. Jones, *Borough Politics* (London, Macmillan, 1969), Ch. 16.
29. See, for example, Alt, op. cit. and Boaden (0000), op. cit. Also see M. Aiken and R. Depre, 'Politics and Policy in Belgian Cities' (Ch. 5 this volume) and Tore Hansen and Francesco Kjellberg, 'Municipal Expenditures in Norway: Autonomy and Constraints in Local Government Activity', *Policy and Politics*, 4 (1976), 25-50.
30. See Wilensky, op. cit., Ch. 1 for an interesting discussion of popular misconceptions about the redistributive effects of public services, especially education .
31. Janet Lewis, 'Variations in Service Provision: Politics at the Lay-Professional Interface', in K. Young (ed.), *Essays in the Study of Urban Politics* (London, Macmillan, 1975), p. 73.
32. As Ken Newton's essay in this volume shows, one important determinant of expenditure patterns is related to the role and functions of towns in the urban hierarchy and the national urban system.
33. Michael Aiken and Guido Martinotti, 'Left Politics, the Urban System and Public Policy', a paper given at the Joint Sessions of the European Consortium for Political Research, Florence, March 1980; and Tore Hansen, 'Transforming Needs into Expenditure Decisions' (Ch. 2 this volume), and Stein Kuhnle, 'Economics, Politics and Policy in Norwegian Urban Communes' (Ch. 4 this volume).
34. Oliver P. Williams and Charles Adrian, Four Cities (Philadelphia, University of Pennsylvania Press, 1963). For a study of the British equivalent of a boosterism city see the study of Croydon by Peter Saunders, *Urban Politics: A Sociological Interpretation* (London, Hutchinson, 1979).
35. Galen A. Irwin, 'Socialism and Municipal Politics in the Netherlands', a paper given to the conference of Parties, Politics and the Quality of Urban Life, Bellagio, June, 1975. A similar point is made by Helga Treiber, 'Once Again, Does Politics Matter?', a paper given at the Joint Sessions, European Consortium for Political Research, Florence, March 1980, p. 4.
36. Lewis, op. cit., p. 63.
37. F. G. Castles and R. D. McKinley, 'Public Welfare Provision in Scandinavia, and the Sheer Futility of the Sociological Approach to Politics', *The British Journal of Political Science*, 9 (1979) 157-71. Also see F. G. Castles, *The Social Democratic Image of Society* (London, Routledge, 1978), Ch. 2; and Douglas Hibbs, 'Political Parties and Macroeconomic Policy', *American Political Science Review*, 71 (1977), 146-87.
38. Christopher Hewitt, 'The Effect of Political Democracy and Social Democracy on Equality in Industrial Societies: A Cross-National Comparison', *American Sociological Review*, 42 (1977), 450-63. Also see F. Parkin, *Class, Inequality and Political Order* (London, MacGibbon & Kee, 1971).
39. D. K. Cameron, 'The Expansion of the Public Economy, A Comparative Analysis', *American Political Science Review*, 72 (1978), 1243-61. For an informative summary of the literature on sub-national and national outputs and its relation to the broader policy-making literature see Richard Simeon, 'Studying Public Policy', *Canadian Journal of Political Science*, 9 (1976), pp. 548-80.
40. Guy Peters, 'Income Inequality in Sweden and the United States: A Longitudinal Analysis', *Acta Sociological*, 16 (1973); Phillips Cutright, 'Inequality: A Cross-National Analysis', *American Sociological Review*, 32 (1967), 562-78.
41. B. Headey, *Housing Policy in the Developed Economy* (London, Croom Helm, 1978).

42. Castles, op. cit.
43. Anthony Downs, *An Economic Theory of Democracy* (New York, Harper, 1957).
44. V.O. Key, *Southern Politics* (New York, Vintage Books, 1949), p. 337.
45. Hansen and Kjellberg, op. cit., p. 21.
46. Godwin and Shepard, op. cit., p. 1129.
47. Brian Barry, *Sociologists, Economists and Democracy* (London, Collier Macmillan, 1970), p. 153.
48. See Wilensky, op. cit.
49. For an example of a comparative study of welfare provision that assumes education expenditure is redistributive, see Arnold Heidenheimer, 'The Politics of Public Education, Health and Welfare in the USA and Western Europe', *British Journal of Political Science*, 3 (1973), pp. 315–40.
50. Lewis, op. cit., p. 76.
51. Ashford (1975), op. cit.
52. See Carl Friedrich, *Constitutional Government and Democracy* (Boston, Ginn & Co., 1950), p. 417.
53. On this point see Douglas Ashford, 'The Effects of Central Finance of the British Local Government System', *British Journal of Political Science*, 4 (1974), p. 313.
54. For an account of the restricted view of the proper scope of government adopted by a local authority whose overwhelming dominant Conservative majority has never been challenged by a socialist opposition, see Dearlove, *The Politics and Policy in Local Government* (London, Cambridge University Press, 1973), pp. 205-225.
55. Maurice Duverger, *Political Parties* (London, Methuen, 1954), p. xxvii.
56. Bryan Keith-Lucas and Peter C. Richards, *A History of Local Government in the Twentieth Century* (London, Allen and Unwin, 1978), p. 115. Also see John Gyford, *Local Politics in Britain* (London, Croom Helm, 1976), Ch. 3.
57. Hansen and Kjellberg, op. cit., p. 25.
58. Stanyer, *County Government in England and Wales* (London, Routledge and Kegan Paul, 1967), pp. 2-3.
59. See Newton and Sharpe, op. cit., for further discussion of this inter-relationship.
60. Hansen, 'Transforming Needs into Expenditure Decisions' (Ch. 2 this volume).
61. There is one unusual result in Table 1.2 which has been carefully checked but which has no obvious explanation. It will be seen that education per pupil has a strong positive relationship with *Labour seats (%)*, but a weaker negative relationship with both years of Conservative and Labour control. This may be because *Labour seats (%)* is quite strongly associated with years of Labour control and collinearity of this sort often produces strange results.
62. See The Registrar General's *Annual Statistical Review of England and Wales* (London, HMSO, 1946–71) Table V.

Annexe

The following table sets out in summary form the extent to which Labour-Party policy can have positive or negative expenditure effects by analysing the major policy changes inaugurated by the Party after it gained a majority for the first time on the council of a small English city (population 110 000 in 1972.

Although the summary illustrates the extent to which in current circumstances recognizably left-wing policies have either nil or negative expenditure effects, it is clear that the conventional assumption that policies of the Left tend to have positive expenditure effects appears at first glance to be confirmed. Out of a total of fifteen major policy changes nine had positive net effects. When the actual amounts are totted up, however, the overall effect is clearly negative since Policy (xii) — the decision not to build a projected urban motorway — saved the city £4.5 m spread over 10 years. Even the big spending projects such as the Park and Ride schemes, the expansion of the house-building programme and the swimming pool did not, in total, approach this figure.

	New policy	*Net expenditure effect*
Education		
(i)	Abolition of corporal punishment in schools	Nil
(ii)	Abolition of scholarships taken up by the city in semi-private grammar schools	Negative
(iii)	Larger expansion of Polytechnic than opponents would have contemplated	Positive
Housing		
(iv)	Expansion of municipilization of private housing	Positive
(v)	Expansion of public house-building programme	Positive
Planning		
(vi)	Abolition of any increase in planning permission for office space	Nil
(vii)	Relocation of non-conforming industrial plants	Positive
Transportation		
(viii)	Subsidized bus fares for old people	Positive
(ix)	Park and Ride schemes	Positive
(x)	Intensified traffic management schemes	Positive
(xi)	Municipally run multi-storey car park	Negative
(xii)	Abolition of urban motorway	Negative
(xiii)	Pedestrianization of central streets	Positive
(xiv)	Increased parking charges	Negative
Recreation and leisure		
(xv)	New swimming pool	Positive

2 TRANSFORMING NEEDS INTO EXPENDITURE DECISIONS

TORE HANSEN

Since 1963, when Dawson and Robinson published their study on the determinants of welfare policies in American States, students of public policy have been preoccupied with the question of the relative importance of socio-economic and political variables as determinants of public expenditures.[1] Dawson and Robinson's conclusion that socio-economic factors are the major — and probably only — determinants of expenditures, have been substantiated by several later studies of other areas of public activities in different institutional and political settings.[2] Although some studies — in particular European ones — have demonstrated significant effects of political factors on expenditure decisions, the general conclusion to be drawn from this research is that socio-economic variables are far more powerful determinants than are political variables.[3]

These findings, which contradict the assertions in traditional political theory on the primacy of politics in explaining public decisions, have inspired a considerable amount of research, most of it aiming at restoring the importance of political factors as policy determinants. In discussing the question of the relative importance of 'politics' and 'economics' as expenditure determinants, Dye points out that

> It is a useful question, despite its oversimplification, if it inspires serious modelbuilding, thoughtful specification of policy-relevant variables and their relationships to each other, careful testing of hypotheses, and then reformation of the original models on the basis of the results achieved.[4]

Although some efforts have been made to refine the models of analysis, most studies so far have been based on the general theoretical approach suggested in the earlier studies, where a simplified version of Easton's general systems model has provided the framework within which the variables have been organized.[5]

Discussions of the findings have focused mainly on the range, reliability and validity of the variables — both dependent and independent — used in these studies.[6] Far less attention has been paid to the way in which the models have been formulated.[7] Only in recent years have there been serious attempts to revise and refine the models of analysis. One such attempt has been the use of path analytical techniques based upon causal models of the relationships between socio-economic, political and expenditure variables.

Lewis-Beck has suggested that

> research efforts to date have failed to assess accurately the relative
> importance of socioeconomic and political variables for public policy,
> in large part because they have relied on statistical techniques inade-
> quate to the task.[8]

Thus, in order to make accurate assessments of the relative importance
of socio-economic and political variables, it is — according to Lewis-Beck
— 'necessary to specify the underlying causal structure and estimate its
parameters'. He suggests the use of 'effects coefficients' which combine
the direct and indirect effects of causal variables. Although his use of this
method gives some insight into the relationships between socio-economic
and political factors, however, the results of his analysis do not reverse
the earlier findings of the primacy of socio-economic over political
variables in determining welfare expenditures. Rather, he concludes that
'socio-economic variables are found to be considerably more important
than political variables'.[9]

Despite its methodological sophistication, causal modelling does not
seem to provide any solution to the basic problem of how socio-economic
factors are converted into expenditure decisions, and what functions
political factors have in this conversion process. In order to discuss this
problem in more detail it may be useful to consider the conventional
formulation of the Eastonian approach to expenditure analysis.

Conventional expenditure models

Despite slight differences as to their precise formulation, the underlying
model applied to most studies of public expenditure decisions may be outlined as in Fig. 2.1. According to this model both socio-economic and
political factors exert a direct impact on expenditure (linkage c and b).
In addition, socio-economic variables influence expenditures indirectly
via the political system (linkage a and b). Although the major elements of
this model — i.e. the three sets of variables — may be regarded as a crude
approximation to Easton's model, the way in which the elements are related
differs at least in one important respect from Easton's formulation. That
is, only relations a and b seem to be in accordance with Easton's general
systems model.[10] The direct relationship between socio-economic variables
and expenditures is not a part of the original model, and it is also difficult
to conceive how such environmental characteristics may produce policy
outputs directly.

The deviation from Easton's model becomes clearer if we consider
the way in which the model has been operationalized mathematically.
Apart from more recent attempts to view the model in terms of a causal

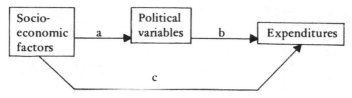

Fig..2.1. Conventional model

structure,[11] the most common way of expressing the model in a mathematical language is shown in equation 1: (1)

$$\text{Exp} = a + b_1\,P + b_2\,S$$

where p = political variables, S = socio-economic variables, a = constant term, and b_1 = regression coefficients.

According to this formulation both political and socio-economic variables are additively related to the expenditure level, and the internal relationships between socio-economic and political variables are ignored or unspecified. In other words, only relations b and c in Fig. 2.1 are included in this formulation, and the equation expresses a model like that outlined in Fig. 2.2.

This model is obviously a mis-specification of Easton's model. In particular it misses Easton's basic idea about the political system as a mechanism for transforming demands into 'authoritative allocations'. Budgetary decisions are made by political bodies, and a social problem has at least to be perceived by the decision makers in order to effect the decisions. Linkage c in Fig. 2.1 implies a deterministic decision-making system, where changes in the socio-economic environment automatically lead to changes in public expenditures. Apart from policy areas where decisions are made according to a set of fixed standards or decision-making criteria based on certain environmental characteristics, there are no such direct causal links between socio-economic factors and policy output. Even within a strictly regulated local-government system, there is always some leeway for the exercise of discretion on the part of the decision-makers.

A common way of interpreting socio-economic factors in expenditure studies is to regard them as aggregate measures of individual needs for public goods and services. Thus, Boaden has divided environmental factors into two distinct groups, namely needs and resources.[12] As Rakoff and Schaefer have pointed out, however, the relationships between individual needs and certain socio-economic characteristics are far more complex than commonly assumed, and any particular environmental problem may give rise to quite different individual needs.[13] Furthermore, to interpret socio-economic factors as expenditure needs implies a 'market view' of

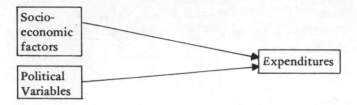

Fig. 2.2. The conventional model operationalized

the public sector, where individual demands are regarded as the basic determinants of public activity. According to this view, public authorities perform a rather passive and reactive role which is quite similar to the role supposedly performed by suppliers of goods in a private, competitive market. As Brown and Jackson have noted, this

> methodological individualism . . . automatically discounts the anthropo-morphic concept of the state as an organic entity which is independent of the citizens that make it up. It also discounts the paternalistic role of the state.[14]

A major justification − at least according to economists − for public activity is that there are no markets for such goods and services, and it is therefore impossible to apply normal market standards in the provision of these goods. In addition, an increasing share of government activity is devoted to the provision of so-called merit goods, goods which people − according to certain values or standards − ought to consume more than they would of their own volition.[15] A substantial proportion of especially redistributive expenditures may be regarded as merit goods, where the government assumes paternalistic attitudes vis-a-vis the public. In such cases the purpose of the public services may be to counteract the satis-faction of individual needs − or wants − rather than passively responding to such needs.[16]

Although this 'needs' approach may reflect a political ideology where choices made by individuals in a competitive market are regarded as superior to collective decisions, such a model does not represent a realistic description of how budgetary decisions are made. In other words, there does not seem to be any theoretical − or practical − justification for including the direct relationship between socio-economic variables (or 'needs') and expenditures in the models of analysis. Socio-economic factors have to be perceived and acted upon by the decision-makers in order to exert an impact upon public expenditures. I have therefore chosen to disregard linkage c in the further discussion.

Turning now to relations a and b in Fig. 2.1, there has been a tendency to interpret these relationships as a causal chain; socio-economic factors cause political factors which in turn cause public expenditures. In commenting on a similar model, Dye argues that

> This particular model assumes that the socio-economic character of a society, that is, any condition defined as external to the boundaries of its political system, determines the nature of its political system. The political system is that group of interrelated structures and processes which functions to authoritatively allocate values within a society.[17]

Although this may be an acceptable observation in a long-term perspective, it cannot possibly apply to annual budgetary decisions. Even if the definition of political factors is broadened from the formal organizational arrangement for decision-making, to encompass political attitudes and policy objectives, it seems unlikely that these will be caused by environmental factors in the short run. Even in the long run, such causal links may be rather complex and conditioned by several intervening factors.

How, then, are we to interpret the relationships between socio-economic variables and political factors? Rather than regarding socio-economic variables as causes of the decisions, it seems more reasonable to treat them as decision-making *criteria* upon which public authorities may act. It is important to notice the difference between a causal factor and a decision-making criterion. While a causal factor is automatically related to the effect variables, the relationship between a decision-making criterion and the decision has to be *established* by the decision-making body. In other words, the decision-makers select the criteria upon which the decision is going to be based, and this selection process will be determined by the political values of the decision-makers.

The relationship between any particular socio-economic problem and policy measures to solve this problem may differ according to political priorities of the decision-makers. To use an example which may be quite familiar: shortage of housing may either lead to increased public or council housing, or to increased building activity in the private-housing market. The solution to this problem will depend on the political priorities of the decision makers. A Labour council will usually give priority to public housing, while a Conservative council is more likely to leave the solution of the problem to the private market. Thus, the way in which this problem — or its particular socio-economic indicator — is related to public expenditures depends on the preferences of the decision makers. Or to use yet another example: expenditures for children's day nurseries may depend on, (1) the number of children in the relevant age groups, (2) the number of mothers entering the labour force, (3) the distribution of family incomes, (4) unattended playground facilities in the housing areas, (5) safety from traffic in the housing areas — and so on. The weights given to these factors in arriving at a decision will depend on political priorities of the decision makers.

In other words, choice of decision-making criteria is a function of political perception, selection and ideology, not a problem of simple causal relationships. Another way of saying this is that socio-economic factors *interact* with political variables in determining the expenditures, or rather that the effect of one particular socio-economic factor on the level of expenditures is conditioned by political factors.[18]

This way of looking at political cleavages differs from the traditional interpretations of inter-party differences, where the focus has been on more general ideological attitudes and policy objectives.[19] Far less attention has been paid to the way in which political ideologies or values serve as a means to 'organize' the socio-economic environment for the decision makers. Thus, party political programmes may be interpreted as 'cognitive maps', within which the decision makers categorize and interpret environmental problems and relate them to certain policy measures. Such differences in 'cognitive maps' are probably of far more practical importance in the determination of public expenditures, than are disagreements over general policy goals. This applies in particular to the local level, where central legislation and scarcity of financial resources restrict the extent to which local authorities may choose their own independent policy objectives.

Political conflicts at the local level tend, therefore, to centre round the choice of decision-making criteria, rather than general political goals. I do not thereby maintain that the parties do not disagree over goals. Rather, this disagreement manifests itself in the selection of premises for the decisions. In other words, selection of a specific set of decision-making criteria implies a choice of a specific policy objective. Furthermore, even in cases where all political parties base their decisions on the same set of decision-making criteria, differences in political values may be reflected in the different weights given to the decision-making criteria.

A reformulation

What consequences does this interpretation of the relationships between socio-economic variables and expenditure decisions have for model formulation? Let us again consider Fig. 2.1 — deleting relation c. Let us now assume that 'political variables' can be interpreted as *decision models* which vary according to political priorities. The model can then be expressed in the following way.[20]

$$P = g(S) \tag{2}$$

$$\text{Exp} = f(P) \tag{3}$$

where g and f denote functional relationships between dependent and independent variables. By substituting for P in equation (3), we get

$$\text{Exp} = f[g(S)] \tag{4}$$

In this model expenditures are expressed as a function of socio-economic variables. The political factors have not disappeared altogether, however; political effects are now expressed through the *shape* of the function, or rather the way in which socio-economic factors are *transformed* into expenditure decisions. Political effects are no longer expressed as variables, but as transformation effects.

Our problem now is how to operationalize this model, or how to express the formulation in an empirical analysis. Here I will demonstrate a simple method, where it is assumed that the major — and only — political dividing line in Norwegian municipalities is between socialists and Conservatives/Liberals. Thus, I assume that municipalities with socialist majorities will apply different decision models in arriving at expenditure patterns than municipalities with Conservative/Liberal majorities. Differences in the decision models applied by these two groups of municipalities will manifest themselves as differences in the weights attributed to each factor — or socio-economic variable — entering the models. Furthermore, I expect the explanatory power of the models to vary according to political majority in the councils. Differing explanatory powers may indicate variations in response to demands — or local problems — between the two groups of municipalities. The method used in testing these propositions is simply to run separate analyses for the two types of municipalities, and then compare the effects of individual variables in the two subsets. If we find significant differences between the coefficients, these differences may be attributed to different political preferences between socialist and non-socialist municipalities.

Before presenting the variables used in this analysis, it may be useful to illustrate the method by using an empirical example from Norwegian municipalities. In this example I have used spending on services for the aged — measured as per capita expenditures in 1976 — as the dependent variable, and percentage of total population aged 70 and over as the independent variable. Three separate regressions have been run; one including all municipalities, one for municipalities with socialist majorities, and one for municipalities with non-socialist majorities. The estimated equations are shown below:

All municipalities: $\quad$ Exp $= 17.2 + 2.68A \quad (N = 430)$

Socialist municipalities: $\quad$ Exp $= 17.0 + 3.36A \quad (N = 142)$

Non-socialist municipalities: Exp $= 14.0 + 2.71A \quad (N = 288)$

where A = percentage aged 70 and over.

Although it should be noted that the explanatory powers of all three models are low, the estimated coefficients display some interesting differences, especially between socialist and non-socialist municipalities. These differences are shown in Fig. 2.3, where the curves — or rather lines — of each equation are drawn.

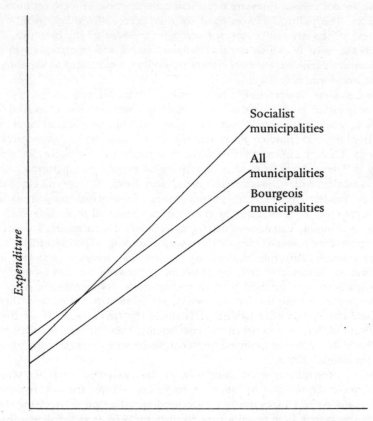

Socialist municipalities

All municipalities

Bourgeois municipalities

Expenditure

Percentage aged 70 and over

Fig. 2.3. Per capita expenditures for the aged as a function of total population per cent aged 70 and over.

While the intercept with the vertical axis does not differ much between the three equations, the slopes of the regressions display some interesting differences. In the first place, the level of expenditures for these services is generally lower in bourgeois municipalities than socialist ones. In the second place, the slope of the regression is steeper in socialist than in bourgeois municipalities. This indicates that socialist councils give more weight to this factor in deciding on such expenditures, than non-socialist communes. Thus, this difference may be interpreted either as a difference in political priorities, or of responsiveness between the two groups of parties, or as differences in the actual content and quality of the services for the aged. A note of caution should, however, be added to this interpretation. As noted above, the explanatory power of the model is rather

poor, and a control for other factors may change the observed relationships, although the regression coefficients in all three equations are significant at a 0.01 level. The purpose of presenting this example has been only
to demonstrate the basic idea behind my formulation of the method of
analysis, and, as we will see later on, political differences in the weights
given to the decision-making criteria in arriving at an expenditure decision
will turn out to be far more dramatic than in this example.

Let me point out, finally, that in using this approach, it is also important
to take the constant term of the estimated equations into consideration.
If the constant terms differ between socialist and bourgeois municipalities,
this may be taken as evidence of a more *general* difference between the
parties in the priorities given to those particular services. In other words,
such differences may be interpreted in a similar manner as the regression
coefficients of political variables in 'traditional' expenditure analyses.

Dependent variables

The analysis which follows is based on budgetary decisions in Norwegian
municipalities in 1976. Both urban and rural municipalities are included in
the analysis. In choosing the service expenditures, the extent to which
local authorities have to comply with central-government legislation in
deciding on the level of expenditures has been taken into consideration.
There are substantial variations in the degree of local autonomy across
various service areas, and even within areas which are regulated, the
regulatory techniques vary. Kjellberg has suggested a distinction between
two dimensions of central regulations, namely (1) regulations of the policy
goals of local authorities and (2) regulations of the means by which local
government pursue their goals.[21] Apart from the regulation of tasks and
financial means of local government activity, however, relatively little
attention has been paid to the way in which the *decision-making models* of
local authorities have been regulated by central government. Although
students of local budgeting acknowledge the importance of national
standards for local service provision,[22] little empirical research has been
done in order to clarify the character of such standards, or to assess how
these standards influence budget decisions.

Although standardization normally takes place within policy areas
where central government has defined specific objectives of local-government activity, standardization may be regarded as analytically distinct
from goal-setting. While goal-setting aims at defining a desired state of
affairs in terms of local-government activity, standardization usually
implies the regulation of the decision-making rules by which these objectives ought to be pursued. To put it differently; while goal-setting aims at
regulating the level of local-government output directly (i.e. the dependent
variable), standardization aims at regulating or defining the criteria, or

the determinants (independent variables), upon which the decisions are to be based. Thus, while central authorities may define certain standards of living for the aged population as an objective of local government activities, standardization serves to specify what problems or rather what criteria a person has to satisfy in order to be entitled to such services.

Goal-setting and standardization are in fact two separate dimensions of central regulations; national legislation may define goals without specifying any standards for the service provision; conversely, central authorities may define standards without setting any goals. The Norwegian building legislation may serve as an example of a situation where procedural rules and technical standards or requirements for building activities — including local planning — have been specified, without setting any goals for the total level of local-government activity within the building sector.

The building or technical sector also exemplifies an area of municipal activities where the local authorities themselves have made significant contributions to the process of standardization by means of local physical planning. Above all, this planning serves to establish a set of decision-making rules or criteria for the future building development both in private and public sector.[23] Also long-term budgeting, corporate planning, and economic planning serve the purposes of establishing decision-making criteria for future allocations of goods and services, thus constraining discretionary power in deciding on individual issues. In the short run, however, although locally determined standards may have similar restrictive effects on local decision makers as national standards, it may, nevertheless, be far easier to alter and deviate from them than national standards. Furthermore, locally defined standards are not uniform across municipalities, and may vary according to the political priorities of the majority parties. In other words, what I previously termed political cognitive maps, serve a similar function as decision-making rules by directing the attention of the decision makers towards specific criteria in deciding on individual issues.

By combining the two dimensions — goal-setting and standardization — and assuming that both dimensions may be dichotomized, we arrive at Table 2.1 which may serve as a classificatory scheme of local-government activities in this study.

In Table 2.1 I have also stated the areas of local government activities to be analysed in this study. Primary education is an area where central authorities have clearly defined both goals and standards for local service provision. Apart from providing clear-cut rules or definitions of who is liable to such services (children aged 7–15), even the actual content of the teaching is defined by central regulations. Local authorities do, however, have some leeway in determining the organization of the local school system, like the number of schools, size of classes, etc., but generally I expect that the budget decisions within this sector will be made on the basis of a fixed set of decision-making criteria which do not vary significantly

Table 2.1

	Regulation of goals	
	Yes	No
Setting of standards		
Yes	Primary education	Public building activities
No	Social welfare	cultural activities

according to political majorities on local councils.

In the area of social welfare activities I expect to find more variations between socialist and bourgeois municipalities in the weights given to different decision-making criteria. Although legislation defines certain tasks for local government to perform, a major purpose of social welfare services at local level is to take charge of those social problems which are not covered by the national insurance scheme. Thus, the tasks of local government within this policy area are partly residual, and there are, consequently, few standards or rules for the service provision.

As already pointed out, central legislation of the local building sector — which includes housing and public works — aim mainly at setting standards and technical requirements. Municipalities are free to choose whether to provide such services or not, but if they are provided, they have to comply with centrally defined standards. In addition, legislation has made physical planning a responsibility of local authorities, although not defining the criteria upon which the plans should be based. Planning may therefore be regarded as a means by which local government establish their own decision-making criteria by socialist and bourgeois municipalities. Thus, planning serves as a means by which political differences between socialist and non-socialist parties are strengthened, although planning in both cases contributes to establish standards for the decision makers.

Cultural activities are probably the least regulated area of municipal activities in Norway, mainly because it has been a major objective of the central government not to set any goals for this area of local activity.[24] Furthermore, there have been few attempts both by central and local authorities to establish any decision-making rules for this sector. This is partly because of the lack of unambiguous goals within the sector, but also because lack of appropriate social indicators has made it difficult to devise any specific set of decision-making criteria for the sector. I do, however, expect political factors to exert an influence on the way in which the socio-economic variables are related to the level of cultural expenditure, which implies that the weight given to each individual factor varies according to political majority in the municipal council. Let me now turn to the selection of independent variables for this analysis.

Independent variables

An obvious consequence of the preceding discussion is that the independent – or explanatory – variables in a study of public expenditure ought to be selected on the basis of a thorough study of party programmes and actual decision-making behaviour in the individual municipalities. Neither time nor resources have made such a procedure possible in this study, therefore, for each expenditure area, I have selected a set of independent variables which I believe may be relevant decision-making criteria. It is therefore possible that the models reflect my own political priorities rather than those of the local decision-makers. It should also be noted that availability of data has restricted the number of variables which can be used in the study.

The purpose of this study has, however, not been to establish 'correct' decision-making models for different local authorities and policy areas, but to demonstrate how the effects of socio-economic factors on local expenditure may be conditioned by the political preferences of the decision-makers.

One may distinguish between three groups of independent variables, namely (a) general contextual factors, (b) service-specific factors and (c) political/administrative factors. Group (a) comprises two variables, population size and population density. These variables may be regarded as indicators of the total range of expenditure 'needs' in a municipality. Both population size and density, however, may also affect the *costs* of providing local government services. In particular, economies and diseconomies of scale in service provision are important in this respect. Such effects will depend on the character of the services provided. In the case of collective goods I expect these factors to be negatively related to the expenditure level, while individual (or divisible) services may display diseconomies of scale. Once again, however, these relationships may be conditioned by the priorities of the decision-makers. In particular, I expect socialist parties to prefer collective to individual services, which would imply negative relationships between these two factors and the level of expenditures.

The selection of service-specific factors has been somewhat more arbitrary. I have settled for two types of variables, one type which measures the number of potential clients within the sector, and another type which may be related only indirectly to needs for services. An example of the first type is number of children of school age (aged 7–15), while the second type is exemplified by the proportion of total labour force employed in primary industries (agriculture, fisheries and forestry). Apart from indicating the industrial structure of municipalities, this variable also characterizes their social structure. In addition, it may be regarded as an indicator of certain cultural characteristics of the community, such as religious attitudes. Thus, such factors may give rise to many different — and often competing — needs within one particular policy area. It is therefore difficult to formulate unambiguous hypotheses on the relationship between them and the level of expenditures, and I will therefore restrain myself from more detailed comments on each individual variable.

The last group of independent variables — political/administrative — needs some comment. In this study the percentage of votes for socialist parties, and the size of the central administration are used as political/administrative characteristics of the decision-making system. As one study of local budgeting has shown, demands arising from within the administration are probably more powerful determinants of the expenditure level than are others (i.e. external) demands.[25] Here I assume that the larger the size of the administration the more 'developed' it is in terms of specialization, planning resources and so on. I further expect that the more 'developed' the more acquisitive is the administration in budgetary matters. Thus I expect to find a positive relationship between size of administration and level of expenditure in all four policy areas. I also expect the political parties, however, to differ in terms of responsiveness to the demands from the bureaucracy. On the basis of more general attitudes towards the public sector, I expect socialist parties to be more responsive to these demands than non-socialist parties. Size of administration is measured as the number (per capita of total population) employed in the central administrative section of the department whose expenditure is under analysis. The central administration excludes field workers (teachers, social workers, technicians, road menders, etc.) who actually deliver services, and includes only those bureaucrats in the central office of the department who are responsible for general administration and budgeting.

The inclusion of percent socialist votes as an independent variable in the analysis may seem quite strange, since I run separate equations for municipalities with socialist and bourgeois majorities. There are two reasons for including this variable in the analysis. In the first place, I want to compare the two subsets of municipalities with a more 'conventional' analysis based on all municipalities. In order to make such a comparison possible, the same variables have to be included in all equations. In the second place, this variable may be interpreted as a measure of inter-party competition, such that values approximating 50 per cent may be regarded as a high degree of inter-party competition. The interpretation of this variable, however, differs between the two types of municipalities. While higher values on the variable imply a low degree of competition in socialist muncipalities, low values on the variable has a similar interpretation in bourgeois municipalities. This different way of interpreting the variable will only affect the sign, not the magnitude, of the relationship between the variable and the level of expenditures.

In Table 2.2 the dependent and independent variables employed in the analysis are listed. A X denotes that an independent variable is combined with a dependent variable in the analysis. I have employed the same set of independent variables for both types of municipalities.

Table 2.2 *Models of analysis*

Independent variables	*Dependent variables expenditure*			
	Primary Education	*Social welfare*	*Housing public works*	*Culture*
Population size	X	X	X	X
Population density	X	X	X	X
Aged 7–15 (%)	X			
Aged 0–15 (%)		X		X
Aged 70 or over (%)		X		X
Pupil : teacher ratio	X			
Single-parent families (%)		X	X	
Women in labour force (%)		X		
Widows & divorced women in labour force (%)		X		
Total (%)		X		
Net migration (%)			X	
Housing built before 1940 (%)			X	
Persons per household			X	
In primary industry (%)				X
In tertiary industry (%)			X	
Size of school administration	X			
Size of technical administration			X	
Size of cultural administration				X
Size of social administration		X		
Percentage socialist votes	X	X	X	X

Findings

To estimate the models, multiple regression analysis has been employed. This estimation procedure is based on the assumption that the relationships between dependent and independent variables may be described in this study. Scale effects in service provision may lead to non-linear relationships, and this applies in particular to the relationship between population size and per capita expenditures. Furthermore, such non-linear relationships may be conditioned by political preferences. While, for example, socialist parties may prefer collective solutions to particular problems, thereby benefiting from economies of scale, bourgeois parties may prefer individual solutions where no such effects are apparent. This example points to a more general problem in assessing differences in expenditure levels between socialists and bourgeois municipalities. Although socialist parties may be more disposed towards a high level of public activity than bourgeois parties, the actual expenditure level may still be higher in bourgeois communes, simply because they prefer individual solutions which are more costly. The sector of housing and public works is a case in point, where the socialist parties in Norway have preferred collective solutions — such as high-rise housing which costs less than the more scattered single-family housing preferred by the conservatives. The possibilities of such differences and the existence of non-linear relationships should therefore be kept in mind when interpreting the results of the analyses.

Let me now turn to the results of the analysis. As a general hypothesis — and on the basis of the previous argument — I expect to find more variation in the regression coefficients across municipalities within so-called autonomous sectors than within the regulated sectors. Furthermore, because of a high degree of standardization of the decision rules, I expect the explanatory power of the models to be highest for the sector most regulated by central legislation (primary education) and lowest for the least regulated sector (culture). The *differences* in explanatory power between the two groups of municipalities, however, are expected to increase as local autonomy increases.

Table 2.3 reports the regression coefficients for primary education. In this and the following tables only the standardized coefficients are reported.[26] I also report the overall explanatory power of the models.

For all three groups of municipalities the explanatory power of the model is fairly high, and highest for municipalities with a socialist majority. The difference in explanatory power may indicate that the socialists are more likely to apply this set of independent variables as decision-making criteria than bourgeois parties, although the difference also may be explained by the lower number of cases in the socialist group of municipalities.

As expected, the regression coefficients do not vary much across the

Table 2.3   *Per capita expenditures for primary education*

Independent variables	Type of municipality		
	All	Bourgeois	Socialist
Population size	−0.022	−0.17	−0.018
Population density	−0.293*	−0.308*	−0.246*
Aged 7–15 (%)	0.305*	0.279*	0.371*
Pupil : teacher ratio	0.408*	0.384*	0.456*
Size of administration	0.252*	0.310*	0.120*
Socialist votes (%)	−0.065*	−0.093*	−0.036
R^2	0.67*	0.63*	0.73*
$N =$	430	288	142

* Significant at 0.05

Table 2.4   *Per capita expenditures for social welfare services*

Independent variables	Types of municipality		
	All	Bourgeois	Socialist
Population size	0.105*	0.125*	0.228*
Population Density	−0.079	−0.037	−0.186
Single-parent families (%)	0.122*	0.168*	0.135*
Aged 70 and over (%)	−0.262*	−0.165	−0.289
Women in labour force (%)	0.087	0.101	0.017
Widows and divorced women (%)	0.117	0.035	0.141
Aged 0–15 (%)	−0.118	−0.065	−0.204
In labour force (%)	−0.058	−0.137	0.162
Size of administration	0.067	0.021	0.164*
Socialist votes (%)	0.113*	0.050	0.037
R^2	0.09*	0.08*	0.13*
$N =$	430	288	142

* Significant at 0.05

two groups of municipalities, thus indicating fairly standardized decision-making procedures operating in all municipalities. It is also interesting to note that the significant coefficients — apart from one — are the same in the three groups. The bourgeois municipalities, however, seem to keep expenditures for such services at a higher level than do socialist municipalities. This is indicated by the negative coefficient for percentage socialist votes in the regression including all municipalities.

In Table 2.4 the results of the regressions for social welfare expenditures are shown. The table reveals greater differences across the municipalities than for education expenditures, although most coefficients are not significant. The explanatory power of the model is also low, not exceeding 13 per cent for any of the three regressions. In other words, there does not seem to exist any uniform decision-making procedures for this sector. Alternatively, the independent variables used here may not reflect the criteria employed in deciding on these expenditures. One coefficient does, however, deserve a comment. While size of administration does not exert any influence on the expenditure level in bourgeois municipalities, this factor has a fairly strong positive — and significant — impact in socialist municipalities. Although care should be taken not to over-interpret this finding, it indicates that the socialists are more likely than the bourgeois to respond positively to the demands brought forward by the administration. This finding also corresponds to observations made in a study of budgeting in Oslo.[27]

Turning now to expenditures for housing and public works, differences between socialist and bourgeois municipalities are more prominent than in the two previous analyses — as revealed in Table 2.5.

First, the model seems to fit much better in socialist than in bourgeois municipalities. Thus, while it accounts for 53 per cent of the expenditure variations in bourgeois municipalities, 73 per cent of the variation is accounted for in municipalities with socialist majorities. In other words, socialist and non-socialist politicians seem to apply different criteria in deciding on these expenditures. Secondly, to the extent the same criteria are applied, they are treated differently across the two groups of municipalities. For two of the variables — population and percentage old housing — the sign of the coefficient changes when we move from bourgeois to socialist municipalities. The negative relationship between expenditures and population size in socialist municipalities suggests that the socialist parties tend to favour collective to individual solutions also within this area of activity. Apart from these two variables which change sign, we also note that while the percentage of single-parent families and number of persons per household apparently do not effect expenditures in bourgeois municipalities, the effects of these variables are significant in socialist municipalities. Finally, the number of significant coefficients for all municipalities supports my suggestion that it is easier to devise standardized decision rules for this sector than, for example, social welfare services.

Table 2.5   *Per capita expenditures for housing and public works*

Independent variables	Type of municipalities		
	All	Bourgeois	Socialist
Population size	0.178*	0.245*	−0.105*
Population density	−0.038	−0.067	−0.027
Single-parent families (%)	0.078*	0.001	0.259*
Persons per household	−0.136*	−0.084	−0.325*
Net migration	−0.069*	−0.56	−0.052
Old housing (%)	−0.006	0.038	−0.097
In tertiary industry (%)	0.080	0.090	0.093
Size of administration	0.670*	0.657*	0.734*
Socialist votes (%)	−0.106*	−0.086	−0.054
R^2	0.57*	0.53*	0.73*
N	430	288	142

* Significant at 0.05

Such rules vary between municipalities, however, and seem to be conditioned by the political priorities of the decision-makers.

In Table 2.6 the findings for cultural services are reported. As expected, the explanatory power of the model is rather poor for all groups of municipalities. It is, however, interesting to note that it is lowest when all municipalities are included in the analysis, and increases for both bourgeois and socialist municipalities. This suggests that both bourgeois and socialist alike apply the same set of decision-making criteria by and large, but that the weights given to each individual criterion differ according to party. As in the previous analyses, the effects of population size differ between the two types of municipalities. Again, this relationship is positive for bourgeois and negative for socialist municipalities. This finding is in accordance with observations made in connection with recent debates in Norway over cultural policies, where the bourgeois parties have expressed preferences for an 'elitist' approach to cultural activities, while the Labour Party give priority to more collective forms of such activities, including certain services for the youth.[28] Such attitudes are partly revealed in the coefficients of the variable 'Aged 0–15 (%)', where there is a significant negative relationship for municipalities with a bourgeois majority and no such relationship for socialist municipalities. It is also interesting to note that, although size of administration exerts a significant positive impact on these expenditures in non-socialist municipalities, this relationship is much stronger in socialist municipalities, where it is the more powerful determinant.

Table 2.6   Per capita expenditures for cultural services

Independent variables	Type of municipality		
	All	Bourgeois	Socialist
Population size	0.100*	0.130*	−0.050
Population density	0.076	0.073	0.023
Aged 70 and over (%)	−0.069	−0.069	0.022
Aged 0–15 (%(	−0.304*	−0.423*	−0.003
In primary industry	0.170*	0.089	0.180
Size of administration	0.282*	0.204*	0.496*
Socialist votes (%)	−0.070	−0.168*	0.051
R^2	0.18⁴	0.25*	0.20*
N	430	288	142

* Significant at 0.05

Concluding remarks

The purpose of this analysis has been to demonstrate an approach to expenditure analysis, where the focus has been on how political factors influence the way in which needs are transformed into expenditure decisions. Rather than treating political variables as additive, marginal effects in determining public expenditure, this approach suggests that political factors determine the effects that socio-economic variables have on expenditures. Thus, socio-economic variables are regarded as decision-making criteria rather than causal factors, and the relationship between political and socio-economic factors in determining expenditures is conceived of as one of interaction.

My point of departure has been the primacy of politics as policy-determinants. I reject the suggestion made in earlier studies that socio-economic factors exert a direct and independent impact on the level of public expenditures for specific services. Any such relationships have to be established by the political decision-making bodies. This suggestion is also supported by the empirical results reported here. Apart from the policy area most regulated by central legislation − primary education − the impact of socio-economic variables on the level of expenditures vary according to the political majority of the municipal councils. For analytical purposes, and on the basis of these findings, it may therefore be an advantage to reformulate the conventional Eastonian approach to expenditure studies. A suggested revision of the model is shown in Fig. 2.4.

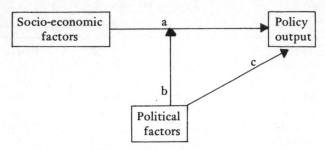

Fig. 2.4   *A revised model*

In this model the interaction between political and socio-economic factors in determining expenditures is denoted by relation b. This implies that relation a is filtered through political factors. In addition, political variables exert a direct independent impact on policy output. Thus, a distinction is here made between political *parameters* and *variables*, where the parameters are the weights given to socio-economic factors in deciding on the level of expenditures, while the variables express the policy objectives of the decision makers more directly.

In their review of local outputs research, Newton and Sharpe have suggested that

> Rather than seeing political and socio-economic factors as in some sense distinct or opposed, it is better to view them as interdependent and mutually reinforcing. It is not a question of 'Do political variables explain more or less than socio-economic ones?' but rather, 'What combinations of political and socio-economic variables are associated with what sorts of expenditure patterns?'[29]

This is exactly what I have attempted to do in this study. Although the differences between socialist and bourgeois municipalities are not great, they make sense in terms of ideological differences between the two groups of parties.

Notes

1. R. E. Dawson and J. A. Robinson, 'Inter-Party Competition, Economic Variables and Welfare Policies in the American States', *Journal of Politics* (1963), 265–89.
2. For an account of this research, see R. C. Fried, 'Comparative Urban Policy and Performance', in F. J. Greenstein and N. W. Polsby (eds.), *Handbook of Political Science* (Reading, Mass., Addison-Wesley, 1976) 305–81;

3. Cf. for example N. Boaden, *Urban Policy Making* (Cambridge, Cambridge University Press, 1971); K. Newton and L. J. Sharpe, 'Local Outputs Research: Some Reflections and Proposals', *Policy and Politics*, 5 (1977), 61–82; C. J. Skovsgaard, *et al., Studier i Dansk Kommunalpolitik* (Aarhus, 1977); F. Kjellberg (ed.), *Den Kommunale Virksombet* (Oslo, Universitetsforlaget, 1980).

4. T. R. Dye, 'Politics Versus Economics: The Development of the Literature on Policy Determination', *Policy Studies Journal*, 7 (1979), 653.

5. See for example T. R. Dye, *Politics, Economics and the Public: Policy Outcomes in the American States* (Chicago, Rand McNally, 1966).

6. Cf. B. R. Fry and R. F. Winters, 'The Politics of Redistribution', *American Political Science Review*, 64 (1970), 508–22; J. L. Sullivan, 'A Note on Redistributive Politics', *American Political Science Review*, 66 (1972), 1301–5.

7. For a discussion of the weaknesses of conventional models, see S. H. Rakoff and G. Schaefer, 'Politics, Policy and Political Science: Theoretical Alternatives', *Politics and Society*, 1 (1970), 51–77.

8. M. S. Lewis-Beck, 'The Relative Importance of Socio-economic and Political Variables for Public Policy', *American Political Science Review*, 71 (1977), 559–60.

9. Lewis-Beck, op. cit., 566.

10. D. Easton, *A Framework for Political Analysis*, (Englewood Cliffs, Prentice-Hall, 1965).

11. Lewis-Beck, op. cit., 559–66.

12. Boaden, op. cit., 21–7.

13. Cf. Rakoff and Schaefer, op. cit., 51–77.

14. C. J. Brown and P. M. Jackson, *Public Sector Economics* (Oxford, Martin Robertson, 1978), 96.

15. For a discussion of 'merit goods', see R. A. Musgrave and P. B. Musgrave, *Public Finance in Theory and Practice* (New York, McGraw-Hill, 1973).

16. Cf. J. M. Buchanan, 'Public Goods and Public Bads', in J. P. Crecine (ed.), *Financing the Metropolis* (Beverly Hills, Sage Publications, 1970), 51–72.

17. Dye, op. cit., 63–97.

18. A similar argument has been put forward by J. Stonecash, 'Politics, Wealth and Public Policy: The Significance of Political Systems', *Policy Studies Journal*, 7 (1979).

19. See L. J. Sharpe, 'Does Politics Matter?' (Ch. 1 this volume).

20. For a more detailed discussion of the model, see T. Hansen, 'Modeller i studiet av offentlig politikk', *Politico* (1978).

21. F. Kjellberg, 'Det kommunale selvstyre i komparativt perspektiv', *Statsvetenskapelig Tidsskrift*, 1974. See also T. Hansen and F. Kjellberg, 'Municipal Expenditures in Norway: Autonomy and Constraints in Local Government Activity', *Policy and Politics*, 4 (1976), 25–50.

22. Cf. F. Kjellberg, 'Politiske konsekvenser av standardisering av kommunale ytelser', in Kjellberg (ed.) op. cit.

23. Cf. T. Hansen, 'The Politics of Local Planning', *International Political Science Review*, 1 (1980), 168–86.

24. For a discussion of Norwegian cultural policy, see Helene Roshauw, *Fra Mesenvirksombet til Velferdspolitikk* (Cand. polit.-dissertation, Oslo, 1980).

25. A. T. Cowart and K. E. Brofoss, *Decisions, Politics and Change. A Study of Norwegian Urban Budgeting* (Oslo, Universitetsforlaget, 1979).

26. Strictly speaking, unstandardized regression coefficients should be used when comparing subsamples. Here I am also interested in the relative importance of the variables, which only may be assessed by using standardized coefficients.

27. See Cowart and Brofoss, *Decisions, Politics and Change*.

28. Cf. Roshauw, *Fra Mesenvirksombet til Velferdspolitikk*.

29. Newton and Sharpe, op. cit., 75.

3 PARTY INFLUENCE ON LOCAL SPENDING IN DENMARK

CARL-JOHAN SKOVSGAARD

Does Politics Matter?

This chapter presents an attempt to show the importance of the local political system, especially the local party system, in Danish municipalities with regard to local-government expenditure. The main theme is that the traditional image of non-partisan politics and neutral or objective decision-making at the local level needs some modifications. Even today it is popularly believed that party political questions do not matter as much in local politics as in national politics. On the other hand, politicians involved in local government often argue that this is not true, claiming that party politics does matter in local government. Thus, it seems reasonable to try to assess the actual role of political parties in local government.

Patterns of Public Expenditure

Before analysing this question, two tables will be presented in order to underline the importance of local government activities for the entire national economy.[1] In the last decade local and regional authorities in Denmark have undergone a series of reforms which have meant important and far-reaching changes in the system of local government and in the national economy. These reforms started in 1970 with a new division of areas which reduced the number of local authorities from 1389 municipalities in 1962, to 277 after the reform, and the number of regional authorities from 24 to 14. In turn, there followed reforms in the distribution of tasks and economic burdens between different levels of government, which have meant that local and regional authorities have taken over an increasing number of responsibilities. These changes have taken place gradually in the 1970s and are not yet finished.

The figures in Table 3.1 leave no doubt that there has been a dramatic change in the distribution of tasks and economic burdens over the last decade. Since 1975 about 30 per cent of public expenditure has been incurred by authorities below the national level, if expenditure financed through refunds and grants is not included.

One of the chief objectives of the reforms was that the right to make a decision should be linked to an obligation to pay the costs following this

Table 3.1 Distribution of public expenditure between the three levels of government, 1966–76

	Central government		Regional government		Local government	
	Net*(%)	Gross*(%)	Net(%)	Gross(%)	Net(%)	Gross(%)
1966/67†	60.6	80.6	2.2	3.1	17.2	36.3
1971/72	46.1	75.9	3.2	..5.1	20.9	48.8
1972/73	48.2	78.3	3.7	5.3	18.0	46.6
1973/74	45.2	77.6	3.9	6.8	18.5	48.0
1974/75	40.7	75.2	4.6	8.0	20.2	51.2
1975/76	35.3	70.3	8.3	11.6	21.4	53.1

Sources: 1966/67 figures: Statistiske efterretninger, nr. 28, 1969.
Other figures: Statistical Yearbook, published annually by Danmarks Statistik.

* In the gross figures state refunds and grants to lower levels of government are included. In the net figures they are not.
† Up to 1977 the local and regional government budgeting year covered the period April 1 to March 31. Since 1977 it has followed the calendar year. The state budgeting year was changed to the calendar year in 1979.

decision. Before the reforms, municipal councils could make decisions on a number of matters, which, to a large extent, were paid by the state through percentage refunds. This meant that local councils could make decisions, knowing that this would not mean an increase in their own financial responsibilities, because the central government had to foot the bill.

This system was criticized for being economically unsound. For instance, 85 per cent of local-government teachers' salaries was paid by the central government. In a number of instances municipalities appointed more teachers than were actually needed. To a large extent, the reforms abolished this system and local government has, for instance, now taken over the full financial burden of employing teachers. In general, one third of public expenditure is now both under the control of, and financed by local government.

To make it clear what is meant by 'refunds' in this context it should be explained that refunds are specific grants which cover a certain proportion of the costs of a service. Before the reforms about ninety different specific grant arrangements existed, the proportion of costs being covered by the central government varying considerably from one arrangement to another.[2] Reform reduced the number of specific grants and replaced them by general grants. The specific grants which remain are mainly found in the social sector, a prominent example being retirement and disablement pensions, which are refunded 100 per cent by the central government. Including grants, more than half of public expenditure is incurred by the municipalities, and 65 per cent by local and regional authorities together. In spite of the fact that half of this expenditure is paid by central government through percentage refunds and general grants there is no doubt that the period since reform has been characterized by a radical increase in the activities of regional and local authorities.

In spite of the fact that such large amounts of public money are spent by authorities below the national level very little is actually known about regional and local government. Thus, it is important not only to analyse the importance of the political factor in regional and local government, as attempted in this paper, but also to investigate the entire set of social, economic, and political forces which determine local policy making.

Patterns of Local-Government Expenditure

Data from all Danish municipalities are available for the year 1972/73, and all 277 municipalities will be analysed together in order to uncover general trends. Data is available only for 1972/73, and thus no trends over time can be traced.[3]

The three main types of municipal expenditures are those for social welfare, primary schools and roads. In several ways, these are the most important services, and they account for 75 per cent of total municipal expenditure. Therefore, these are the sectors which will be analysed.

The expenditure will be analysed by splitting municipalities into four groups according to population size. Each group is characterized by a number of social, economic and political differences, some of which are shown in Table 3.2, which illustrates several points. It shows, first, that Denmark is a rather urbanized country, since even in the group with the lowest urbanization percentage, more than 50 per cent of the population live in urban areas; secondly that the larger the municipality, the more urbanized and industrialized it is; thirdly that these factors also correlate with Socialist strength.

Table 3.3 reveals two clear spending patterns.[4] It seems that the larger the municipality is, the higher is the total expenditure and the lower is its expenditure on roads. The table also shows that social welfare expenditure makes up more than half of the total municipal expenditure. Unlike some other European countries the greatest part of local revenues derives from income taxes which are levied by local government, almost without any limits imposed by the central government. Of the total municipal income, 34 per cent is income tax, 3 per cent property tax, and the rest specific and general central government grants (1976/77 figures).[5]

Table 3.2   *Characteristics of municipalities, by size, 1972/73*

	Inhabitants				
	<10 000	10–19 999	20–99 999	>100 000	Average
Average inhabitants	6640	13835	40467	290906	18077
Urbanization*	51.7%	64.9%	90.0%	95.2%	61.9%
Industrialization†	74.3%	80.7%	94.2%	97.0%	79.4%
Socialist strength‡	32.7%	36.5%	50.3%	59.6%	37.0%
N (277)	(161)	(66)	(46)	(4)	

* Per cent of population living in urban areas (200 inhabitants).
† Per cent of population working in industry and commerce.
‡ Per cent of votes for Social Democrats, Socialists, and Communists in local government election 1970.

Table 3.3   *Municipal current expenditures in selected sectors, 1972/73 (Dkr. per capita)*

Expenditures	Inhabitants				
	<10 000	10–19 999	20–99 999	>100 000	Average
Total net	4820	4992	5368	6297	4973
Social welfare	2925	2904	2801	3640	2910
Schools	591	604	708	589	614
Roads	238	209	162	102	216
N (277)	(161)	(66)	(46)	(4)	

Political Sensitivity of Local Government Expenditure

In Danish municipal councils there is a tradition for a rather clearcut political dividing line between Socialist and non-Socialist parties. By far the most important of the Socialist parties is the Social Democratic Party, which is represented in every municipal council in the country. While all Socialist parties attracted 37 per cent of the local-election vote in 1970, the Social Democratic Party alone accounted for 35.6 per cent of the poll. This clearly shows that the Social Democratic Party is much stronger in municipal politics than the Socialist parties.

Traditionally, in only a very few municipalities do the Social Democrats make any pre-election agreements with other parties over the sharing of votes in the proportional distribution of council seats. This procedure is used by the non-Socialist parties in about 75 per cent of the municipalities in order to secure as many seats as possible. Thus, in general, Socialist

Table 3.4   *Strength of parties taking the post of the Lord Mayor*

	Majority over 50%	Largest party no majority %	Second-largest or weaker %	Total %
Social Democratic Party	43	53	4	100
Radical Party	0	0	100	100
Liberal Party	19	54	27	100
Conservative Party	17	30	53	100
Average	20	34	46	100

Source: Danske Kommuner, No. 4, 1978.

strength is an important determinant of the political complexion of the municipalities.

Socialist Strength and Social Welfare Expenditure

In the following tables, municipalities will be organized into three groups: those with Socialist voting strength below the national average of 37 per cent; those with a Socialist vote of between 37 and 50 per cent; and those with an absolute Socialist majority. Since the Social Democrats rarely make electoral pacts, they must usually have an absolute majority in order to control the Lord Mayor's office. This is demonstrated in Table 3.4 which shows that in the municipalities where the Social Democrats have taken over the post of mayor since the 1970 local election, in 43 per cent of the municipalities they have the majority, in 53 per cent of the municipalities they are the strongest party, and in only 4 per cent of the municipalities are they the second-largest or weaker party. Table 3.4 also shows that this pattern is not shared by other parties, which hold the Lord Mayor's post, even though they are not the largest party.

Table 3.5   *Total social welfare expenditure, 1972/73 (Dkr. per capita), by Socialist strength*

Socialist strength	(N)	Inhabitants				Average
		<10 000	10–19 999	20–99 999	>100 000	
<37%	(151)	2941	2874	2641	–	2907
37–50%	(78)	2894	2872	2988	–	2903
>50%	(48)	2899	3072	2768	3640	2929
Average		2925	2904	2801	3640	2910

Traditionally, the Socialist parties in Danish national politics are said to be more positive towards social welfare expenditure than non-Socialist parties, but is this true at local government level? Table 3.5 does not indicate any clear trends with regard to the importance of the political factor for the *level* of social welfare expenditure. Instead of looking at the level of social welfare expenditure, it might be useful to take a look at the proportion of the total municipal expenditure used for social welfare, that is at the *priority* it is given as an expenditure item (Table 3.6).

Table 3.6   *Social welfare's proportion of total expenditure, 1972/73, by Socialist strength*

Socialist strength	Inhabitants				
	<10 000	10-19 999	20-99 999	>100 000	Average
<37%	58.3	55.9	48.6	–	57.2
37–50%	57.0	56.2	53.5	–	56.3
>50%	54.9	55.9	52.7	58.3	54.3
Average	57.8	56.0	52.1	58.3	56.4

As in Table 3.5, Table 3.6 shows no clear trends with regard to the priority given to social welfare expenditure. The totals seem to indicate that increasing Socialist strength means that the social welfare expenditure's proportion of the total expenditure goes down. The left-hand column of Table 3.6 indicates that the small municipalities spend a lot of social welfare. This is to be expected because the average taxable income in municipalities with less than 10 000 inhabitants is 13 000 Dkr. whereas in the large municipalities it is 18 500 Dkr. In the small municipalities one might thus expect a high need for social welfare services. On the whole, however, Table 3.6 does not suggest a high Socialist priority for social welfare services. Before reaching this conclusion, though, a little more examination of the figures is necessary.

As mentioned above, total social welfare expenditure includes expenditure on pension payments which are refunded 100 per cent by the central government through specific grants. No self-determination is thus left to local government over a high proportion of the social welfare expenditure. When discussing the role of local politics it will be of much greater interest to look at total social welfare expenditure *without* pension payments.

Contrary to Table 3.5, Table 3.7 shows a trend with regard to the importance of the political factor. It seems that stronger Socialist influence means higher welfare expenditure. At the same time there is an even clearer indication that the larger municipalities have a high welfare expenditure. Thus the heavy burden of social welfare expenditure in the small municipalities indicated by Tables 3.5 and 3.6 must be mainly pension

Table 3.7   *Total social welfare expenditure minus pensions, 1972/73 (Dkr. per capita) by Socialist strength*

	Inhabitants				
Socialist strength	<10000	10-19999	20-99999	>100000	Average
<37%	454	484	540	–	466
37–50%	491	526	613	–	519
>50%	528	536	547	788	561
Average	469	504	563	788	498

payments which are actually paid by the central government (Table 3.8).

When looking at the proportion of the total municipal expenditure (Table 3.8) it also seems that a higher priority is given to social welfare expenditure in municipalities with a large Socialist vote. At the same time the influence of population size is not nearly as strong as in Table 3.7.

With these findings in mind it might be useful to analyse the same data with a different technique in order to see if this will change or accentuate the results. We will therefore move from grouped data and cross tabulations to beta coefficients. This will be done by constructing a model for social welfare expenditure minus pension payments and subjecting it to regression analysis (Fig 3.1).

Table 3.8   *Social welfare minus pensions as a proportion of total expenditure, 1972/73, by Socialist strength*

	Inhabitants				
Socialist strength	<10000	10-19999	20-99999	>100000	Average
<37%	9.5	9.8	9.7	–	9.6
37–50%	10.0	10.4	11.2	–	10.3
>50%	10.7	10.4	10.4	12.3	10.6
Average	9.7	10.1	10.4	12.3	10.0

The model is based on the assumption that local-policy output is determined by local needs, resources and political preferences.[6] A second assumption is that it is possible to operationalize variables which can be used as indicators for these dimensions.

The model is based on theoretical considerations. It involves indicators which are both few and general but is the best of a number of models which have been tried. Furthermore, the problem of multicollinearity has been checked and was found not to present any serious difficulties in connection with the model chosen.

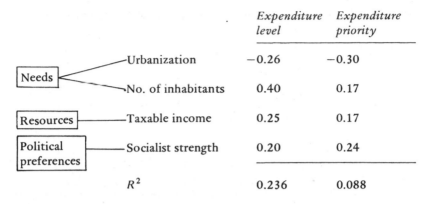

		Expenditure level	Expenditure priority
Needs	Urbanization	−0.26	−0.30
	No. of inhabitants	0.40	0.17
Resources	Taxable income	0.25	0.17
Political preferences	Socialist strength	0.20	0.24
	R^2	0.236	0.088

Fig. 3.1.   A Social welfare expenditure model (beta coefficients which are significant at the 0.05 level.)

Less than 24 per cent of the variance in expenditures, and as little as 9 per cent of the variance in expenditure priority is statistically explained by the chosen independent variables. Thus the major part of the variation is left unexplained, and little can be said for certain about the coefficients reported in the figure. The coefficients do seem to reinforce the most interesting finding in the above tables, however; namely that the political factor does have some influence which is statistically significant.

In Tables 3.5–3.7 only total welfare expenditure has been analysed. In order to take a closer look at the importance of local decision making it might be useful to disaggregate total expenditure into *specific* types of social welfare expenditure, as L.J. Sharpe suggests in chapter 1. In particular, expenditure without state refunds, or with only a low percentage, are an obvious choice for closer examination, for such expenditures leave more room for local decision-making. This, in turn, might result in policy and expenditure variations from one municipality to another.[7] This argument is based on the fact that two conflicting values may be attributed to the existence of the local government, i.e. equal treatment of citizens regardless of where they live, on the one hand, and local autonomy, which logically implies the possibility of differences in the treatment of citizens in different municipalities, on the other hand.

One such social welfare expenditure is payments to the aged, which are designed to help them stay as long as possible in their own homes instead of placing them in institutions. This expenditure covers payment to day-centres, day-care activities, help in the home, nursing in the home, and so on.

Table 3.9 leaves no doubt that the political strength of the Socialist parties in the municipal council has a marked influence on the level of expenditure, especially in municipalities with relatively few old people.

Table 3.9   Home-care payments for the aged (Dkr. per 65 years old and over), by per cent of aged

Aged (%)*	Socialist strength				
	<30%	30–45%	>45%	Average	(N)
<9	788	905	1270	1040	(52)
10–14	702	796	935	811	(144)
>15	648	668	708	675	(81)
Average	691	788	948	814	
(N)	(80)	(103)	(94)		(277)

Source: Ulrik Rhomassen, Kommunernes ældreomsorgspolitik, Specialeopgave, Insti-
for Statskundskab, januar 1978.
* Aged (%) = per cent of the population aged 65 years and over.

It is thus obvious that in this case local autonomy is given a higher priority than equal treatment of citizens in different municipalities. Similar analysis concerning the expenditure for institutions for the aged shows the same general results, although political influence is not quite as strong in this case.[8] Analysis concerning other specific types of expenditure have not yet been carried out, but with these results in mind, it seems to be an obvious candidate for further consideration.

Socialist Strength and Road Expenditure

Just as the Socialist parties are said to be more positive towards social welfare expenditure in politics at the national level, they are traditionally said to be inclined to prefer support for public transport, whereas the non-Socialist parties are said to be more positively disposed towards private transport and road expenditure.[9]

It is thus an obvious idea to take a closer look at municipal road expenditure. Furthermore, local governments in sparsely populated, geographically large municipalities, which are often non-Socialist dominated, have been accused of over-spending on roads.

In Table 3.10 a clear trend seems to emerge, which supports the hypothesis that Socialist parties are less inclined to spend on roads. It is also clear, however, that the larger the municipality is, the lower its road expenditure. There is a possibility, therefore, of factors which make the influence of the political factor a spurious one. Before examining this possibility with the help of regression analysis, however, it might be of use to look into the question of what proportion of the total expenditure of the municipalities is used for road purposes (Table 3.11).

Table 3.10   Road expenditure (Dkr. per capita), by Socialist strength

| Socialist strength | Inhabitants | | | | |
	<10 000	10-19 999	20-99 999	>100 000	Average
<37%	242	225	243	—	238
37-50%	237	197	142	—	212
>50%	193	170	142	102	154
Average	238	209	162	102	216

Table 3.11 does not add much to Table 3.10, in that the trends are much the same, and show a clear tendency for road expenditure to decline as a proportion of total expenditure as Socialist strength increases.

The procedure followed in connection with the analysis of social welfare expenditure will be used again, but this time it will be used in an attempt to discover whether the negative relationship between road expenditure and Socialist strength is true, or if it is spurious. The model shown in Fig. 3.2 is somewhat better than the social welfare expenditure model. Around 35 per cent of the variance of both expenditure measures are explained by the chosen independent variables. It seems that expenditure levels and priorities are determined to some extent by the amount paid in specific grants by the central government, but it also seems that the more rural municipalities spend relatively heavily on roads. Fig. 3.2 also shows that the political factor does have some influence, and that non-Socialist dominated councils are more inclined to spend on roads. This is the same as the British pattern suggested by L.J. Sharpe in his essay in this volume.

Table 3.11   Road expenditure as a proportion of total municipal expenditure, by Socialist strength

| Socialist strength | Inhabitants | | | | |
	<10 000	10-19 999	20-99 999	>100 000	Average
<37%	5.1	4.6	4.4	—	4.9
37-50%	4.9	4.1	2.7	—	4.3
>50%	4.0	3.4	2.7	1.8	3.0
Average	5.0	4.2	3.0	1.8	4.4

		Expenditure level	Expenditure priority
Needs	Urbanization	−0.15	−0.14
	No. of commuters	0.2**	0.12
Resources	Taxable income	0.30	0.13
	Road grants	0.46	0.46
Political preferences	Socialist strength	−0.15	−0.18
	R^2	0.326	0.351

*Fig. 3.2   A road expenditure model (beta coefficients are significant at the 0.05 level, except one marked **.)*

Socialist Strength and School Expenditure

In contrast to the two previous sections this one does not start with a hypothesis about the relationship between the political factor and the expenditure type. In fact, it may be that partisan politics will have a comparatively low influence, because no marked differences between Socialist and non-Socialist parties seem to exist in Danish communes with regard to school expenditure.[10]

In Table 3.12, although the figures for the average in the right hand column suggest a tendency for socialist strength to be accompanied by high education expenditure, when the figures in the main body of the table are examined, it is apparent that this tendency works in the small, but not in the large communes.

Table 3.12   *School expenditure, 1972/73 (Dkr. per 6 to 17 years old), by Socialist strength*

	Inhabitants				
Socialist strength	<10 000	10–19 999	20–99 999	>100 000	Average
<37%	3263	3397	4739	—	3383
37–50%	3585	3854	4243	—	3752
>50%	4197	3455	4510	4634	4242
Average	3409	3537	4485	4634	3636

Table 3.13 *School expenditure as a proportion of total municipal expenditure (per cent), by Socialist strength*

| | Inhabitants | | | | |
Socialist strength	<10 000	10-19 999	20-99 999	>100 000	Average
<37%	12.1	12.1	13.6	–	12.2
37–50%	12.5	12.8	11.4	–	12.4
>50%	14.4	10.8	14.0	10.1	12.9
Average	12.4	12.1	13.3	10.1	12.4

The picture presented in Table 3.12 is not altered much in Table 3.13. Socialist influence means a higher priority for school expenditure in the smallest communes but this trend is not to be found in the larger ones, which show no general trends.

Tables 3.12 and 3.13 did not give any clear picture of the variation in school expenditure. Therefore a model will be constructed and subjected to regression analysis (Fig. 3.3). One problem should be noted, expenditure level is based on expenditure per pupil, whereas expenditure priority can be based only on expenditure per capita. Thus the dependent variables are not directly comparable.

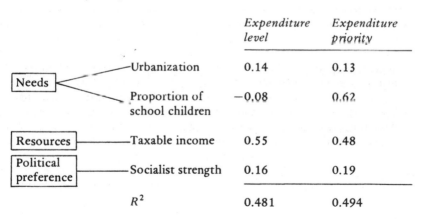

		Expenditure level	Expenditure priority
Needs	Urbanization	0.14	0.13
	Proportion of school children	−0.08	0.62
Resources	Taxable income	0.55	0.48
Political preference	Socialist strength	0.16	0.19
	R^2	0.481	0.494

Fig. 3.3. A school expenditure model (beta coefficients which are significant at the 0.05 level.)

Both with regard to the expenditure level and the proportion of expenditure spent on schools the resource situation is clearly an important factor. The political factor has a weaker influence than either resources or needs, but it still has influence which is statistically significant. It might therefore be useful to try to isolate this influence which will be done by looking at Socialist strength alone, controlled for all other variables in the model.

Table 3.14 shows that the rather weak overall influence of the political factor covers large variations in communes of different size. In fact, the Socialist effect is particularly notable in the forty-six communes with a population of between 20 000–99 999.

Table 3.14   *Socialist strength in municipal councils and primary school expenditure (partial correlation coefficients)*

	Inhabitants			
	< *10 000*	*10–19 999*	*20–99 999. >10 000*	*Average*
Expenditure level	0.206	−0.079	0.420	−	0.181
Expenditure priority	0.187	−0.043	0.387	−	0.141

It is interesting to note that in the group with 10 000–19 999 inhabitants, the results differ widely from the other results. The influence of the political factor is low and the coefficients indicate that growing Socialist strength means lower school expenditure. This result underlines the importance of the political factor for municipal expenditure, and at the same time illustrates the complexity of the problem.

In the group with 10 000–19 999 inhabitants forty-nine out of sixty-six municipalities (74 per cent) have a non-Socialist mayor, compared with the size group with 20 000–99 999 inhabitants, which has eighteen out of forty-six municipalities (39 per cent) with a non-Socialist mayor. The 10 000–19 999 group seems to differ from the others in the sense that a number of municipalities have a non-Socialist mayor in spite of considerable Socialist strength on the council.

It is to be expected that the party affiliation of the mayor is of some importance for decisions made by the municipal council, for the mayor may be able to exercise independent influence which can be used either to counteract or reinforce the power of large minority socialist groups of council members.

Table 3.15 shows that this does, indeed, seem to be the case. In municipalities where Socialist strength is the same, the party affiliation of the mayor makes a difference to school expenditures, Socialist mayors encouraging higher spending. It should be said, however, that there are relatively few Socialist mayors in communes of this size. At the same time it is also clear, when looking at the figures in the top row of the table that the problem is quite complex. Further research which goes deeper into the role of the mayor might therefore produce some interesting results.

Table 3.15 *Mayor's political affiliation and school expenditure in munici-*
palities with 10–19 999 inhabitants (Dkr. per 6 to 17 years old

	Socialist strength				
	<37%	37–50%	>50%	Average	N
Socialist mayor	4375	4136	3455	3750	17
Non-socialist mayor	3369	3724	–	3464	49
Average	3397	3854	3455	3537	

Conclusion

In this chapter municipal expenditures in Denmark has been discussed in order to show the importance of the local political system, the starting point of the analyses being the popular argument that local politics does not matter. Three types of expenditure: social welfare, road, and primary school expenditure, have been discussed. Throughout this chapter Socialist strength has been used as the most important political variable, but in addition, the party affiliation of the mayor has also been used as a political variable. It has been suggested that different combinations of party strength and the political affiliations of the mayors may produce different outputs in local councils.

The results of the analysis show that local politics does matter. This is especially true when looking at disaggregated expenditure instead of total expenditure. Thus social welfare expenditure was disaggregated to expenditure categories over which local councils have some autonomous control. Further research might disaggregate other service expenditures in similar ways. Another possibility would be to analyse sectors with a comparatively high degree of local self-determination, such as libraries and culture; as does Hansen in chapter 2.

Two output measures have been employed in the analyses: expenditure level and expenditure priority. Both of these are financial measures, and future research might also include other kinds of output measures, such as pupil-teacher ratios, pupils per classroom, number of places available in old-people's homes, and the like. In some instances, the proportion of the total budget consumed by a specific service is a useful output measure. It does, however, suffer from two limitations. First, the priority given to any specific service is influenced indirectly by expenditure on other services, so that the full range of services should be analysed, in theory. Secondly, as Figure 3.3 illustrates, it is not possible to make any direct comparisons of expenditure per pupil, and education expenditure as a proportion of the total budget.

As mentioned above a limited number of political variables have been used in these analyses. The need for further research on the role of the mayor has been mentioned, and others have recommended a number of alternative political variables,[11] to which may be added grassroots and community organizations, as well as the environmentalist groups which have recently risen to prominence. In general, there is every reason to continue to investigate the role of politics in local government, so far as these results for Denmark are concerned.

Notes

1. F. Bruun and C.-J. Skovsgaard, 'Local Determinants and Central Control of Municipal Finance: The affluent Local Authorities of Denmark' in L.J. Sharpe (ed.), *The Local Fiscal Crisis in Western Europe: Myths and Realities* (London, Sage, 1981, forthcoming).
2. *Statens refusioner af kommunernes udgifter. Betænkning nr. 471* (Copenhagen, Statens trykningskontor, 1968), 16.
3. All data is drawn from a municipal data bank at the Institute of Political Science, University of Aarhus, if no other source is given.
4. Similar trends are found in other countries in Western Europe, see K. Newton, *et. al., Balancing the Books* (London, Sage, 1980), 159–83.
5. Bruun and Skovsgaard, op. cit.
6. This way of setting up the model was originally inspired by N. Boaden, *Urban Policy-Making* (Cambridge, Cambridge University Press, 1977).
7. C.-J. Skovsgaard, *et. al., Studier i dansk kommunalpolitik* (Aarhus, Forlaget Politica, 1978), 114–16.
8. U. Thomassen, *Kommunernes ældreomsorgspolitik* (Aarhus, Institut for Statskundskab, 1978) is a local-government output study of municipal expenditure for the aged.
9. P.E. Mouritzen, *Byrdefordelingsreformen* (Aarhus, Institut for Statskundskab, 1976) is a local-government output study of municipal road expenditure.
10. C.-J. Skovsgaard, *Kommunestørrelse og effektiv serviceydelse* (Aarhus, Institut for Statskundskab, 1974) is a local-government output study of municipal primary-school expenditure.
11. K. Newton and L.J. Sharpe, 'Local Output Research: Some Reflections and Proposals', *Policy and Politics*, 5 (1977), 61–82.

4   ECONOMICS, POLITICS, AND POLICY IN NORWEGIAN URBAN COMMUNES

STEIN KUHNLE

Initial Questions

What factors account for variations in the expenditure profiles of Norwegian urban municipalities? Does the political composition of town councils have a significant effect on the scope of economic activity, or on levels of expenditure for educational and social welfare purposes? How is level of economic development related to municipal economic activity and expenditure patterns — in general, and when controlling for political composition?

These questions have been asked and tentatively answered in a number of studies in various national contexts.[1] As a rule, analysis has been of a synchronic design: many units compared at one point in time. In our inquiry, we compare data for two timepoints, 1962 and 1966, thus contributing to a dynamic perspective on two main questions: in which urban settings are changes in the political composition of town councils most likely to occur, and how do changes in political composition from one election period to the next affect economic activity and policy orientation?

Norwegian studies of municipal expenditures

Studies of policy processes and policy outputs in the US during the 1960s spurred parallel efforts in Norway, and over the last 10 years, a number of studies of policies or policy-outputs at all administrative levels — municipality, province, and nation — have materialized.

The first analysis of variations in municipal expenditures in Norway appeared in 1967 when Eldrid Nordbø compared local efforts in the social sector and found, as in many other studies that urbanization and level of economic development appeared to be more crucial explanatory variables than the political composition of the local-government councils.[2] A study of data from 1966 and 1970 confirmed the basic finding of Nordbø's analysis, but also indicated a somewhat more active social policy in municipalities run by socialist majorities.[3] J. E. Kolberg also undertook a major review of social welfare payments across regions and types of communes, and found gross variations,[4] while a highly sophisticated model for the analysis of budgetary policies in an urban setting has been suggested and tested on the case of Oslo.[5] A most promising and interesting approach to the study of municipal expenditures has also been published by F. Kjellberg and T. Hansen.[6] Starting with a four-fold typology of local activities based upon degree of autonomy (from central authorities) in terms of the definition of *goals* and of the control over *means*, they found that areas in which local authorities enjoy some degree of autonomy from central control are the social sector and the educational sector. Their analysis of budget data from 1966 for all municipalities showed that resource variables best explained levels of expenditures in all sectors, but they were also able to point to a strong positive relationship between socialist votes and social expenditures, as well as a weak independent effect of socialist votes on educational expenditures.

The first important *historical* study of change in policy outputs at the local level was recently completed by Terje Sande.[7] This study covers a period (1913-23) of explosive growth, and substantial variations in local expenditures which was also the time of entry of the Labour Party into Norwegian local politics.[8] Sande concluded that the Labour Party seemed to have been an important initiator and supporter of local public-sector growth, since strength of the party is consistently related to high levels of taxation. But he also found variations in both resource and in spatial location to be important explanatory variables. Expansion in local expenditures was also related to rapid economic growth.

Studies of local budget data in Norway were further encouraged by the establishment of the Norwegian Social Science Data Services in 1975; a large file, rich with information on all municipalities, has been built up and is continuously updated.[9] The data file is available for computer analysis at all four university sites in Norway, and a number of established scholars and graduate students are exploiting its potential. The present inquiry is based on this file and represents the first analysis concentrating on the *urban* municipalities as a distinct subset of all municipalities. The extent to which patterns of local activity and policy outputs differ in Norwegian urban and rural settings is not examined here, but some of the results may be compared with Kjellberg and Hansen's study of all municipalities. A hypothesis to guide such a comparison might be that such urban-rural differences are less pronounced in Norway than in larger European nations.

A conceptual scheme

Kjellberg and Hansen discuss a proposition raised by many local politicians, namely that local self-government has been reduced to such an extent that local authorities are now no more than subordinate branches of central government. Possibly it can be shown that municipalities have grown less and less autonomous in recent decades vis a vis the central government. In part this may be because national authorities — government, legislature,

and bureaucracy — often set common standards of policies for all municipalities, thereby binding substantial proportions of the revenues at the
disposal of municipal councils. Limits on local taxation policies are also
set by central government. But, on the other hand the simple fact that
observable differences in expenditure patterns do exist between local
units may also be used to sustain the view that some leeway for autonomous local initiatives is available.[10] The analysis in this paper rests on this
assumption, and focuses on two of the sectors that Kjellberg and Hansen
found to be relatively autonomous: education and social welfare.

Let us spell out our basic propositions about the relationships between
level of economic development, economic activity and policy orientation,
and the political composition of town councils, in both a static and a
dynamic perspective. Relative level of economic development is conceived
to be a fundamental factor accounting for variations in scope of municipal
economic activity and expenditure profiles.[11] Municipal revenues per
capita are used as an indicator of level of economic development — possibly
more correctly called level of economic wealth. This indicator might seem
to be one of local tax effort, but since the tax rate on personal income
varies little between towns,[12] and since direct-income taxes make up most
of the revenues, it can be justified as an indicator of level of economic
development.

The richer the town, the more it can spend on public, collective goods,
and the more it can spend on purposes for which there is a great demand
and widespread support among its electorate. Presumably, education,
social welfare — at least certain aspects of welfare policy — and health
investments are targets of high priority; the more active the economy, i.e.
the more investments per capita, or the proportionally larger the investments, the higher the level of economic development is likely to be at a
later point in time, thus constituting a positive-feedback loop, though it
is not suggested that *all* public (or private) investments have positive
effects on the economy. There are likely to be variations in levels of municipal economic activity and in policy priorities and outputs, however,
holding level of economic development constant. In the 1960s in Norway
these variations were unlikely to be large: among other things, the
generally high level of prosperity and the development and consolidation
of the modern welfare state are thought to have brought about a high
degree of political consensus during this time period compared, for
example, with the period before the Second World War, or further back
in time.

To account for such variations as did exist in economic activity and
policy orientation, indicators of the political composition of local councils
can be introduced. First of all, a distinction can be drawn between towns
with an absolute Labour Party majority, and towns run by either a coalition
of non-socialist parties, or a coalition of the Labour Party and Socialist
People's Party and/or the Communist Party. As an alternative indicator,

the percentage of Labour Party representatives on the council can be used. These indicators are different from that used by Kjellberg and Hansen, in that stress is laid on majority constellations in the town councils, not on the proportion of votes for socialist parties. Another difference is that while Kjellberg and Hansen used the socialist/non-socialist distinction, we shall resort to the Labour Party/non-Labour Party division. The major reason for this is that among urban municipalities during the period 1959–63, only three out of forty-seven towns had non-socialist majorities.[13]

The split between Labour and non-Labour may also be justified on theoretical grounds. One might expect town councils with absolute Labour Party majorities to favour greater total public economic activity, and to spend relatively more on education and social welfare than towns with some kind of socialist or non-socialist coalition. The rationale for this proposition is that the Labour Party — nationally and locally — is supposedly more favourable towards public economic activity and redistributive policies, and an absolute majority (as L. J. Sharpe suggests in Chapter 1) would provide the party with the political control and stability necessary for the implementation of its programme. A coalition of socialist parties would also presumably favour public economic activity, but it might be hypothesized that such a constellation would generate more conflict over policies and budget decisions than a Labour Party with an absolute majority. In a situation where the Labour Party had to rely on support from other parties, policy-making is likely to be more unpredictable, because majorities would tend to differ from issue to issue, and 'horse-trading' would enter to a larger degree than under one-party rule.

Although party platforms and programmes have not been studies in this context, the rationale for this proposition is not very different from those of other studies of this kind, and is based on an everyday conception of the ideological differences between social democratic (and socialist) and non-socialist parties. It may well be that such differences should not be taken for granted, or at least that differences have become so marginal in modern times as to leave the distinction blurred. It may also be that parties may differ in terms of intent, but not in terms of practical politics, or maybe splits other than those between socialist vs non-socialist or Labour vs non-Labour would be more revealing. None of these questions can be satisfactorily answered in this essay, and the following analysis should be considered as a first step, with indicators of party differences that are adequate for their present purposes.

Figure 4.1 lays out in simple terms our general notion of the dynamic relationships between economic development, economic activity and policy orientation, and the political composition of decision-making bodies. Though no data on voter perceptions are furnished here, the diagram suggests how changes in political compositions may come about. Voters are more likely to respond by voting for another party or coalition

Level   Voter perception of,
of economic   and satisfaction with,
development   political performance
(wealth)

Municipal economic   Political composition
activity and   of town council
policy
orientation   marginal
                           effect

Fig. 4.1.   *A simple conceptual model of factors influencing economic
            activity and policy orientation*

at the next election when economic activity is low in absolute terms, or
lower than expected — i.e. low relative to other towns, or the town's total
resources and potential. A change in the political composition of the town
council is expected either when:

(1)   level of economic development is relatively low, thus resulting in low
      economic activity, or
(2)   level of economic development is relatively high, but economic
      activity is relatively low.

In the first instance change comes about because the means for economic
activity are lacking (for either economic or political reasons) and in the
second instance, because the means are present, but not used 'properly' —
for some political reason.

Just as changes in political composition are more likely to occur in
towns rating relatively poor on output measures, changes in political
compositions are likely to be followed by relatively large positive changes
in output measures.

Indicators, data and some limitations

The indicators and variables included in the analysis are explicated in
Table 4.1. To some extent, data availability has guided the selection of
variables. We have worked with a few, simple indicators of level of economic development, local public economic activity, policy output priorities,
political composition, and change/stability of political composition from
one election period to the next. Municipal elections were held in 1959

Table 4.1   *Overview of indicators and variables used in the analysis*

Indicators	Variables	Years covered	Name of variables in text and tables
Level of economic development (wealth)	Municipal revenues per capita, N kr.	1962, 1966	Revenues per capita 1962, 1966
Level of economic activity	Total municipal investments per capita, Nkr.	1962, 1966	Investments per capita 1962, 1966
	investments as a proportion of total municipal expenditures	1962, 1966	Investment proportion 1962, 1966
Policy orientation (policy output pattern)	Proportion of investments for educational purposes	1962, 1966	Education investment 1962, 1966
	Proportion of total expenditures for social welfare purposes*	1966	Social expenditures 1966
	Proportion of social welfare expenditures for social aid*	1966	Social aid expenditures 1966
	Proportion of total investments for the health sector*	1966	Health investment 1966
Political composition of town	Labour representatives as a proportion of all representatives	1959–1963 1963–1967	Percentage Labour Party representatives 1959–63, 1963–67
	Dummy: code 1: The Labour Party has an absolute majority on the town council	1959–1963 1963–1967	Labour Party majority 1959–63=1, 1963–67=1

Table 4.1 *(contd)*

Indicators	Variables	Years covered	Name of variables in text and tables
Stability and change in political composition	*Dummy:* code 1: change from an absolute Labour majority to a Labour minority on the town council or vice versa	1959–1967	Political change either way
	Four-way split[†]	1959–1967	Political change:
	(a) towns which change from a Labour to a non-Labour absolute majority;		from Labour to non-Labour majority
	(b) towns which change from a non-Labour majority to a Labour majority		from non-Labour to Labour majority
	(c) towns with a stable non-Labour majority;		stable non-Labour majority
	(d) towns with a stable Labour majority.		stable Labour majority

Note: The variables listed as 'dummy' variables are also used to define various sub-sets of towns, in tabular analysis.

* Comparable data not available for 1962.
† By 'Labour Party majority' is meant absolute majority.

and in 1963. All budget data are from 1962 and 1966, which, within each of the election periods, make up the third, of the span of four, budget years. The rationale for selecting these particular years is that if any effect of political composition or political change is to be found at all, such effects are likely to be detected within three years of the take-over of power.

In our conceptual scheme, as well as in our selection of variables, indicators of *needs* for investments or for expenditures of certain kinds are lacking. The concept of need is problematic, not simply because of the difficulties of aggregating individual needs to community needs,[14] but because the definition of need varies according to time and context, and one can easily — although not necessarily — run the danger of tautological arguments of proof for a hypothesis.

A factor which has not been controlled for is the proportion of social welfare expenditures which are fixed from one year to another as a consequence of established institutional arrangements. Large shares of local social welfare expenditures are transfers to the national insurance and pension scheme in accordance with regulations established by national legislation.

In the educational sector, size of investments may vary from one year to another depending upon the year in which a comprehensive school system was introduced. To overcome this problem a useful measure would have been average level of investments over 4-year periods. Unfortunately these data were not available. A further possible source of misinterpretation is a general one in this kind of study, namely that the budget years selected are not 'representative' for the whole period under study. Until data bases are more complete, this is a problem we will have to live with, although we have no reasons for believing that the selected years are atypical. In spite of these problems, and the range of possible interpretations of the results of the analysis, the present study should add to our knowledge about variations in municipal economic activity and expenditure patterns in Norway for four main reasons:

(1)   for the first time, focus is exclusively on the urban municipalities
(2)   the time period 1959-66 (1962-6) has not been studied in the manner proposed
(3)   the whole set of political indicators used has not been employed before
(4)   the study focuses not only on variations at one point in time, but consideration is also given to factors causing changes in political composition, and the effects of political change and stability on policy output patterns.

Analysis

Economic development, economic activity, and politics

Correlational analysis confirmed our expectation that total economic activity — as measured by investments per capita — would be strongly and positively correlated with level of economic development. Table 4.2 shows the significant correlation coefficients between per capita revenues and per capita investments. To show that these relationships hold, whatever the political characteristics, coefficients for various subsets of towns are

Table 4.2. *Pearsonian correlation coefficients between revenues per capita and investments per capita: All towns and subsets of towns by political characteristics*

All towns (N = 47)		Investments per capita 1962	Investments per capita 1962
Revenues per capita 1962		0.86*	0.55*
Revenues per capita 1966		0.72*	0.78*
Subsets of towns			
Stable non-Labour	1962	0.91*	0.42*
majorities (N = 20)	1966	0.86*	0.74*
Stable Labour	1962	0.83*	0.69*
majorities (N = 18)	1966	0.63*	0.86*
Towns with political	1962	0.74*	0.79*
change either way	1966	0.54*	0.83*
(N = 8)			

* Significant at the 0.05 level.

also given. The other indicator of economic activity — investments as a proportion of municipal expenditures — was less clearly related to level of economic development. The towns which changed their political composition in the 1963 election, however, show a distinct pattern: the Pearson correlation coefficient between revenues in 1962 and investment proportion in 1966 is 0.46, and between revenues in 1966 and investment proportion in 1966 it is 0.44. A weaker relationship between revenues and investment proportion in 1966 (r = 0.39) was found for towns with a stable Labour majority, while no consistent pattern at all could be observed in towns with stable non-Labour majorities (r = 0.11). This could indicate that change in political composition over time as well as political composition at a given point in time have a bearing on scope of economic activity. In other words it is not sufficient to know level of economic development in order to predict the proportion of total expenditures used for investments, but level of economic development is a good predictor of total per capita investment.

Level of economic development, policy orientation, and politics.

The proposition relating level of economic development and policy orientation is not conclusively supported in this section of the paper. While health investments and social aid expenditures tend to be positively related to level of economic development, the opposite tendency is true of social-sector spending, and no distinct tendency at all is apparent for education investment figures.

In an effort to test the proposition that towns with Labour Party majorities spend relatively more than other towns in these three policy areas, we applied simple multiple regression equations, with economic activity and policy output variables as the dependent variables, and with level of economic development, political composition, and change in political composition as the independent variables. The analysis did not suggest any clear-cut patterns of the type hypothesized. Generally, the political indicators turned out to be of only marginal importance for the policy output variables. One-way analysis of variance on towns with the different political characteristics indicated some differences, but F-values significant at the 0.05 level were not discovered. It is worth reporting some of the empirical results, however, in spite of the weakness of many of the statistical relationships.

Health Investments
The proportion of investments for health purposes was found to be positively correlated with level of economic development. The correlation between revenues per capita in 1962 and health investments in 1966 is 0.44*[15] and between revenues in 1966 and health investments in 1966, is 0.35*. For various subsets of towns, positive correlations were most marked in towns with stable non-Labour majorities: revenues 1962 and health investments 1966: $r = 0.54$*; revenues 1966 and health investments 1966: $r = 0.58$*. For the subset of towns with a change in political composition, no significant correlation appeared, while a coefficient of 0.39 was found between revenues in 1962 and health investments in 1966 in towns with a stable Labour majority.

Social expenditures
The results did not confirm the hypothesis that the richer towns spend proportionally more. The overall correlation coefficient between revenues in 1966 and social expenditures in 1966 was -0.11. Among towns with a change in political majority in 1963, a more marked negative coefficient appeared: -0.47, and -0.58 between revenues in 1962 and social expenditures in 1966, both coefficients being almost significant at the 0.05 level. Poor towns with political change spend relatively more on social welfare purposes than rich towns with political change. Among the towns with a stable Labour Party majority, the correlation coefficient between revenues in 1966 and social expenditures in 1966 was again negative and insignificant (-0.13), while the correlation was even lower among stable non-Labour towns in 1966 ($r = -0.007$). But we found a coefficient of 0.33 between revenues in 1962 and social expenditures in 1966 in these towns.

On the other hand, social-aid expenditure as a proportion of total social expenditures present a different picture. Although no coefficients are of remarkable magnitudes, one positive and statistically significant relationships with level of economic development were found, this being the figure of 0.26* between revenues in 1962 and social-aid expenditures in 1966. In towns with a change in political majority the coefficient between revenues in 1966 and social-aid expenditure in 1966 was 0.29, and a similar strength of association between revenues in 1962 and social-aid expenditures in 1966 occurred in towns with a stable non-Labour majority (the correlation of 0.35 is almost significant at the 0.05 level). Though these relationships are weak, at least they suggest that social aid expenditure is a positive function of economic development (or wealth).

Educational investments
No general or systematic relationships between the proportion of investments for educational purposes and per capita revenues are apparent. No relationships were uncovered, moreover, for the various sub-sets of towns with different political compositions or which experienced political change.

Economic development, economic activity, and politics

As one moves from correlations between the various sets of economic variables and policy output variables to direct correlations between these variables and political indicators, the strengths of associations are considerably reduced. Of the twelve relationships between Labour representation 1959–63 and 1963–7 on the one hand, and level of economic development and level of economic activity, on the other, only one was significant — which is not very impressive. In order to shed more light on the significance of political indicators for patterns of economic activity, however, we shall present the means for the per capita measures, and for the investment and investment-proportion measures. The means are unweighted — i.e. the figures listed in Tables 4.3 and 4.4, and 4.6 and 4.7, represent the average mean for all towns within each category.[16]

Tables 4.3 and 4.4 show that towns with Labour majorities tended to be richer in 1962, than towns with a different party composition, while practically no difference is observable in 1966. The tables also show that:

(1) Towns with a change in political composition in the 1963 election had relatively low investments per capita in 1962, compared to politically stable towns. At the same time towns changing from a Labour to a non-Labour majority had conspicuously low investment proportions in 1962, while towns changing from a non-Labour to Labour majority had the highest proportions of all. The proposition that political change would occur in relatively poor towns and/or

Table 4.3   Comparison of means for indicators of level of economic development and economic activity, by political characteristics of towns

Indicators of level of economic development and economic activity	Indicators of political composition			
	Labour Party majority 1959-63 (N = 21)	Labour Party majority 1963-67 (N = 23)	Non-Labour Party majority 1959-63 (N = 26)	Non-Labour Party majority 1963-67 (N = 24)
Revenues per capita 1962	1543		1273	
Revenues 1966		2425		2407
Investments per capita 1962	418		348	
Investments per capita 1966		584		590
Investment proportion 1962	27.4		27.4	
Investment proportion 1966		23.8		24.2

towns with relatively low economic activity is not generally supported, therefore.

(2)   Towns with a Labour majority had higher investments per capita in 1962 than towns with a non-Labour majority, but this pattern was reversed in 1966.

(3)   In terms of proportion of expenditures used on investments practically no difference existed — neither in 1962 nor 1966 — between Labour and non-Labour towns.

(4)   The investment proportion dropped between 1962 and 1966 in towns which changed from non-Labour to Labour majorities in the 1963 election, but increased in towns with a political change in the opposite direction. This is contrary to our expectation about the effect of a Labour Party majority on levels of economic activity.

Table 4.4   *Comparison of means for indicators of level of economic development and activity, by characteristics of change and stability in political composition*

Indicators of level of economic development and economic activity	Indicators of stability and change in political composition			
	Stable Labour Party majority (N = 20)	*Stable non-Labour majority* (N = 20)	*Political change from Labour to non-Labour majority* (N = 3)	*Political change from non-Labour to Labour majority* (N = 6)
Revenues per capita 1962	1619	1350	1084	1017
Revenues per capita 1966	2513	2412	2370	2160
Investments per capita 1962	463	356	152	323
Investments per capita 1966	581	602	506	594
Investment proportion 1962	29.2	26.6	16.8	29.8
Investment proportion 1966	22.7	24.8	20.4	26.9

Note: The third column of figures is based on only three cases.

Policy orientation and political composition

Table 4.5 spells out the surprising fact that education investments are not related to Labour Party strength. This may be because investments vary a great deal from year to year, in which case the two budget years of 1962 and 1966 may not be representative of the whole election period. Consequently long time-series would seem necessary to assess the importance of political composition — especially for the educational investment data. One should also bear in mind that, at the national level, the Labour Party had a majority until 1965, and it was a Labour Government that introduced a trial comprehensive-school system in 1959–60, leaving the decision on the introduction of this sytem to the municipalities. It seems reasonable to assume that towns led by the Labour Party would be both more enthusiastic in bringing the reform into practice, and more loyal to

Table 4.5   Correlations between indicators of policy orientation and political composition (All towns)

	Indicators of political composition	
Indicators of policy orientation	Labour representatives 1959–63 (%)	Labour representatives 1963–67 (%)
Education investments 1962	−0.19	−0.16
Education investments 1966	−0.24	−0.05
Social expenditures 1966	0.26*	0.12
Social aid expenditures 1966	0.28*	0.18
Health investments 1966	0.20	0.18

Table 4.6   Means for indicators of policy orientation, by political characteristics of towns

	Indicators of political composition			
Indicators of policy orientation	Labour Party majority 1959–63 (N = 21)	Labour Party majority 1963–67 (N = 24)	Non-Labour Party majority 1959–63 (N = 26)	Non-Labour Party 1963–67 (N = 23)
Education investments 1962	15.1	16.8	19.6	18.3
Education investments 1966	22.2	25.4	27.8	25.1
Social expenditures 1966	17.3	16.7	15.8	16.3
Social aid expenditures 1966	11.7	11.4	8.7	8.7
Health investments 1966	2.4	2.1	1.4	1.6

political guidelines established by the national party, than towns in which the Labour Party did not enjoy absolute control. Thus investment data for each year between 1960 and 1966 would be required to make a balanced judgment on differences between towns under different party control.

On the other hand, Table 4.5 does indicate an expected relationship between Labour Party strength, social expenditures, and social aid expenditures, plus some positive but insignificant associations between Labour Party strength and health investments.

The comparison of the means of proportion of education investments, social expenditures, and health investments in towns with different political characteristics is provided in Tables 4.6 and 4.7. A striking result is that towns with non-Labour majorities consistently spent proportionally more on education than towns with Labour majorities. A tempting interpretation is simply that municipalities without Labour majorities gave priority to the educational sector during the first half of the 1960s but in the absence of information about such things as the number of schoolchildren and other demographic features, this conclusion remains uncertain. It should also be noted that the most marked increase in investments for educational purposes from 1962 to 1966 took place in towns which changed to a Labour majority in the 1963 election.

Table 4.7 *Means of indicators of policy orientation by characteristics of change and stability in political composition*

Indicators of policy orientation	Indicators of stability and change in political composition			
	Stable Labour majority (N = 18)	Stable Labour majority (N = 20)	Change from Labour to non-Labour majority (N = 3)	Change from non-Labour to Labour majority (N = 6)
Education investments 1962	15.5	19.2	12.2	20.7
Education investments 1966	23.0	26.3	17.7	32.8
Social expenditures 1966	17.1	16.0	18.2	15.3
Social aid expenditures 1966	11.9	8.4	10.6	9.9
Health investments 1966	2.6	1.7	1.1	0.4

Social welfare, social aid, and health investment data for 1966 all emphasize the distinctly different policy output profiles in towns with different political characteristics. The figures show that Labour towns spent relatively more on these services than other towns. Though the differences are not overwhelming, they are consistent for all three indicators, and the findings are in accordance with our proposition.

Finally, Table 4.8 shows the increase in revenues per capita and investments per capita from 1962 to 1966 in politically stable and changing towns. The table offers some support for the proposition that towns undergoing change in political composition increase their economic activity and improve their level of economic development.

Table 4.8   *Increase in municipal revenues per capita (Nkr) and in municipal investments per capita (Nkr), 1962 to 1966 by stability and change in political composition*

	Stable Labour Party majority (1959-67)	Stable non-Labour majority (1959-67)	Change from Labour to non-Labour majority (1963 election)	Change from non-Labour majority (1963 election)
	(N = 18)	(N = 20)	(N = 3)	(N = 6)
Increase in revenues	894	1062	1284	1143
Increase in investments	118	246	354	271

Summary and suggestions for further research

Some of our propositions are partially confirmed by this exploratory analysis, while others stubbornly refuse to comply with the empirical data. The trends uncovered among Norwegian urban municipalities in the 1960s are:

(1)   Investments per capita are strongly and positively correlated with revenues per capita.

(2)   Proportions of expenditures for health investments are positively correlated with revenues per capita.

(3)   Proportions of expenditures for social aid are weakly and positively correlated with revenues per capita.

(4)   Expenditures for social sector, social aid, and health investments are higher in towns with absolute Labour majorities.

(5) Change in political composition is more likely in relatively poor towns and in towns with a relatively low rate of economic activity.

(6) Expenditures for health investments correlated positively with political stability. Total economic activity correlates positively with the strength of Labour Party representation in 1962, but not in 1966.

(7) Towns experiencing a change in political composition in the 1963 election show the most marked increase in economic activity — as well as in revenues per capita — between 1962 and 1966.

(8) Expenditures on education were higher in towns in which the Labour Party did *not* hold absolute power.

(9) Expenditures on the social sector correlate negatively with revenues per capita.

More refined analysis, using more variables and path analytical models, may place political indicators in a different perspective, producing stronger relationships, and a better account of differences in policy output patterns. But as Tables 4.6–4.8 show, the differences between towns with different political characteristics are *not dramatic*. This is perhaps because the political climate in Norway in the 1960s was rather placid. One might also speculate that a *high degree of consensus* between contenders for political power had developed, not only about the scope of public activity but also about policy priorities. The 1960s — half a generation after a devastating war — marked a period of mature, consolidated economic growth in a country already highly industrialized, and steadily preparing for decisive steps to bring about the transformation of the country into a fully-fledged, modern welfare state.

A working hypothesis could be that politics play a vital role in certain crucial periods — for example, in periods of fundamental changes in local administration, periods when new parties emerge, or when new issues are raised by parties or pressure groups at the national level. It may be that over the past 10–12 years, we have witnessed a trend in which political issues are raised to a greater extent than before outside popularly elected assemblies — by pressure groups, bureaucracies, or the mass-media.[17] Parties will most probably differ in ability (and willingness) to adopt new issues introduced in the political arena, and in a period of embryonic growth of the party system; this may result in measurable differences in policy orientation.

When interpreting similarities and variations in levels of economic activity and policy orientation at the local level, we should probably also take into consideration the political composition at the national level, and its changes over time.[18] The greater the stability at the national level, the greater the tendency may be for convergence in policy orientation among political contenders at lower decision-making levels, because important principles and 'rules' of public activity are defined and implemented at the national level in such a way as to make both a direct and indirect effect on municipal policy-making.

A final word on research design. It is both necessary and valuable to combine this type of quantitative, aggregate study with survey research at the mass and the elite levels, and with more qualitatively oriented studies of law texts and public documents. Else Øyen, for example, has carried out a detailed study of how new social legislation and principles of social care are interpreted and put into practice by members of social services committees in Norwegian municipalities.[19] This kind of work is important for understanding the processes of ideology formation, ideology diffusion, and ideology maintenance, and thus furnishes us with knowledge about the basis and principles on which policies and decisions are concerned and implemented. The study of such processes over time can also equip us with insights about how ideologies are developed and sustained within various settings.

The other useful study is that carried out by Johan P. Olsen on budgetary behaviour in one Norwegian municipality.[20] Based on detailed interviews with elected representatives on the municipal council, Olsen concludes that important parts of the budgetary process can be understood as ritual rather than decision-making. His study indicates that the majority party on a municipal council is probably less important than the pattern of negotiations between the local administration and council members. But has budgetary behaviour always been a ritual? Is it more of a ritual in periods of economic progress? And can the spread of knowledge about the budgetary process as a ritual lead to a repoliticization of the process? What forces turn the budgetary process into a ritual and back again? Many questions remain to be answered — and the Olsen study provides an excellent background against which to place further inquiries of municipal economic and political activity.

Notes

1. For an overview, see L. J. Sharpe, Chapter 1 this volume. See also Robert C. Fried, 'Comparative Urban Performance', in Fred. I Greenstein and Nelson W. Polsby (eds.), *Handbook of Political Science* (Reading, Mass., Addison Wesley, 1975), vol. 6, 305–81.
2. Eldrid Nordbø, *Kommunenes ytelser i sosialsektoren* (mag. art. thesis, Institute of Political Science, 1967, mimeo).
3. Arvid Viken, *En analyse av variasjoner: kommunale sosialytelser* (Cand. polit. thesis, Institute of Political Science, Oslo 1974, mimeo).
4. Jon Eyvind Kolberg, *TrygdeNorge* (Oslo, Gyldendal, 1974).
5. Andrew Cowart, Tore Hansen and Karl-Erik Brofoss, 'Budgetary Strategies and Success at Multiple Decision Levels in the Norwegian Urban setting', *American Political Science Review*, 69 (1975), 543–58.
6. Francesco Kjellberg and Tore Hansen, 'Municipal Expenditures in Norway: Autonomy and Constraints in Local Government Activity', *Policy and Politics*, 4 (1976), 25–50.

7. The Norwegian Labour Party is equivalent to the Social Democratic Parties of Denmark, Finland, Germany, and Sweden, and to the Labour Party in Britain.

8. Terje Sande, *A decade of Local Government Boom, Norway 1913-1923* (Cand. polit. thesis, Institute of Sociology, Bergen, 1976, mimeo.)

9. The Norwegian Social Science Data Services was established, and is financed, by the Norwegian Research Council for Science and the Humanities. For an overview of data holdings and services, see Stein Rokkan and Bjørn Henrichsen, 'The Norwegian Social Science Data Service, *Research in Norway 1976* (Oslo), 11-15. For a description of the data file used for this analysis, see Bjørn Henrichsen and Stein Rokkan, *Kommunedatabanken: en handbok for brukere* (Norwegian Social Science Data Service, Bergen, 1977).

10. Although local variations may alternatively be due to central-government policy of redistributing resources and equalizing services between areas. Redistribution schemes exist in Norway, indicating central-government control of local expenditures, but with reference to the study by Kjellberg and Hansen, op. cit. local variations in expenditure patterns in some policy fields more than others may be considered consequences of local priority setting.

11. By 'relative' is meant relative to other municipalities at one point in time.

12. Maximum municipal tax rate is fixed by Parliament. In recent years, all municipalities have decided to adopt the legally accepted maximum rate. We have not had access to taxation data for 1962 and 1966 — the budget years analysed below. But in 1961, thirty-nine out of the forty-seven towns had a tax rate varying between 17 and 18 per cent, while seven had a rate of 16.5 per cent, and one single town a rate as low as 15.5 per cent and in 1965, thirty-five towns had the maximum rate of 19 per cent, seven towns had the rate 18.5 per cent, four towns 18 per cent and one town a rate of 17.5 per cent. Since variations in tax rates are fairly small, and since it is difficult to arrive at one single, good indicator, we have decided to settle for municipal revenues as an (indirect) indicator of level of economic development.

13. Fifty-eight towns and communes with a town status existed in the period 1959-63, while only forty-seven existed in the period 1963-7 due to changes in the town-definition and administrative status of some communes. In this analysis, the forty-seven units have been used as basis throughout the period 1959-67. Also, the size of population changes occurring as a result of boundary changes has been taken into account, such that a transfer of 10 per cent or less of a population from one commune to another has been accepted. Larger transfers would have given us missing data on a number of variables.

14. Kjellberg and Hansen, op. cit., have made attempts to develop indicators of needs, and suggest, among others: industrialization, population size, population density, proportion of old people, unemployment, level of education, average income.

15. The asterisk will mark, throughout, all correlation coefficients which are statistically significant at least at the 0.05 level. No asterisk will indicate that the coefficient is not significant at the 0.05 level.

16. A *weighted* measure would be (for example): the aggregate revenues for all towns of a special political characteristic divided by the aggregate population of the same towns. Though this might be an interesting control measure, it would not be very meaningful for this analysis.

17. A similar point is suggested by M. Aiken and M. Depre in chapter 5 in this volume.

18. This is also suggested by Ken Newton and Jim Sharpe, 'Local Outputs Research', *Policy and Politics*, 5 (1977), 75.

19. Else Øyen, *Sosialomsorgen og dens forvaltere* (Oslo, Universitetsforlaget, 1974).

20. Johan P. Olsen, 'Local Budgeting, Decision-Making or a Ritual Act?', *Scandinavian Political Studies*, 5 (1970).

SECTION 2

URBAN SYSTEMS AND PUBLIC SERVICES

5 THE URBAN SYSTEM, POLITICS, AND POLICY IN BELGIAN CITIES

MICHAEL AIKEN and ROGER DEPRE

The Problem

Increasing attention has been given in recent years to questions of public policy analysis in comparative urban studies – how policies are formulated, the nature of the service delivery systems through which they are distributed, and their impact on, and consequences for, target populations. The emphasis in comparative studies of local politics seems to have shifted from a concern with the form of power to its consequences. While much research in the US in the 1950s and 1960s was concerned with the more informal aspects of urban political systems,[1] comparative research in the 1970s was more concerned with the mechanisms through which policies are generated and applied, meaning that the role of local governmental instrumentalities has become a critical focus of an increasing number of studies.[2]

The model often used in policy research is that resources, conceived as inputs, are transformed into outputs through authoritative decisions and actions and are distributed to consumer units within a system.

Without readily accessible measures of services and their quantity, quality, and extent, much policy-oriented research at the local level has used expenditures for various functional categories as a surrogate. In attempting to account for variations in expenditure patterns among cities, a 'resource' or 'environmental' model is often juxtaposed against a political one.[3] With a few exceptions, research on local government expenditures, both in the US and in a number of European nations, has shown that political variables are not the most important determinants of expenditures.[4] Until a few years ago, most studies, except for some in England, had found that political variables had little or no influence on public policies of local governments, leading at least one student of this subject to ponder the role of politics.[5] His conclusion may have been premature, however, in the light of some recent studies in France, Italy, Denmark, Norway, and Sweden, showing that Social Democratic or left-wing control of local government results in higher levels of expenditures and services.[6]

The exact way in which environmental or resource attributes of cities affect policy formulation, services, and their delivery is often not satisfactorily explained, however. Further, many studies have not used measures of political process that would best show the influence of politics on policy, and few investigators have been sensitive to historical change and its effect on politics and policy formulation.

In this paper we address part of this general question of determinants and correlates of local government expenditures among 196 Belgian cities. We attempt to avoid the weaknesses we have noted in some previous studies by developing a framework for understanding the ways in which environmental factors are transformed into public policies, by examining how population change of cities has historically affected public policy formulation, and by devising several detailed measures of the political process and examining how these affect public policy outputs. Our major concern will be to determine the exact role of politics on public policy and how politics compares with 'environmental' or 'resource' factors in affecting public policies.

Hypotheses

The Urban System

The cities in a nation-state are conceived here as consisting of an interdependent network of economic units. We refer to this interdependent network as the *urban system*. The concept of the urban system, which has become an increasingly important one in recent years, reflects an image of interdependencies and linkages among the urban units within a nation-state.[7] The territory of the Belgian nation-state, like most European nations, is divided into relatively autonomous, self-governing communal units. In 1970 there were 2 585 of these communal units, although there are now less than 500 because of fusions of communes during the mid-1970s. While Belgian municipalities generally have the same political status, they are by no means equal in terms of the ecological and economic functions they perform in the urban system. Some cities have concentrated within their borders the headquarters of the largest economic and financial institutions of the nation-state while others are the location of the administrative bureaucracies of the national and provincial governments; some are the location of major productive forces of the economy; others are centres of consumption and cities that offer and distribute goods and services on a national and regional basis; still others are less central to the economic life of the nation-state and have a more dependent status such as bedroom communities or outlying retail centres. Hence, the urban system can be conceived as an essentially hierarchically organized, interdependent network of cities.

There are two ways in which cities in the urban system can be hierarchically ranked to reflect their centrality in the urban system: the first is primarily a regional ranking while the second is primarily a national ranking. The first aspect of centrality is derived from central place and human ecological theory.[8] In this perspective cities are considered to be service-rendering units which vary in terms of the extensiveness of services offered as well as in the area over which they offer these services. A nation-state is conceived in terms of a set of regions, each with a centre providing the most highly specialized and greatest range of services. Other cities within a given region can be ranked in terms of their dependence on this central city of the region as well as in terms of their own degree of centrality and influence over cities in sub-regions of the larger region. We use the concept of *ecological centrality* to reflect the degree to which cities are central to a region of the nation-state in terms of providing services of consumption and production. The conceptualization here emphasizes the ranking of cities in terms of their service-rendering activities, but does not make any assumption about symmetrical spatial manifestations of this ranking such as some central place theorists have made.

In considering the functions of local governments in general, and specifically those in Belgium, and how these relate to the phenomenon of ecological centrality, we start with the assumption mentioned above that local governments provide three critical kinds of functions:

(1) *co-ordination* of diverse units and activities within its borders;
(2) *social control* of units and persons under its jurisdiction; and
(3) the *provision of a range of basic services* to clients and consuming units — citizens, businesses, organizations, and other entities — under its jurisdiction.

We further assume that the greater the degree of ecological centrality of a city, the greater will be problems of co-ordination, social control, and need for basic services with which political decision makers in local government must contend. Beyond simply servicing its resident or night-time population, cities with a high degree of ecological centrality must also provide co-ordination, social control, and other services for a daytime population commuting to it for purposes of work or consumption.[9] A considerable part of the expenditures of local governments is for the provision of such services, either directly or indirectly. Hence, a further assumption is that local governments are likely to vary considerably in their expenditures because of variations in the degree of ecological centrality. In cities where problems of co-ordination, social control, and need for basic services are greatest, expenditure patterns will be highest; in cities where these problems are less acute, expenditures will be comparatively less. Following our assumption that the need for such services will be highest in cities with a high degree of ecological centrality, we hypothesize:

Hypothesis 1: *The greater the degree of ecological centrality of a city, the greater will be the expenditures by the local government of the city*

While ecological centrality reflects centrality within regions, the second type of centrality of the urban system reflects the ranking of a central city and its metropolitan region in terms of the degree to which the dominant economic activities of the nation-state are located within its borders. Specifically, we are concerned with the degree to which the headquarters of the largest multi-local organizations — corporations, banks, and other financial institutions — are located in cities within the urban system.[10] Pred has suggested that regional inequalities are to a great extent a function of the assymmetry in the location of the headquarters of the largest economic institutions in a nation-state, and he has given an explanation as to why this assymmetry persists. Drawing on organizational theory, he suggests that locational decisions by top economic institutions are made in the context of the information that is available to decision makers.

While Pred's argument is more extensive than this, we extrapolate from his reasoning to suggest some implications of the second type of centrality in the urban system — the degree to which the top financial and economic organizations of a nation state are located within a city. Such activities are typically concentrated in a few cities, although there is some variation among nation-states in the degree of this concentration.[11] We use the concept of economic concentration to refer to this second type of centrality, and we define *economic concentration* as the degree to which the control function (headquarters) of the largest multi-local economic organizations are concentrated within a city.

We assume that problems of co-ordination, social control, and need for basic services are also likely to be greater in cities in which the largest economic and financial institutions of the nation-state are concentrated. Such cities have a disproportionately large number of high-status managers and other personnel who are likely to make demands of specialized services on the central city of the metropolitan area. In addition, these large economic organizations themselves are likely to place additional demands for services on local government. The environment of local governments of such cities then is more complex and presents more problems of co-ordination and social control. This means that expenditures by a local government are likely to be greater, leading to our second hypothesis:

Hypothesis 2 :   *The greater the degree to which a city is economically dominant in the urban system, the greater will be the expenditures by the local government of the city.*

Social Class

The social composition of a city is also expected to have an effect on expenditure patterns of local governments. Cities with more high-status citizens are likely to have greater demands placed on local government for a variety of specialized services than are cities with fewer higher-status citizens. This is particularly true in a nation-state like Belgium where the central cities of the very largest metropolitan centres are disproportionately high-status cities, unlike the American pattern. Cities with many high-status citizens are likely to provide a variety of specialized services such as libraries, museums, and artistic activities, and the like, with the result that the expenditures of local government are likely to be greater. The third hypothesis, therefore is:

Hypothesis 3: *The higher the social status of the citizens of a city, the greater will be the expenditures by the local government of the city.*

Political Competition

The form of the political process in a city is also expected to be a key factor in explaining expenditure patterns, especially for politically sensitive categories of expenditures such as public assistance, public education, and religion. Form refers to the degree of political competition in the city. Specifically, it implies that there is a diversity of political parties or groups in the city; that voting strength is relatively dispersed among these parties or groups; that no single party has sufficient seats on the city council to dominate the executive committee, meaning that a coalition controls the committee; and that there is considerable turnover in the parties or groups controlling the executive committee.[12] To the extent that a city has a diversified, competitive, dispersed, and unstable political system, we assume that a city will have greater social, economic, and political cleavages. There are the basic cleavages of class, religion, and language in Belgium and these are reflected in various political parties and groups. We assume further that these pressure groups make demands on the city government, and that those in control of local government are likely to develop a wide range of programmes and services in an attempt to mollify such pressure groups. This chain of reasoning leads to our fourth hypothesis:

Hypothesis 4: *The higher the degree of political competition in a city, the greater will be the expenditure by the local government of the city.*

We would expect that this hypothesis will be most highly supported for expenditures in functional categories.

Ideological Orientation of the Dominant Party

As discussed at the outset, the content of the political process is expected to be another important factor in explaining expenditure patterns. By *content*, we mean the ideological orientation of the party controlling the local government, which in the Belgian case is the executive committee.

Either the Catholic Party or the Socialist Party was disproportionately successful in holding majority control of the executive committees of the cities included in this analysis, and a proper understanding of the argument here requires some discussion of the historical origin and ideology of these two dominant parties.[13]

With the enfranchisement of the working classes in 1893, the leaders of the Belgian Workers' Party (Parti Ouvrier Belge (POB)), now the Socialist Party, saw the conquest of local government as a means to establish political bases in their fight for power at the national level. They reasoned that they would follow the same strategy to gain power at the national level that was used by the bourgeoisie when the nation was occupied by foreign powers prior to independence in 1830.[14]

Hence it was in the city halls that the working classes would prepare its emancipation from the bourgeoisie.[15] Even before it had a significant foothold in local governments, the POB programme displayed a significant commitment to using the mechanism of local government for delivering services to all citizens, and especially the working class. In the campaign of 1911, their 'minimum programme' for cities included: (a) a variety of family programmes such as free maternity care, nurseries, and orphanages; (b) educational reforms, libraries, and parent–teacher councils; (c) city public welfare programmes such as unemployment compensation, programmes to prevent and combat poverty and misery; and (d) distribution of communal services such as transportation, street lighting, water, and garbage disposal to all citizens.[16]

With the arrival of universal suffrage in 1919 and the success of the Socialists in the national parliament and their extensive victories at the local level, the implementation of social programming in city governments controlled by them was possible. Given the tendency toward stability in Socialist control of local governments, once it has taken over, as well as the tendency toward incrementalism in budget-making and expenditure patterns, we would expect Socialist controlled cities to have higher expenditures than other cities. This chain of reasoning leads to our fifth hypothesis:

Hypothesis 5:   *The greater the degree of Socialist control of the local government of a city, the higher will be the expenditures by the local government.*

We expect to find the effect of Socialist party control strongest among expenditure categories that reflect social-welfare expenditures such as public assistance and public education.

We now raise the question of how Catholic control of local government affects expenditure patterns. For several reasons, our expectation is that Catholic control of local government will be associated with lower levels of expenditures. With the arrival of the working-class social movements near the end of the nineteenth century and the success of the Socialists in recruiting workers to their ranks, the Catholic church launched a counter-offensive in an attempt to protect its members, especially workers, from the evils of the de-Christianization by the Socialists. The vehicle for this was 'Christian socialism'.[17] The result was the creation of a network of Catholic-controlled organizations such as labour unions, mutualities, welfare organizations, schools, recreational groups, and newspapers. It was to the advantage of the Catholics to keep this network of organizations outside the control of the local government since, given the vagaries of politics, it could always fall under the control of another political party. In essence, the Catholics had their own private service delivery system outside of local government. Our sixth hypothesis, therefore, is:

Hypothesis 6:　*The greater the degree of Catholic control of local govern-*
　　　　　　　　ment in a city, the lower will be the expenditures by the
　　　　　　　　local government.

Population Stagnation

The final factor which we hypothesize will have an effect on the level of expenditures is the degree of population stagnation. Between approx-imately 1830 and 1880, Belgium became an industrialized nation. During this period the industrial centre of gravity shifted from Flanders to Wallonia, and the basic industry shifted from textiles to iron and coal production. Many of these rapidly growing cities reached the apogee of their growth near the end of the nineteenth century, but with the decline in the coal and steel industries in recent decades, many cities in Wallonia have experienced population stagnation or decline.[18] In the last few decades, Flanders has experienced rapid industrialization as the conse-quence of the location of plants there by multinational corporations, although a few cities in Wallonia have also participated in this 'second' industrial revolution. The result has been rapid population growth in a number of Flemish cities, and a few Walloon ones as well.

But how does population growth or stagnation affect the level of expenditures of local governments? Our expectation is that cities that have experienced population stagnation or decline will have higher local govern-ment expenditures than cities that have experienced rapid population increase. The reasoning for this expectation is essentially political. In a highly competitive context such as is the case of Belgian cities, there is pressure for the political leadership to develop new programmes and services. Hence, even though a city may have had a stable population, its leaders would nevertheless have incentives to develop programmes and services, in hopes of retaining favour in the next election. This means increased expenditures; and if this process were to go on for some time it would mean increasing per capita expenditures. Alternatively, if cities are growing rapidly, it is likely that their needs will outstrip their ability to raise monies to meet those needs. Certainly the communal fund would be of only limited help since the formulas used there tended to favour cities with stagnant populations. We expect rapidly growing cities, therefore, to have lower expenditures. To a considerable extent, this variable of population change is a surrogate for region. Cities in the Brussels agglomeration had the least growth from 1900 to 1964, cities in Wallonia were next, and cities in Flanders had the most growth. As will be shown below, this ordering also reflects the magnitude of local government expenditures, i.e. expenditures in the Brussels agglomeration are highest and those in Flanders are lowest. This reasoning permits us to state formally our seventh hypothesis:

Hypothesis 7:   *The more a city has tended toward stagnation or decline in its population size in this century, the higher will be expenditures by local government.*

We discuss below our findings about each of these hypotheses. Before doing so, however, we first describe the various measures used in this study.

Methods and Data

This study is based on data for the 196 Belgian cities with populations of 10 000 or more on 31 December, 1968. Of the 196 cities, 116 were in Flanders, 61 in Wallonia, and 19 in the Brussels agglomeration.

Expenditure Measures

The expenditure data reported here are for the years 1965 and 1966 and were obtained from the National Institute of Statistics in Brussels. The data for the thirteen categories of expenditures were obtained for each of these 2 years, standardized by the population size of the city at the beginning of the year, and then the 2 years were averaged.

The thirteen expenditure categories are divided into five general categories for ease of interpretation:

(1)   *Administration*: general administration; pensions and social security, i.e., administration and services in the past.
(2)   *Social control*: police.
(3)   *Social welfare*: public assistance; public education.
(4)   *Other basic services*: hygiene and public health; roads and public works; municipal enterprises; real estate and city properties; art, popular education, and leisure.
(5)   *Miscellaneous*: religion; deficit; other.

Construction of the Index of Ecological Centrality

Five items are used to construct the index of ecological centrality. These were selected after extensive investigation determined that they were both related to expenditures and had face validity as measures of this concept. Each was taken from either the 1961 Census of Population or the 1961 Census of Commerce and Industry.

Central City Status
The central city status of a city was based on a study by J. A. Sporck which defined nineteen cities at first- and second-order central cities in Belgium.[19] Each of the agglomerations of which these cities were the central place had a population size of at least 30 000 and each had at least 80 000 persons in the active labour force within its zone of influence.

Employment-Residence Ratio
The employment–residence ratio is a ratio of the active population working in a city to the active population living in the city.[20] It reflects the degree to which the work force in a city is greater or less than the work force which actually resides within its boundaries. A figure of less than 1.00 means a net out-migration of workers on a daily basis, as in the case of a bedroom community; a figure greater than 1.00 reflects a net gain in the daily working population.

Percentage of the City's Labour Force in Services
Cities with a high percentage of their labour force in services are likely to be specialized service centres, or centres of consumption for territorial areas beyond their boundaries. In such cities the daily population using the facilities of the city is likely to be greater than the resident population, meaning that local government has to co-ordinate, control, and provide basic services for a population larger than its resident population. Hence, this measure is similar to the employment–residence ratio, except it refers primarily to consumption, not production, activities.

By services we mean only that part of the tertiary sector which includes recreational, personal, administrative, public, social, religious, and other such services. We have used the percentage of the active labour force living in the city rather than that working in the city because the 1961 Census of Population gives more complete information for it.[21]

Percentage of Dwelling Units that are Non-Owner Occupied
This is a measure of the metropolitan character of a city. Because of the scarcity, and consequently high price, of land in Belgium, especially in areas of high density such as metropolitan agglomerations, home owner-ship is considerably less than in more rural areas. Additionally, in the factor analysis of the five variables reflecting ecological centrality, this

measure was found to have a consistently high relationship with each of the other four.

The Number of Economic Establishments in a City
This is a measure of the degree to which a city is structurally differentiated. The greater the number of economic establishments, the greater we assume the problems of co-ordination, social control, and need for basic services to be.

These five characteristics were factor analysed using a principal components solution. The first factor extracted explained 52.9 per cent of the variance in these items; each of these five variables had a factor loading of 0.550 or higher. Subsequent factors had an eigenvalue less than 1.00, obviating any rotation procedure. The index of ecological centrality was constructed using the complete estimation method, that is, by multiplying the standardized value of each variable times its factor weight, then adding these products. The reliability of the resulting scale was established by calculating the coefficient of alpha of Cronbach, which was 0.777, meaning there was a relatively high degree of internal consistency in this scale. The validity of the scale was verified through item analysis, that is, by calculating the correlation coefficient between each item and the overall scale.[22] The item-to-total correlation coefficients between each item and the overall scale varied between 0.55 to 0.85.

Construction of the Index of Economic Concentration

Three types of data were used in constructing the index of economic concentration.

The number of headquarters of the top one hundred commercial and industrial corporations located in a city
The number of headquarters of the one hundred largest commercial and industrial corporations located in a city in 1965 and 1966 was taken from *Enterprise*, a French magazine similar to *Fortune*.[23] Since there was some variation in the data for these two dates, the average number of headquarters in 1965 and 1966 was used in constructing this index. The city of Brussels had the largest number of headquarters of such organizations with 34.5 followed by Antwerp (12.0) and then Liege (6.0).

The number of bank headquarters
There were seventy-four independent banks in Belgium in 1968 as reported by *Kompass Belgium*.[24] The measure used here is simply a count of the number of such bank's headquarters located in each city in our study. Once again Brussels had the largest number of bank headquarters with thirty-two followed by Antwerp (fourteen) and then Liege (six).

The number of headquarters of insurance companies
Kompass Belgium also reported the number of headquarters of (first-party) insurance companies in Belgium.[25] Once again Brussels had the largest number of this kind of financial institution followed by Antwerp, Ghent, Bruge and Liege.

These three items were factor analysed using a principal-components solution. The first factor extracted explained 96.6 per cent of the variance in these items; each factor had a factor loading of 0.977 or higher. Since subsequent factors did not have an eigenvalue of 1.00 or higher, no rotation was performed. The index of economic concentration was constructed using the same method as in the case of the index of ecological centrality. Cronbach's alpha was 0.991, and the correlation coefficients between each item and the overall scale was 0.98 in each instance.

The Index of High Social Class
The following measures of educational, occupational, and income characteristics of cities were used in constructing the index of high social class:

Ratio of the number of persons completing a high-school education to the population age 14 and older
This first measure reflects the degree to which the citizens of a community have a *lycee* (high school) education. It was taken from the 1961 Census of Population.

Percent of the active labour force residing in the city with high occupational status
This second measure, which was also taken from the 1961 Census of Population, reflects the percentage of the active labour force residing in a city with white collar, managerial, or professional occupations.

Median income
The third measure reflects the median income of adults residing in the city.

These three measures were also factor analysed using a principal components solution. The first factor extracted explained 62.5 per cent of the variance in these items; the second factor did not have an eigenvalue of 1.00 or higher, and hence no rotation was performed. The index of high social class was constructed using the same procedures as described above, i.e. by multiplying the standardized value of each variable times its factor weights and then adding these products. Cronbach's alpha for this scale was 0.692. The correlation coefficient between each item and the overall scale varied from a low of 0.66 in the case of occupational status to a high of 0.94 in the case of the educational measure.

Construction of the Index of Political Competition

The data used in the construction of the index of political competition, as well as the data used to measure the two indices of ideological orientation, were taken either from the files of the Minister of the Interior in Brussels or from the archives of various provinces. In a number of instances, officials of cities were questioned in order to resolve inconsistencies or ambiguities in the data. The measures included in this index are explained below.

The average number of parties or lists entering the communal elections of 1946, 1952, 1958, and 1964
The measure reflects the degree of political diversity in local elections in each city.

The Index of Political Fractionalization
This measure of political diversity was computed by using the following formula:

$$\text{Fract} = 1 - \sum_{i=1}^{k} P_i^2$$

where P_i is the proportion of votes for the ith party or list.[26] This index can theoretically vary between 0 (low political fractionalization in which a single party got all the votes) and 1.00 (high political fractionalization). The more parties in an election and the more the votes are equally divided, the higher the score. The index was computed for each city for each of the four elections between 1946 and 1964, and then the average for the four elections was computed.

The Index of Instability or Turnover in the Control and Composition of the Executive Committee
This index reflects the degree to which the control and composition of the executive committee was unstable between 1946 and 1970. In some cities the political composition of the executive committee (*college*) did not change, while in others it changed from 1946 to 1952, 1952 to 1958, and 1958 to 1964. If there was a turnover in the control and composition of the *college* for each of these periods, a city received a score of 3.0; if there was no turnover, a city received a score of 0.

The Number of Times a Coalition Ruled the Executive Committee
If a single party or list did not have enough votes on the city council to

control the executive committee, two or sometimes three parties or lists formed a coalition. The percentage of cities having two or more parties on the executive committee following the communal elections of 1946, 1952, 1958 and 1964 varied between 21 and 35 per cent, respectively. Cities were coded 1 for presence of a coalition and 0 for absence of a coalition. Cities could vary on the measure from 4 (a coalition after each election) to 0 (no coalition).

These four variables were also factor analysed using a principal components solution. The first factor extracted explained 65 per cent of the variance; each variable had a factor loading of 0.738 or higher on this first factor. We used the criteria of Kaiser and retained only this factor, obviating the necessity of rotation.

The index of political competition was constructed using the same procedures as described previously, that is, the complete estimation method in which the standardized value of each variable was multiplied by its factor weight and then summed. We also used the same measures of reliability and validity. Cronbach's alpha was 0.819, meaning a relatively high degree of internal consistency in this scale. The item-to-total correlations varied from 0.74 to 0.87.

Measures of Ideological Orientation

We developed two indices to reflect the ideological orientation of the party or parties controlling the executive committee.

The Number of Times the Christian Social Party Controlled the Executive Committee

This is a measure of the number of times following these four elections that the Christian Social (Catholic) Party had majority control of the executive committee.[27] The Catholic Party controlled the executive committee at least three times out of four in 63 per cent of the Flemish cities, but only in 7 per cent of those in Wallonia.

The Number of Times the Belgian Socialist Party Controlled the Executive Committee

This is a measure of the number of times following these four elections that the Belgian Socialist Party had majority control of the executive committee. Seventy-five per cent of the Walloon cities were controlled at least three times out of four by the Socialist Party, while this was true for only 8 per cent of Flemish cities.

Measure of Stagnation in Population Size

This measure reflects the degree to which the population size of a city tended toward stagnation between 1900 and 1964. It is a ratio of the population size in 1900 to the population size in 1964. If a city had a score greater than 1.00, its population size in 1964 was smaller than in 1900; if a city had a score less than 1.00, its population size in 1964 was greater than in 1900. Cities varied from a low of 0.046 on this index (reflecting high growth) to 1.36 (reflecting considerable decline in population). Seventeen of the 196 cities experienced a decline in population over this period. It is noteworthy that 11 of the 61 Walloon cities experienced such a decline, but only 4 of the 116 Flemish cities.

Regional Variations in City Expenditure Patterns

Because regional diversity has historically been one of the most distinguishing characteristics of Belgian national life,[28] it is appropriate to ask whether expenditure patterns of Belgian cities reflect regional differences.[29] Per capita expenditures are highest among cities in the Brussels agglomeration, next highest among cities in Wallonia, and lowest among cities in Flanders, with exceptions for categories of municipal enterprises; roads and public works; art, popular education, and leisure; and a miscellaneous other category. Walloon cities spent on the average 50 per cent more per capita than did Flemish cities. Cities in the Brussels agglomeration spent twice as much per capita as Flemish cities, and approximately one-third more per capita than Walloon cities.

Such regional differences in per capita spending are not a recent phenomenon. While the average per capita spending increased among these cities by more than 40 per cent from 1961–2 to 1965–6, and by almost 175 per cent from 1947–65/6, the same regional differences in spending rates per capita were present in those earlier years.[30] There has been little change in the relative spending patterns of these cities over this period. The correlation coefficient between per capita city expenditures in 1947 and 1965/6 was 0.92 among all cities, 0.90 among Flemish cities, 0.89 among Walloon cities, and 0.97 among cities in the Brussels agglomeration. The mere fact that there is an unusually strong relationship between city expenditures at the beginning and end of this twenty-year period, however, tells us nothing about the causal forces which account for variations in these expenditure patterns.[31]

Findings

The zero-order correlation coefficients between each of the seven hypothesized relationships and total city expenditures are shown in Table 5.1. There are strong zero-order relationships between the index of ecological centrality and overall expenditures in each of the three regions and among all cities. In fact, this single index can explain between 53 and 76 per cent of the variance in overall city expenditures. Each component of the index

Table 5.1.   *Zero-order Pearsonian correlation coefficients between selected city characteristics and total per capita city expenditures, 1965-6, among 196 Belgian cities of size 10 000 or more on 31 December 1968, by region*

	All cities (N=196)	Flanders (N=116)	Wallonia (N=61)	Brussels agglom- eration (N=19)
A. Ecological centrality				
Central city of a metropolitan area	0.58***	0.56***	0.71***	0.83***
Employment- residence ratio	0.51***	0.42***	0.58***	a
Per cent of the labour force employed in services	0.35***	0.32***	0.32**	0.08
Per cent of dwelling units that are non- owner occupied	0.64***	0.59***	0.60***	0.56**
Number of economic establishments (natural logarithm transformation)	0.68***	0.67***	0.71***	0.70***
Index of ecological centrality	0.77***	0.73***	0.80***	0.87***
B. Economic concentration				
Number of head- quarters of industrial corporations 1965–6	0.60***	0.81***	0.69***	0.86***
Number of bank headquarters, 1968	0.71***	0.80***	0.82***	0.87***
Number of insurance company head- quarters, 1968	0.66***	0.88***	0.82***	0.86***
Index of economic concentration	0.67***	0.85***	0.82***	0.87***

Table 5.1 (*contd.*)

	All cities (N=196)	Flanders (N=116)	Wallonia (N=61)	Brussels agglom- eration (N=19)
C. *High social class*				
Percentage completing high school	0.25***	0.24**	0.27**	−0.37
Percentage with white collar occupations	0.16*	0.14	0.28**	−0.08
Median income	0.28***	0.19*	0.26*	−0.53*
Index of high social class	0.29	0.26**	0.34**	−0.36
D. *Political competition*				
Average number of lists in the communal elections, 1946–70	0.59***	0.58***	0.56***	0.46*
Index of political fractionalization, 1946–70	0.36***	0.23**	0.43***	0.13
Index of instability in the control and com- position of the executive committee, 1946–70	0.15*	0.13	0.21*	−0.26
Number of times a coalition ruled the executive committee, 1946–70	0.43***	0.34***	0.50***	0.22
Index of political competition	0.47***	0.40***	0.53***	0.19
E. *Ideological orientation*				
Number of times the Christian Social Party (Catholic) had majority control of the executive committee 1946–70	−0.27***	−0.13	−0.05	−0.14

Table 5.1 (*contd.*)

	All cities (N=196)	Flanders (N=116)	Wallonia (N=61)	Brussels agglom- eration (N=19)
Number of times the Socialist Party had majority control of the executive committee, 1946–70	0.18**	0.09	−0.10	0.03
F. *Population stagnation* Index of population stagnation (1900 pop- ulation size as a proportion of 1964 population size)	0.40***	0.35***	0.32**	0.74***

[a]The employment-residence ratio for each of the nineteen cities in the Brussels ag- glomeration was not given in the 1961 Census of Population, although it was given for all nineteen together. Cities in the Brussels agglomeration were assigned the val- ue of the metropolitan area, but a correlation could not be computed here with a constant.

* P < 0.05, one-tail test of significance.
** P < 0.01, one-tail test of significance.
*** P < 0.001, one-tail test of significance.

of ecological centrality has strong relationships with overall city expendi- tures as well.

There are also strong zero-order relationships between the index of economic concentration and total expenditures among all cities and among cities within each of the three regions. Each of the three components of economic concentration also has a strong relationship with total expendi- tures. It should be noted that the correlation coefficient between ecological centrality and economic concentration is 0.41. While they are moderately related, they are not identical, meaning we can expect each to have independent effects on local government expenditures when considered simultaneously.

The index of high social class has positive relationships with total expenditures among all 196 cities and among cities in the regions of Flanders and Wallonia, but the relationship is insignificant and reversed among the nineteen cities in the Brussels agglomeration. A comparable observation can be made about each of the three components of this index. The magnitude of the relationships between this index and its components and total expenditures is considerably less than ecological centrality and economic concentration, however.

The zero-order relationship between the index of the political competition and overall expenditures is also relatively strong in Flanders, Wallonia, and among all cities, but not among the cities in the Brussels agglomeration. The zero-order relationship between control of the executive committee by the Catholic Party and overall expenditures is negative and moderately strong among all cities, but these relationships do not hold up within regions. Finally, the index of population stagnation is moderately to strongly related to overall expenditures among cities in the various subsets of cities, but particularly among the cities in the Brussels agglomeration.

Each of the seven hypotheses is supported among all cities, but only three — ecological centrality, political competition, and population stagnation — are related to expenditures as hypothesized among cities within each of the three regions, although the indices of high social class and political competition have statistically significant relationships among cities in Flanders and Wallonia.

The obvious problem with these findings is that, (1) we have not disaggregated these expenditures, and (2) we have not established the net effects of each of these variables. It may be that there are great variations in these relationships within various expenditure categories. In addition some of the independent variables are themselves interrelated (see Table 5.2). Therefore we have also disaggregated overall expenditures and examined the net effect of each variable on each of the various expenditure categories. The results for all cities are shown in Table 5.3. We also carried out separate analyses among Flemish and Walloon cities, although we do not show the results here.

Looking first at the results for the index of ecological centrality, we see in Table 5.3 that this variable is strongly related not only to total expenditures, but also to twelve of the thirteen functional categories. Only expenditures for religion do not have a significant beta coefficient with ecological centrality. The same general findings are true when these regressions are run within Flemish cities and Walloon cities, although we do not show the results here. The beta coefficients are particularly strong for the categories of administration and social control. It is precisely these expenditure categories that most directly reflect expenditures for co-ordination and social control activities. The figures provide support for our first hypothesis that the degree of ecological centrality is associated with greater expenditures by local government.

The index of economic concentration is also strongly related to total expenditures, and it also is positively and significantly related to twelve of the thirteen expenditure categories as shown in Table 5.3. Only the result for the category of expenditures for religious activities is not consistent with our hypothesis.

Table 5.2   *Zero-order correlation coefficients among predictors of city expenditures among 196 Belgian cities of size 10 000 or more on 31 December 1968*

	1	2	3	4	5	6	7
1. Index of ecological centrality							
2. Index of economic concentration	0.41***						
3. Index of high social class	0.47***	0.11					
4. Index of political competition	0.53***	0.28***	.39***				
5. Index of Socialist control of the executive committee, 1946–70	0.04	-0.05	-0.13*	-0.03			
6. Index of Catholic control of the executive committee, 1946–70	-0.12*	-0.06	-0.23***	-0.68***			
7, Index of population stagnation	0.33***	-0.21**	0.21**	0.07	0.38***	0.21**	

*   P < 0.05, one-tail test of significance.
**   P < 0.01, one-tail test of significance.
***   P < 0.001, one-tail test of significance.

These results provide considerable support for our hypotheses about the role a city plays in the urban system — both in terms of its intra-metropolitan and inter-metropolitan rank — and the effect this has on expenditures by local governments. These results are also consistent with our assumption that problems of co-ordination and social control and the need for basic services are greater in such cities, thus necessitating greater expenditures.

The results shown in Table 5.3 provide little or no confirmation for our third hypothesis which argued that cities with many high status citizens would have greater expenditures. The hypothesized relationship occurred for only two of the fourteen categories shown in Table 5.3.

The hypothesized relationship between the degree of political

Table 5.3　*Regression of various expenditure categories, 1965–6, on selected independent variables among all 196 cities of size 10 000 or more on 31 December 1968*[a]

				Indices of			
Expenditure categories	Ecological centrality	Economic concentration	Social class	Political competition	Socialist control	Population stagnation	R^2adj.
Total city expenditures	0.517***	0.423***	-0.011	0.080	0.152***	0.085*	0.7778
Administration							
General administration	0.582***	0.133**	0.127*	0.097*	0.169***	0.095*	0.6714
Pensions and social security	0.521***	0.421***	0.062	0.075*	0.172***	0.104**	0.8344
Social control							
Police, security and fire	0.628***	0.342**	0.028	0.073*	-0.004	0.078*	0.8204
Social welfare							
Public assistance	0.361***	0.406***	0.067	0.113*	0.178***	0.145**	0.6470
Public education	0.392***	0.322***	-0.007	0.045	0.416***	0.045	0.5783
Other basic services							
Hygiene and public health	0.536***	0.243***	0.106*	0.104*	0.082*	0.067	0.6484
Roads and public works	0.233*	0.275***	0.121	-0.040	-0.028	-0.057	0.1817
Municipal enterprises	0.281**	0.299***	-0.134	0.080	-0.032	0.040	0.2395
Real estate and city properties	0.493***	0.242***	0.041	0.055	0.089	0.133*	0.5391
Art, popular education and leisure	0.472***	0.164**	0.003	0.049	-0.063	0.191**	0.4333
Miscellaneous							
Religion	0.028	-0.138*	0.103	-0.109	-0.086	0.364***	0.0879
Deficit and past debt	0.362***	0.380***	0.050	0.019	0.002	0.031	0.4192
Other	0.216**	0.120*	0.110	0.064	0.276***	0.299***	0.3965

[a] The figures shown here are standardized regression coefficients.

*　　P < 0.05, one-tail test of significance
**　P < 0.01, one-tail test of significance
***　P < 0.001, one-tail test of significance.

competition and the level of expenditure also does not fare well. The beta coefficients are statistically significant for only five expenditure categories — general administration, pensions, police, public assistance, and public health, but these relationships are not very strong. The same weakness in findings for this variable occurs when Flemish and Walloon cities are examined separately. Hence, the fourth hypothesis receives only limited support.

The fifth hypothesis argued that the ideological orientation of the party in control of the executive committee would have an effect on the level of city expenditures.[32] As shown in Table 5.4 there is confirmation for this hypothesis among all cities for total city expenditures, and particularly public education,[33] as well as for hygiene and public health. In addition, we find that Socialist control also affects expenditures for general administration, which we interpret to mean expenditures for both current and past administrative services. Socialist control also has statistically significant relationships with expenditures for real estate and city properties and other expenses, although we have no particular explanation for these findings. It should be noted that, with the exception of expenditures for real estate and city properties, the partial correlations noted here are stronger than the zero-order relationships. In other words, it is only after controlling for the effects of factors such as ecological centrality, economic concentration, and the other variables that we find such strong relationships.

These findings are generally even stronger among sixty-one Walloon cities, the region in which Socialist control of city governments is most pronounced. Among the 116 Flemish cities, where the Catholic hegemony is greatest, we find relationships only in the case of expenditures for the social-welfare categories of public assistance, pensions and social security, and expenditures in support of religious activities.

The findings for the variable of general administration are understandable since greater activities in welfare programming also create greater problems of administration.

The sixth hypothesis argued that expenditures, especially for social-welfare programmes and services, would be less in Catholic-controlled cities because of the penchant of the Catholic Church to provide social services through a private network. This hypothesis also receives support as shown in Table 5.4. We find strong negative partial correlations for total expenditures and for expenditures on the two categories of social welfare, the two categories of administration, and for the other category. Catholic-controlled cities do indeed spend less on social-welfare programming and past and present administrative activities. These relationships generally held up when we recalculated the partial correlations within the Walloon and Flemish regions as also shown in Table 5.4.

Finally, in the seventh hypothesis we argued that cities in which the population had been stagnant or declining since the turn of the century

Table 5.4   *Partial correlation coefficients between the index of socialist control of the executive committee, and the index of Catholic control of the executive committee and various expenditure categories, controlling for other variables,*[a] *by region among 196 Belgian cities*

Per capita expenditures in 1965–6	All cities (N = 196)		Flemish cities (N = 116)		Walloon cities (N = 61)	
	Socialist control	Catholic control	Socialist control	Catholic control	Socialist control	Catholic control
Total city expenditures	0.29***	-0.31***	0.09	-0.27**	0.47***	-0.41***
Administration						
General administration	0.26***	-0.26***	0.14	-0.17*	0.25*	-0.30*
Pensions and social security	0.37***	-0.37***	0.16*	-0.27**	0.53	-0.45***
Social control						
Police, security and fire	-0.01	-0.09	-0.07	-0.14	0.22	-0.14
Social welfare						
Public assistance	0.27***	-0.26***	0.32***	-0.22**	0.28*	-0.10
Public education	0.51***	-0.48***	0.18	-0.21*	0.40**	-0.39**
Other basic services						
Hygiene and public health	0.13*	-0.10	0.14	-0.04	0.15	-0.08
Roads and public works	-0.03	0.08	-0.05	0.01	-0.04	0.11
Municipal enterprises	-0.03	0.03	-0.08	-0.06	0.14	-0.12
Real estate and city properties	0.12*	-0.11	0.12	0.10	0.19	-0.21
Art, popular education and leisure	-0.08	-0.03	-0.04	-0.25**	0.16	-0.24*
Miscellaneous						
Religion	-0.08	-0.05	-0.20*	-0.07	-0.24	0.14
Deficit and past debt	0.00	-0.05	-0.11	-0.11	0.23*	-0.32**
Other	0.31***	-0.27***	0.09	-0.11	0.37**	-0.25*

a   The variables that were controlled were the index of Ecological Centrality, the Index of Economic Concentration, the Index of Social Class, the Index of Political Competition and the Index of Population Stagnation.

*	P < 0.05, one-tail test of significance
**	P < 0.01, one-tail test of significance
***	P < 0.001, one-tail test of significance

would have higher expenditures because of political leaders expanding programmes and services in search of electoral support. This hypothesis receives support for total city expenditures and for eight of the thirteen expenditure categories as shown in Table 5.3. It receives support in the two categories of administration, the category of police, the category of public assistance, in two of the five basic services, and in two of the three miscellaneous categories. Hence, population stagnation is associated with higher expenditures by local governments, even when the variables of ecological centrality, economic concentration, social class, political competition, and ideological orientation are statistically controlled.

While the effect of this variable is strong among all cities, it does not hold up when these regressions are computed separately for Flemish and Walloon cities. Among Flemish cities, there is a significant net effect of this variable only for debt and other expenditures, while among Walloon cities, there is only a significant net effect for police, public assistance, religious activities, and other expenditures. We noted previously that population stagnation since 1900 was greatest for cities in the Brussels agglomeration, than for cities in Wallonia, and lowest for cities in Flanders. This variable is in part a surrogate for region, which means that when we run the regressions within each of these two major regions we find less of an effect. Given this qualification, we nevertheless conclude that Hypothesis 7 receives some support, but mainly among all cities.

There are several additional observations we can make about these findings. First, the measures of ecological centrality, economic concentration, social class, political competition, ideological orientation, and population stagnation explain 78 per cent of the variance in total per capita expenditures, meaning that they provide a reasonably efficient explanation of overall expenditures.

Secondly, these variables explain more variance within subsets of cities than among all cities. These variables explained 88 per cent of the variance in overall expenditures among the nineteen cities in the Brussels agglomeration, 85 per cent among the sixty-one Walloon cities, and 86 per cent among the 116 Flemish cities.

Thirdly, the proportion of variance explained was greatest for expenditures on administration, social control, social welfare, public health, and real estate and city properties. We were the least successful in explaining traditional basic services offered by city governments.

Fourthly, the two measures of the role of a city in the urban system — the index of ecological centrality and the index of economic concentration — are the most powerful variables considered here in terms of explaining variance in city expenditures. Ecological centrality alone can explain 59 per cent of the variance in overall expenditures among all 196 cities, while economic centrality alone can explain 40 per cent of overall expenditures. Among the nineteen cities in the Brussels agglomeration ecological centrality alone can explain 76 per cent of the variance while economic concentration alone can explain the same amount of variance. Among the sixty-one Walloon cities the percentages are 64 and 67, respectively, while the percentages for Flemish cities are 53 and 72 respectively.

Fifthly, the political and other variables can explain some additional variance in some expenditure categories, but they are clearly not as powerful as the urban system measures.

Finally, in spite of the limited explanatory power of the political variables, they nevertheless do make important contributions to explained variance for some categories of expenditures, specifically in the case of public education, general administration, pensions and social security, public assistance, and overall expenditures. Hence, while political variables are not the factors that account for the most variance in expenditures, they do have a significant impact.

Summary and Conclusions

In examining the findings for each of the seven hypotheses about the determinants of city expenditures — or policy outputs — we have found some support for all seven hypotheses. The strongest and most consistent support, however, was for the hypothesis about the role a city plays in the urban system and the effect of this on city expenditures. Specifically, cities that have a high degree of ecological centrality, meaning they are centres of production and consumption for a surrounding region, and cities in which the headquarters of the largest financial and economic institutions of the Belgian state are concentrated, were found to have higher expenditures in every category of expenditures with one exception, and that one exception constitutes in most instances a budget category with no more than 1 per cent of the total budget of these cities.

Population stagnation was also found to be associated with higher expenditures for most categories. As political leaders of local government anticipate periodic elections, they add on programmes and services, meaning they increase expenditures, even if the city's population base is stable or declining. The longer the period of time that this process has been taking place, the more programmes and services the political leaders are likely to have added, and the higher the expenditure levels of local government. The degree of population stagnation is to a great extent a result of the economic expansion or decline of a region, at least in the Belgian case, and is a reflection, albeit an indirect one, of the evolution of the economic system, at least in its effects on city growth or decline.

Political variables were also shown to have independent effects on some expenditure categories. Politically competitive cities had higher expenditures for some categories, but the overall effect of this factor was neither very strong nor very extensive. The other political variables — control of the executive committee by either the Catholic or Socialist

Party — had an influence on expenditures for social welfare, administration, 'other' expenditures, and total expenditures, but not on the remaining expenditure categories. The finding that party control primarily affects expenditures for social welfare activities rather than all expenditure categories was consistent with our expectations, given the evolution and ideological orientation of these parties. We had not anticipated the effect of this variable on expenditures for current administration and administration and services in the past (as reflected by expenditures for pensions and social security), but upon closer examination of this finding, it is consistent with our arguments since these expenditures are for previous administrative services. These results are generally consistent with earlier findings about the effect of Labour Party control of local governments in England and with more recent findings about the effect of control of local governments by the Social Democratic Parties in Denmark, Norway, and Sweden, the effect of control of local governments by Socialists or Communists in Italy, and the effect of control of local governments by the Communist Party in France. In each of these nations, and in Belgium, Social Democratic or leftist control has resulted in higher levels of services and expenditures for public welfare and education. A study of expenditures and services in fifty seven West German cities found little support for the effect of control by the Social Democratic Party on various policy outputs, but it did show that control by the Christian Democratic Union (the Catholic party) had a negative effect on many categories of policy outputs.[34]

The hypothesis about the relationship between the concentration of high-status citizens in given cities and expenditures by local government was generally not supported, neither among all the cities in our study nor when cities in Wallonia and Flanders were examined separately.

Consistent with many of the previous findings about political variables and policy outputs, we conclude first that the political variables are not the most important predictors of city expenditures in Belgian cities. The role a city plays in the urban system — both in terms of ecological centrality and economic concentration and, to a lesser extent, population stagnation are clearly the most important predictors of expenditures. Secondly, consistent with some previous studies, we observe that the effect of political variables is not uniform, that is, political variables are more important for some kinds of expenditures — particularly social welfare and administration — than for others. Thirdly, this observation should not obscure the fact that party control does nevertheless have an important impact on social welfare and administrative expenditures, the reasons for which were linked to the historical evolution and ideologies of the Catholic and Socialist parties.

What conclusions do we draw from these results? If we want to conclude that other factors are more important than political ones, as some researchers have, these results would certainly justify that conclusion. If, on the other hand, we want to make the very strong point that political factors make an independent contribution to the explanation of social welfare, education, and some other expenditures, our results support that conclusion as well. It depends somewhat on one's point of view, what one wants to emphasize, and what one is trying to prove.

But why do we find greater support in Belgium for the hypothesis that political variables have an impact on city expenditures, when some earlier research in other countries has not? Is there something unique about the political climate, cleavage structure, system of local government, and, thus, the spending patterns of cities in Belgium? Is it because we have used an alternative theoretical explanation for expenditures, and hence, have selected in some cases alternative environmental, resource, or ecological variables in explaining city expenditures? Even so, one must admit that our variables of ecological centrality, economic concentration, and population stagnation were efficient predictors. Is it because we have used more sensitive measures of the political process than simply votes for parties, as some studies of this kind have done? Our variables reflect both the form of local politics (the degree of diversity, competition, coalition formation, and turnover) and the content of local politics (the nature of party control over a twenty-five year period). Or is it because we have used a much larger range of cities? We have included all cities over 10 000 while many previous studies have been restricted to cities of 50 000 or 100 000 or more. There may well be unique aspects to the subset of the very largest cities that limit the generalizability of findings from such studies to smaller cities.

There does not exist any study of sufficient depth in terms of number of cities examined, sufficient breadth in terms of the range of political variables considered, and sufficient generalizability in terms of the number of nations covered to answer these questions satisfactorily. Further, theoretical models to explain the mechanisms whereby 'environmental' or 'resource' factors affect levels of services and expenditures have not been sufficiently developed to provide a coherent and theoretically meaningful reason for including some variables and excluding others. While we do not pretend to have developed the best models, nor to have measured our theoretical concepts in optimum ways, we nevertheless have only included variables for which we could give a theoretically meaningful explanation for their expected effects.

At minimum these findings, together with the recent findings from a number of other Western European nations, suggest that political factors should not be dismissed and that any sounding of the death knell of the impact of politics on public policy is premature. At the same time, we should not exaggerate expectations about the importance of political factors in determining service and expenditure levels in cities. As we have tried to demonstrate in this analysis, the levels of city services and expenditures are to a great extent explainable by the need for local government leaders to solve problems of co-ordination, social control, and delivery of basic services. Their task is more a technocratic than an ideological one. Ideological proclivities are not without influence in the formulation of public policies of local governments; however, effects of such ideological proclivities are most likely to occur in some areas of expenditures, such as social welfare and welfare-related activities, than in others.

In other words, the debate about whether politics matters or not is a silly debate. Of course politics matters both in the political process that goes into the making of decisions and in the outcomes of those decisions, although only some outcomes show this clearly. On the other hand, the results of this study clearly suggest that students of public policy should probably spend more time trying to understand the historical and contemporary processes that underly our findings about the role a city plays in the urban system and its relationship to public policy formulation.

Notes

We would like to express our appreciation to Roger Friedland, Robert Lineberry, Ken Newton, Michel Quevit, and John Walton for their helpful comments on previous drafts of this chapter. We also acknowledge the support for computer facilities provided by the Center for Demography and Ecology, University of Wisconsin. This is a revised version of an earlier paper that appeared in *Politics and Policy*, January, 1980.

1. For some standard works, see Michael Aiken and Paul E. Mott (eds.), *The Structure of Community Power* (New York, Random House, 1970); Charles M. Bonjean, Terry N. Clark, and Robert L. Lineberry, *Community Politics: A Behavioral Approach* (New York, Macmillan, 1971).
2. Cf. John J. Kirlin and Steven P. Erie, 'The Study of City Governance and Public Policy Making: A Critical Appraisal', *Public Administration Review*, 32 (1972), 173–82. The most extensive review of this literature can be found in Robert C. Fried, 'Comparative Urban Performance', in Fred I. Greenstein and Nelson W. Polsby (eds.), *The Handbook of Political Science, Policies and Policymaking*, vol. 6, (Reading, Mass., Addison-Wesley, 1976).
3. Some of the earlier expenditure studies were Amos H. Hawley, 'Metropolitan Populations and Municipal Expenditures in Central Cities', *Journal of Social Issues*, 7 (1951), 100–8; Solomon Fabricant, *The Trend of Government Activity in the U.S. since 1900* (New York, National Bureau of Economic Research, 1952); Harvey Brazer, *City Expenditures in the United States* (New York, Bureau of Economic Research, 1959). See Fried, in Greenstein and Polsby op. cit., and Kirlin and Erie op. cit., for reviews of this literature.
4. A number of studies of American political units found the political variables to be unimportant, especially after resource or environmental variables had been controlled. For example, see Richard E. Dawson and James A. Robinson, 'Inter-Party Competition, Economic Variables, and Welfare Policies in the American States', *Journal of Politics*, 25 (1965), 265–89; Thomas R. Dye, *Politics, Economics and the Public* (Chicago, Rand McNally and Co., 1966); Thomas R. Dye, 'Governmental Structure, Urban Environment, and Educational Policy', *Midwest Journal of Political Science*, 11 (1967), 353–80; Richard I. Hofferbert,

'The Relations between Public Policy and Some Structural and Environmental Variables in the American States', *American Political Science Review*, 60 (1966), 73–82; Ira Sharkansky, 'Economic and Political Correlates of State Government Expenditures: General Tendencies and Deviant Cases', *Midwest Journal of Political Science*, 11 (1967), 173–92; Roger Hollingsworth, 'The Impact of Electoral Behavior on Public Policy', unpublished paper, Department of History, University of Wisconsin, 1973. The unimportance of political variables has been challenged by other studies. See Ira Sharkansky, 'Government Expenditures and Public Services in the American States', *American Political Science Review*, 61 (1967), 1066–77; Ira Sharkansky and Richard I. Hofferbert, 'Dimensions of State Politics, Economics, and Public Policy', *American Political Science Review*, 64 (1971), 508–22; Robert L. Lineberry and Edmund P. Fowler, 'Reformism and Public Policies in American Cities', *American Political Science Review*, 61 (1967), 701–16; Charles F. Cnuddle and Donald J. McCrone, 'Party Competition and Welfare Policies in the American States', *American Political Science Review*, 63 (1969), 858–66.

Turning to studies of expenditures and public policies in other countries, perhaps the most work has been done in England, but the results are somewhat mixed. Some studies show that political variables make a difference for some types of expenditures: James E. Alt, 'Some Social and Political Correlates of County Borough Expenditures', *British Journal of Political Science*, 1 (1971), 48–62; Noel T. Boaden and Robert R. Alford, 'Sources of Diversity in English County Boroughs', *Public Administration*, 47 (1969), 203–23; Noel T. Boaden, *Urban Policy-Making: Influences on County Boroughs in England and Wales* (Cambridge, Cambridge University Press, 1971). Others provide no support for the contention that political variables make a difference, especially after controlling socioeconomic variables: Peggy Crane, *Enterprise in Local Government: A Study of the Way in Which Local Authorities Use Their Permissive Power* (London, Fabian Publications, 1953); and F. R. Oliver and J. Stanyer, 'Some Aspects of the Financial Behaviour of County Boroughs', *Public Administration*, 47 (1969–79), 169–84.

Studies of Italy by Robert Fried, 'Communism, Urban Budgets, and the Two Italies: A Case Study in Comparative Urban Governments', *Journal of Politics*, 33 (1971), 1008–51; and Georgio Galli and Alfonso Prandi, *Patterns of Political Participation in Italy* (New Haven, Yale University Press, 1970), 227–54, conclude that party is either not the most important factor in shaping policy (although it is among the most important), and party makes no difference, respectively. In a study of city expenditures in West Germany, Austria, and Switzerland, Robert C. Fried, 'Politics, Economics and Federalism: Aspects of Urban Government in Mittel-Europe', in Terry N. Clark (ed.), *European Communities* (Beverly Hills, California, Sage Publications, 1974), concluded that party was not the most important factor shaping city policy, although it was sometimes important, and the direction of party impact was sometimes contrary to expectation.

It should be noted that various commentators on this and related literature do not always draw the same conclusions from these studies; this difference seems to arise from whether one argues that politics makes no difference or whether politics is not the principal factor shaping policy outputs. For some reviews and commentaries of this, see Fried (1976), op. cit.; John Fenton and Donald W. Chamberlayne, 'The Literature Dealing with the Relationships between Political Processes, Socio-economic Conditions and Public Policies in American States: A Bibliographical Essay', *Policy*, 1 (1969), 388–404; Herbert Jacob and Michael Lipsky, 'Outputs, Structure, and Power: An Assessment of Changes in the Study of State and Local Politics', *Journal of Politics*, 30 (1968), 510–38; Hugh Heclo, 'Policy Analysis', *British Journal of Political Science*,

2 (1972), 83–108; Dennis D. Riley, 'Party Competition and State Policy-Making: The Need for Reexamination', *Western Political Quarterly*, 24 (1971), 510–13.
5. Fried (1976), op. cit.
6. The studies referred to are as follows:
France: In a study of expenditures among the local governments of 221 French cities, Kobielski found that cities with Communist mayors had significantly higher expenditures for social services and education than did cities with non-Communist left or moderate to Conservative mayors, and this effect remained even when other factors were statistically controlled. The effect of left-wing politics was limited primarily to 'social-welfare' expenditures. Jose Kobielski, 'Tendance Politique des Municipalities et Comportements Financiers Locaux', paper prepared for presentation at the Conference on Politics, Policy and the Quality of Urban Life, Bellagio, Italy, June 1975. In a study of forty or so smaller cities in the northern part of France, Becquart found that cities with leftist mayors tended to have more amenities and services. Jeanette L. Becquart, 'French Mayors and Communal Policy Outputs: The Case for Small Cities', paper presented at the meetings of the European Consortium for Political Research, London, England, April 1975.
Italy: In a study of fifty-seven provincial capitals in the northern and central regions of Italy, Brosio found some evidence that leftist controlled cities had higher expenditures. In a more extensive study of expenditures among 325 Italian cities of size 20 000 or more in 1961, Aiken and Martinotti found rather strong evidence that cities in which the ruling 'junta' was controlled by a coalition of leftist parties (primarily Communists and Socialists), expenditures for education and culture, social services, general administration, and capital equipment were considerably higher, even when a variety of other city attributes were controlled. Michael Aiken and Guido Martinotti, 'Left Politics, the Urban System, and City Expenditures: An Analysis of 325 Cities in Italy', unpublished paper, Department of Sociology, University of Wisconsin, 1977.
Denmark: In a study of 277 Danish communities in 1972–3, Skovsgaard found that voting strength of the Socialist Parties in the 1970 municipal election was positively related to expenditures for primary education and one category of expenditures for social welfare — assistance for the aged. See Carl-Johan Skovsgaard, chapter 3, this volume.
Norway: In a study of 460 Norwegian communes, Hansen and Kjellberg found that the Socialist Party's share of the total votes in the 1963 municipal election had made a net contribution to the explanation of expenditures for social welfare and to a lesser extent education, even when a variety of other variables were controlled. In another study of forty-six Norwegian cities, Kuhnle also found 'the Social Democratically-led towns spend relatively more on social welfare measures than non-Social-Democratic towns'. He noted, however, that among his cities these differences were not 'dramatic', but they were nevertheless there. Tore Hansen and Francesco Kjellberg, 'Municipal Expenditures in Norway: Autonomy and Constraints in Local Government Activity', paper presented at the Conference of Politics, Policy, and the Quality of Life, Bellagio, Italy, June 1975; and Tore Hansen, chapter 2, and Stein Kuhnle, chapter 3, this volume.
Sweden: In a study of social services in a stratified sample of thirty-six Swedish communes, Birgersson found that leftist-controlled local governments (Social Democrats, in some cases together with Communists) scored consistently higher on an index of ten communal services including social assistance, housing, day nurseries, play schools, old age homes, home help, town planning, streets and roads, leisure activities, and libraries. He found that Socialist communes generally have the most extensive services of this kind. He also noted that 'the non-Socialist

communes to a greater extent than the Socialist communes devote resources to other services than those influencing the service index'. Unfortunately, Birgersson's index includes six 'social welfare services' and found more traditional basic services. One wonders if his results would have been even stronger, given the evidence cited above, if the analysis had been restricted only to social welfare services. Because he finds that non-Socialist communes tend to spend money on services other than those in his services index, he draws the conclusion that 'local-government activity' is mainly a non-political activity! If he is looking for a political effect on all types of expenditures, this would be a reasonable conclusion, but the data seem to be consistent with that cited above, which suggests that politics has an effect primarily on social welfare services. Hence, this last conclusion seems unjustified. See Bengt Owe Birgersson, 'Services in Communes of Different Types: The Impact of Financial Resources and Political Majority in Swedish Communes', paper presented at the Conference on Politics, Policy, and the Quality of Life, Bellagio, Italy, June 1975.

A recent study of fifty-seven West German cities by Fried is not consistent with the studies cited above. Fried does not find that control of a city by the Social Democratic party has an effect on expenditures in general or even on welfare-type expenditures. However, Fried never controls for the kinds of variables employed in this study, and it may well be that in West German cities, as in Belgian ones, the impact of party emerges only after one controls for the degree of ecological centrality in a city. See Robert Fried, 'Party and Policy in Western German Cities', *American Political Science Review*, 70 (1976), 11–24.

7. For a discussion of this concept, see Brian J. L. Berry, 'Cities as Systems Within Systems of Cities', *Papers of the Regional Science Association*, 13 (1964), 147–63; L. S. Bourne and J. W. Simmons, *Systems of Cities: Readings on Structure, Growth, and Policy* (New York, Oxford University Press, 1978); Allan Pred, *City-Systems in Advanced Economies* (New York, John Wiley and Sons, 1977); David Barker, 'A Conceptual Approach to the Description and Analysis of an Historical Urban System', *Regional Studies*, 12 (1978), 1–10.

8. See, for example, Brian J. L. Berry and William L. Garrison, 'Recent Developments of Central Place Theory', *Papers and Proceedings of the Regional Science Association*, 4 (1958), 107–20; Brian J. L. Berry and Allan Pred, *Central Place Studies: A Bibliography of Theory and Applications* (Philadelphia, Regional Science Research Institute, 1965); K. S. O. Beavon, *Central Place Theory: A Reinterpretation* (New York, Longman, 1977). Human ecological theory also provides a theoretical foundation for this conceptualization of the urban system being constituted by a set of metropolitan areas with dominance over their surrounding hinterland. See for example Amos H. Hawley, *Human Ecology* (New York, The Ronald Press, 1950). See also O. D. Duncan *et al.*, *Metropolis and Region* (Baltimore, The Johns Hopkins Press, 1960).

9. In a study of expenditures in central places in the United States, Kasarda found that expenditures of local governments varied directly with the population of their surrounding suburbs. See John Kasarda, 'The Impact of Suburban Population Growth on Central City Service Functions', *American Journal of Sociology*, 77 (1972), 1111–24.

10. The conceptualization of this aspect of the urban system is derived largely from the work of Allan Pred, especially his *City-Systems in Advanced Economies*.

11. See Leif Ahnstrom, *Styrande och Ledande Verksambet i Vasteurope* (Stockholm, Ekonomiska Forskningsinstitutet, 1973), and Pred op. cit. for a discussion of headquarters location.

12. Since voting is mandatory in Belgium, we cannot include a measure of voting turnout as do some studies of public policy of local government.

13. For an overall discussion of political parties in Belgium, see Maynaud, Ladriere, and Perin, *La decision politique en Belgique*; Lorwin, 'Belgium: Religion, Class,

and Language in National Politics'; and Carl-Henrik Hojer, *Le regime parlemen-
tarie Belge de 1918 a 1940* (Brussels, Centre de Recherche et d'Information
Socio-Politiques, 1969). For specific discussions of the Socialist Party, see
M. A. Pierson, *Histoire de socialisme en Belgique* (Brussels, Institut Emil Van-
dervelde, 1953) and Leo Delsienne, *Le Parti Ouvrier Belge des origines a 1894*
(Brussels, La Renaissance du Livre, 1955). For a background on the Catholic
Party, see Chanoine A. Simon, *Le Parti Catholique Belge: 1830-1945* (Brussels,
La Renaissance du Livre, 1958). For an excellent discussion of citizen par-
ticipation in political parties in Belgium, see L. Huyse, *L'apathie Politique*
(Brussels, Editions Scientifiques Erasme, 1969).

Still other sources that are helpful include Luc Huyse, *Passiviteit pacificatie
en verzuiling in de Belgische politiek* (Antwerp, Standard, 1970), and A. Van-
denbrande, 'Elements for a Sociological Analysis of the Impact of the Main
Conflicts on Belgian Political Life', *Res Publica*, 9 (1967), 437–70.

14. *Rapports*, Congres National du Parti Ouvrier Belge, 16–17 avril, 1911, 3.
15. *Le Socialisme Communal* (Brussels, Parti Ouvrier Belge, 1894).
16. *Rapports*, Congres National du Parti Ouvrier Belge, 16–17 avril 1911, 4–5.
    See also J. Destree and E. Vandervelde, *La Socialisme en Belgique* (Paris, V.
    Giard and E. Briere, 1898).
17. See Rudolf Rexsohazy, *Origines et Formation du Catholicisme Social en Belgique*
    (Louvain, Publications Universitaires de Louvain, 1958); Val Lorwin, 'Segmented
    Pluralism', *Comparative Politics*, 3 (1971), 141–74 and Luc Huyse, *Passiviteit
    Pacificatia en Verzuiling in de Belgische Politiek.*
18. For accounts of the economic history of Belgium see H. Vander Linden, *Bel-
    gium: The Making of a Nation* (Oxford, Clarendon Press, 1920); Allan H. Kittell,
    'The Revolutionary Period of the Industrial Revolution: Industrial Innovation
    and Population Displacement in Belgium: 1830–1880', *Journal of Social History*,
    1 (1967), 119–48; Lorwin, 'Linguistic Pluralism and Political Tension in
    Modern Belgium'; F. Baudhuin, *Histoire Economique de la Belgique, 1914–
    1938* (Brussels, E. Bruylant, 1944); F. Baudhuin, *Belgique 1900–1960: Ex-
    plication Economique de Notre Temps* (Louvain, 1961); M. A. G. Van Meer-
    haaghe, *De Economie van Vlaanderen* (Leiden, Stenfert Kroese, 1965); and P. M.
    Olyslager, *De Lokalisering der Belgische Nijverheid* (Antwerp, Standard, 1947).
19. J. A. Sporck, 'Hierarchie des Villes at Leur Structuration en Reseau', Seminaire
    de Geographie, University of Liege, June 1966. We are indebted to Professor
    Jean Remy of the Catholic University of Louvain for bringing this study to our
    attention.
20. The 1961 Census of Population provides the employment residence ratio for
    the Brussels agglomeration, but not for each city within the Brussels agglom-
    eration. We assigned the value of the metropolitan agglomeration to each of
    the nineteen cities which compose it.
21. The category of 'services' includes the following specialized activities:

    (a) services furnished to enterprises, such as accounting and technical services;
    (b) recreational services, such as cinemas, theatres, and sports;
    (c) personal services, such as restaurants, hotels, beauty parlours, laundries,
        and cafes;
    (d) administrative services of the state, the provinces, and communes.
    (e) national defence including military career officers;
    (f) other public services such as police and gendarmerie;
    (g) education, scientific institutes, libraries;
    (h) social workers;
    (i) religious organizations;
    (j) professional associations, unions, and mutualities;
    (k) other private services such as lawyer offices, notaries, and architect offices;

(l) international organizations

22. The formulas used in computing these measures can be found in George W. Bohrnstedt, 'A Quick Method for Determining the Reliability and Validity of Multiple-Item Scales', *American Sociological Review*, 34 (1969), 542–8.

23. The data for 1965 were taken from *Enterprise*, 589 (22 December 1966), 39–45; the 1966 data were taken from *Enterprise*, 641 (22–28 December 1967), 61–64.

24. *Kompass: Register of Industry and Commerce of Belgium and Luxembourg* (Bruxelles, Kompass Belgium S. A., 1968), 1365–9.

25. Ibid., 1247–57.

26. This formula is suggested by Douglas W. Rae and Michael Taylor, *The Analysis of Political Cleavages* (New Haven, Yale University Press, 1970), but it is the same formula described by Stanley Lieberson, 'Measuring Population Diversity', *American Sociological Review*, 34 (1969), 850–63, which has a rather lengthy history among sociologists.

27. We include in this measure only those cities that were formally linked to the Christian Social Party (CVP). There were seven cities in the Province of Limburg (Diepenbeek, Heusden, Koersel, Zonhoven, Bree, Houthalen, and Overpelt) which usually had several Catholic lists in their elections and in which a Catholic list always controlled the executive board. Since these Catholic lists were not officially part of the CVP, however, they were not counted as being controlled by the Christian Social Party. The effect of this decision would, if anything, detract from the findings of this study, for these are low expenditure cities. Had they been included, the effect would probably have been to increase the negative relationship between CVP control and expenditures.

28. Heisler, 'Institutionalizing Societal Cleavages in a Cooptive Policy: The Growing Importance of the Output Side in Belgium'.

29. The city of Eupen is in the German-speaking area of Belgium, but officially a part of Wallonia. We include it among the sixty-one Walloon cities for the purpose of this analysis.

30. More detailed information about service expenditures, party control, and regional variations is provided in Aiken and Depre, 'Policy and Politics in Belgian Cities', 83–9.

31. We, of course, are not the first to raise questions about the incremental perspective and its failure to explain *why* political units vary in expenditure patterns. See, for example, Robert L. Harlow, 'Sharkansky on State Expenditures: A Comment', *National Tax Journal*, 21 (1968), 215–16. Also see Sharkansky's reply in the same issue, 217–19.

32. In Table 5.3, we include only Catholic control of local government. Given the very high degree of association between the index of Catholic control and the index of Socialist control ($r = -0.69$), we included only one of these in these regression equations. If one substitutes Socialist control for Catholic control, similar findings for ecological centrality, political competition, and population stagnation occur and we explain approximately the same amount of variance for each expenditure category.

33. It should be noted that these expenditures on public education do not include most expenditures for elementary and secondary education. Many such schools in Belgium are run by the Catholic Church, although most of the financial resources come from public sources, and others by the state. These expenditures for public education here are primarily for city-run elementary schools, but these expenditures account for only a small proportion of overall expenditures for elementary and secondary education in Belgium.

34. Fried (1976), op. cit.

6   CENTRAL PLACES AND URBAN SERVICES

KEN NEWTON

The purpose of this essay is to try to explain the public expenditure patterns of cities in England and Wales. In other words, the intention is to explain variations in expenditure patterns of the biggest urban authorities in England and Wales in terms of how much they spend on public services, and how they divide their budgets between these services. There have, of course, been many attempts to explain the public expenditure of local authorities both in Britain and in many other countries in Western Europe and North America, but the approach used in this paper diverges from the main body of literature and explores a new way of analysing the problem.[1] The first task, therefore, is to explain why a new approach is necessary.

Most research on city expenditure uses the standard technique of compiling a list of dependent variables, usually per capita expenditures on a range of local services and relating these to a set of independent variables which describe the social, economic and political characteristics of the cities. For example, it might be hypothesised that the poorer the population of a city, the more it is likely to spend on personal social services and housing, while the wealthier a city the more it is likely to spend on such things as parks, libraries, and cultural facilities. Normally, however, particular hypotheses of this kind are not advanced but, instead, a likely looking set of independent variables is run against the expenditure items to see what comes out as statistically significant.

For the most part this approach has not worked particularly well; not only are the empirical results generally rather poor, but there is no general theory to help us interpret them, or to direct our attention to potentially more fruitful ways of tackling the problem. Let us examine the empirical results before turning to the absence of a general theory. Although the method works better in some countries than in others, its results are generally disappointing in the sense that the correlations and percentage of the variance explained are generally rather low. For example, at the end of a thorough, empirical analysis of British cities, Danziger concludes that the approach 'provides a weak and generally unsatisfactory explanation of the inter-unit variation in county borough resource allocation'.[2]

Danziger's conclusion is amply supported by the results of the present research which correlated a set of twenty three independent variables describing the social and economic characteristics of county boroughs in England and Wales with a series of seventeen expenditure variables in 1960–1. The independent variables ranged over a wide variety of community characteristics, including social class, type and value of property, population size and density, age, housing tenure, daily inflow and outflow of population, and the industrial, commercial, and agricultural nature of the local economy. The expenditure variables also dealt with precise service headings, rather than the broad categories often used in this kind of research. In spite of the ample supply of good and detailed data, the results were rather poor. Out of a total of 374 correlations, only 92 (25 per cent) were statistically significant at the 0.05 per cent level, and even when statistically significant the great majority were substantively small. Fewer than a third of the significant variables explained 10 per cent or more of the variance in expenditures. Moreover, the significant figures were distributed in a random way which suggested no theoretically or empirically meaningful patterns.

This brings us to the second major deficiency of urban expenditure studies, namely their largely atheoretical nature. Robert Fried has already made this point in his overview of the urban performance literature. After summarizing the results of many empirical studies in a wide variety of countries he concludes: 'the variables that have been found to possess strong predictive value are different for each function, each country, and each time. Rather than a comparative theory of performance, we seem to be laying the foundation for another monument to "adhockery".'[3]

It seems, therefore, that we must search for a new approach to expenditure studies. This, of course, is not an easy task which is likely to be accomplished overnight, but the remainder of this paper will explore some points which may help towards the construction of such a theory. It must be stressed that it is a tentative and interim research report which is a preliminary to more detailed and comprehensive empirical work.

The starting point for this theory-building attempt might be the observation that conventional expenditure studies assume that local expenditure can best be explained in terms of the characteristics of local authority populations. Therefore they set out to collect a detailed file of information describing the characteristics of urban residents. In other words, they collect information about city populations on the assumption that cities can be understood and analysed as the sum of their individual parts. In strong contrast to this assumption it might be argued that cities are not simply the sum of their individual parts, and that they have important features which are not necessarily reduceable to, or deduceable from, the social and economic characteristics of their individual residents. The dominant characteristics of a suburban dormitory town, for example, is not derived solely or primarily from its middle-class population, but from its relationship to the nearby city for which it provides workers and consumers. On the other side of the coin, some of the major features of cities such as New York, London, and Paris are not produced by their residents so much as by the huge and various populations which visit them on a daily, weekly, or seasonal basis each year. Similarly, seaside resorts, spas, and county towns have their special attributes, as do the capitals of large urban-industrial connurbations, and the industrial cities on their perimeters. In the phrase coined by Brian Berry, it may be helpful to view 'cities as systems within systems of cities'.[4]

There is one well-developed body of work about systems of cities which may serve as a starting point for the explanation of urban spending patterns, and this is the work of geographers on central-place theory and the urban hierarchy. At the heart of this work is the idea that urban places exist to provide services and facilities not only for their own residents, but also for the populations of their hinterlands. Thus: 'one of the main functions of a town — or any service centre — is to supply the needs of the population around it'.[5] Clearly it is impossible for all cities to provide a complete range of services and facilities, for to do so each and every one would have to have a vast range of expensive and specialised provisions. Consequently, there is an urban division of labour between the highest-order central places which cater for an extensive range of specialized demands, and successively lower-order places which provide a range of successively less-specialized services.

Central place theory thus conceives of the urban system as a nested hierarchy in which each city provides all the services and facilities of cities which are below it in the hierarchy, plus an additional range of more specialized services and facilities.[6] Urban places can therefore be ranked from low-order central places, such as market towns, which serve a rather small population with a fairly narrow range of services and facilities, to the very highest central places, such as New York, London, Paris, and Tokyo, which provide the most specialized and costly range of services, in addition to all these provided by lower-order central places.[7] Cities at the top of the urban hierarchy, therefore, have a wide variety of inter-related characteristics. They are often large in terms of population and area: they provide a wide range of shopping facilities; they are centres for entertainment and leisure; they are also centres for professional and commercial services; they are regional or national headquarters for private and public organizations such as banks, insurance companies, chain stores, trade unions, professional, business, and voluntary organisations; they are often government centres; and lastly, because they are centres of business and pleasure, they attract large numbers of commuters and visitors.

But what does all this have to do with the public expenditure of city governments? The answer is that a city's position in the urban hierarchy may affect its public expenditure in two main ways. First, city governments are themselves likely to provide a range of specialized services in accordance with their city's importance as a central place. High order central places are likely to have large and specialized municipal cultural centres, an extensive range of parks and recreational facilities, and a variety of specialized schools and educational institutions.[8] To this extent, it might be hypothesised that the higher the city ranks in the central-place hierarchy the more it is likely to spend on the public services which form part of the city's function as a service centre. While central place theory was initially developed by economists and geographers in order to explain the distribution of private sector facilities and services, it may be possible to adopt the theory to explain the distribution of some public-sector service as well.

Secondly, the higher a city's rank in the urban hierarchy, the more likely it is to attract commuters and visitors who make demands upon public services. Planning and maintaining a clean and effective road and public transport system is likely to be expensive,[9] the public health standards of private hotels and restaurants, and of public facilities, will have to be maintained, large quantities of litter and refuse will have to be moved, parks and open spaces will have to be provided, and large crowds and population movements will have to be regulated. Consequently, the more important the central place, the more it is likely to have to spend on roads, public transport, public health, parks, refuse, and police.

Although all this is speculative there is American and Belgian evidence to support the main thrust of the argument. In the USA, Kasarda has investigated the relationship between suburban population size and growth, and the cost of central city public services in 168 SMSAs, and concludes that the former are crucial determinants of central city expenditures on police, fire, highways, sanitation, recreation, and general administration.[10] And in the preceding chapter in this volume Aiken and Depre convincingly demonstrate that 'ecological centrality' is closely associated with the service expenditure patterns of Belgian cities. The Belgian research and the work on British cities reported in this chapter were carried out completely separately, but by chance, it turns out that they converge on the same general mode of explanation, for it is clear that what Aiken and Depre call 'ecological centrality' is closely akin to the geographers' notion of 'central place'.

There is evidence, therefore, that central-place theory may help to explain the expenditure patterns of county boroughs in England and Wales. The next step is to rank or group the county boroughs according to their position in the urban hierarchy, and to see if their expenditures vary accordingly. Fortunately, two geographers have already done this, so it is possible to build upon their work.[11] The first, Carruthers' study of the major shopping centres of England and Wales (outside London) in 1961, scores cities according to three aspects of their shopping patterns: amount and type of trade; provision of a range of selected shopping facilities; and estimated net trade gained or lost across administrative boundaries.[12] These scores can be used separately, or added together to give an overall weighting for each city, the highest being Manchester, and the lowest Merthyr Tydfil. It is to be expected that the composite score, consisting of the three separate measures, is less likely to suffer from the difficulties of any one of them.

A second source is Smith's classification of English county boroughs in 1965 into eighteen categories according to a wide variety of central place characteristics, including the number of banks, cinemas, post offices, markets, chain stores of various kinds, grammar and comprehensive schools, newspapers, hospitals, hotels, rail depots, theatres, and League football clubs.[13] While Smith's classification is thus based upon a much broader range of items than Carruthers', its utility for present purposes is blunted by the fact that it groups county boroughs into only eighteen categories, while Carruthers has provided a more finely and precisely weighted measure of shopping activity. On the other hand, as has already been pointed out, Carruthers' hierarchy is based upon only one dimension of centrality, as opposed to the many different properties which combine to make a central place. Consequently the two approaches are unlikely to be in full agreement, and, moreover, neither is likely to capture the full complexity of the urban hierarchy.

Whatever the difficulties and deficiencies of these central place measures, however, Tables 6.1 and 6.2 make it clear that they are, in fact, closely associated with spending on many urban services. The tables report the simple correlations between the four urban hierarchy measures, and a set of seventeen service expenditures which are identical to those discussed by Sharpe in the first essay in this volume. Two different years are analysed in order to minimize the danger of picking an unusual year, and in order to explore changes and stability in spending patterns over time. Four main points about the tables are worth stressing briefly.

1. The urban hierarchy seems to be at least as strongly associated with urban service expenditures as any of the social and economic variables mentioned earlier. Of the total of 85 correlations in each year, almost half (47 and 45 per cent) are significant at the 5 per cent level, and quite a high proportion are substantively significant in that they explain at least 10 per cent of expenditure.
2. The pattern of correlations is relatively stable over time, suggesting a consistent effect which is not peculiar to a particular year.
3. The pattern makes theoretical sense in that it is largely consistent with the set of expectations discussed earlier in the paper: the higher the position of a city in the urban hierarchy the more it is likely to spend on libraries, refuse, and police, and on planning (in 1968/69). At the same time, the urban hierarchy does not appear to be strongly related to spending on education in general (as opposed to special education), sewage, personal health, welfare, or housing, and this is also consistent with the theory. On the other hand, parks, public health, planning (in 1960/61), and total expenditure do not have significant correlations by them, as the theory suggests they should

Table 6.1   *Zero-Order Correlations between Smith and Carruthers Central Place Measures and Service Expenditures of County Boroughs in England and Wales, 1960/61*

	Smith ranking	Carruthers' Measures		
	(1–18)	Shopping facilities	Amount/ type of trade	Net gain/ loss of trade	Total score
Per capita *expenditures*					
Education					
Libraries	0.47***	0.47***	0.47**	0.45***	0.49***
Sewage					
Refuse	0.20*	0.34***	0.26*		0.25***
Parks	0.19*				0.20*
Public health					
Personal health	0.21*				0.20*
Children	0.25*	0.26*	0.28**	0.20*	0.29**
Welfare		0.23*	0.28**		
Housing					
Planning	0.27*				
Highways					
Fire	-0.43***	-0.38***	-0.42***	-0.34**	-0.40***
Police		0.22*	0.19*	0.22*	0.25*
Total				.0.22*	0.25*
Education per child	0.22*			0.38*	0.26*
Children per child	0.29**	0.24*	0.27**	0.28**	0.32**
(N)	(74)	(78)	(78)	(73)	(73)

*	= Significant at 0.05 using a one-tailed test.
**	= Significant at 0.01 using a one-tailed test.
***	= Significant at 0.001 using a one-tailed test.

have, while, for reasons which are not clear, children and fire do.

4. The measure which is most closely related to spending is the sum of the three separate measures computed by Carruthers, and for this reason the rest of the analysis will restrict itself to this measure of the urban hierarchy, on the assumption that to substitute any one of the other four measures used in Tables 6.1 and 6.2 would not change the results to any great extent.

Table 6.2   *Zero-Order Correlations between Smith and Carruthers Central Place Measures and Service Expenditures of County Boroughs in England and Wales, 1968/9*

	Smith ranking		Carruthers' measures		
	(1–18)	Shopping facilities	Amount/ type of trade	Net gain/ loss of trade	Total score
Per capita expenditures					
Education					
Libraries	0.48***	0.27**	0.38***	0.40***	0.37***
Sewage					
Refuse	0.26*	0.45***	0.34**	0.22*	0.37***
Parks					
Public health					0.23*
Personal health					
Children	0.32**	0.25*	0.32**	0.23*	0.30**
Welfare					
Housing					
Planning	0.41***		0.30**	0.34**	0.30**
Highways					
Fire	-0.32**	-0.32**	-0.31**	-0.29**	-0.31**
Police	0.28*	0.31**	0.34**	0.13***	0.49**
Total					0.27*
Education per child	0.23*			0.26*	
Children per child	0.38*	0.22*	0.35***	0.33**	0.34**

*   = Significant at 0.05 using a one-tailed test.
**   = Significant at 0.01 using a one-tailed test.
***   = Significant at 0.001 using a one-tailed test.

These, however, are only bi-variate results which tell us nothing of the net effects on expenditures of the urban hierarchy: the 'real' effect may be concealed by intervening variables, and equally the significant correlations reported so far prove to be spurious, and removed after controlling for other variables. If, as the theory claims, position in the urban hierarchy is a central feature of cities, then one would expect it to be associated with a whole cluster of urban characteristics. This is indeed the case, as Table 6.3 shows. This table reports the statistically significant, simple correlations between the urban-hierarchy measure and a set of social, economic, and

Table 6.3   *Zero-Order Correlations between the Urban Hierarchy and a Selection of the Social, Economic and Political Characteristics of County Boroughs, 1960/61, and 1968/69*

| | Urban Hierarchy | |
	1960/61	1968/69
Overcrowding		
Households without hot water		
Standardized mortality rate		
Manual workers		
Owner Occupiers		
Retail-trade turnover per capita	0.32**	0.32**
Density	0.42***	0.43***
Rateable value per capita	0.35***	0.41***
Domestic property (%)	−0.26**	−0.23*
Office property (%)	0.78***	0.72***
Industrial property (%)		
Old people (%)		
Population inflow	0.24*	0.24*
School population		
Log. population	0.74***	0.74***
Conservative seats, 1959 (%)		
Number years Labour control 1955−9		
Number years Conservative control, 1955−9		
Turnout	−0.21*	0 27*
Uncontested seats		

The Urban Hierarchy measure used in this table is the sum of Carruthers three shopping measures.
*   = Significant at 0.05 using a one-tailed test.
**   = Significant at 0.01 using a one-tailed test
***   = Significant at 0.001 using a one-tailed test

political variables which have proved to be closely associated with expenditures. These variables were derived in the way described in Sharpe's essay in this volume (see pp. 13−15), and therefore represent a short-list of the most powerful social, economic, and political variables so far as county borough expenditures are concerned. In other words, to test the net effects of the urban hierarchy against these variables is to subject it to the most stringent and conservative test; if the urban hierarchy continues to be related to service spending while controlling for these variables, then there is good reason to believe that it has explanatory power of its own.

Table 6.3 is not concerned with the general features of the urban hierarchy, but with those features which are also related to spending on urban services. It shows that higher order cities typically have a high retail-trade turnover, a high density, a high rateable value per capita, a small proportion of domestic property but a high proportion of offices, and that they are generally large cities. None of this is at all surprising, given the general thrust of central place theory, but two particularly large correlations present problems of collinearity for regression analysis — those concerned with office property and city size — and these have been removed from the regressions which follow. The grounds for doing so are as follows. While it is clear why central places have a high proportion of office property, it is not clear why offices, as such, should generate a need for some forms of public expenditure. For example, to refer back to Tables 6.1 and 6.2, there is no special reason why library expenditure should be associated with office property, although there is good reason why central places should spend relatively heavily on this central-place service. In other words, on *a priori*, theoretical grounds we may expect library expenditure to be more of a feature of central places than of concentrations of office property, even though central places and offices are closely linked by definition.

Population size is removed from the regressions on the same sort of grounds. Repeated attempts have failed to uncover systematic or theoretically meaningful links between urban service costs and city size.[14] Economies and diseconomies of scale do appear to operate, but the shape of the cost curves varies enormously from one sub-service to another, and the population threshold at which economies are transformed into diseconomies, and *vice versa*, also varies enormously. Besides, there are a good many reasons why spending on urban services may tend to increase with city size, and economies and diseconomies of scale are only two of them.[15] Many of the others, such as population movement, and specialized public services, are connected with the urban hierarchy, rather than population size *per se*. Consequently, it is argued, size is something of a surrogate for centrality, and the problems of collinearity which it raises can be solved, for the time being, by removing it from the list of independent variables. Future research may try to sort out the independent effects of size and centrality, although they are so closely related that this may be difficult to do.

After this brief methodological diversion we can return to the regression analysis. Table 6.4 shows the statistically significant standardized regression coefficients (beta weights) between the urban hierarchy measure and service expenditures in 1960/61 and 1968/69. Five points should be made about this table.

1. The results are generally good in the sense that there are a fairly large number of significant beta weights. In 1960/61 no other social, economic or political variable was related to as many service expenditures

Table 6.4   *Multiple Regression of Urban Hierarchy Measure on Service Expenditures of County Boroughs in England and Wales, 1960/61, and 1968/69*

	1960/61	*1968/69*
Per capita expenditures		
Education		
Libraries	0.38***	0.28*
Sewage		
Refuse	0.36**	0.48***
Public health		
Local health		
Children	0.38**	
Welfare		
Housing		
Planning		
Highways	−0.24*	
Fire	−0.47*	−0.58***
Police	0.30**	0.26*
Total		
Education per child		
Children per child	0.37**	

This table reports standardized regression coefficients
*   = Significant at 0.05 using a one-tailed test.
**   = Significant at 0.01 using a one-tailed test.
***   = Significant at 0.001 using a one-tailed test.
N   = 73.

as the urban hierarchy measure, even though the other variables were carefully chosen for their explanatory power. In 1968/69 the urban-hierarchy measure is related to only four service expenditures, but even so this is exceeded by only three other variables — domestic property, population density, and council housing. In other words, the urban hierarchy measure proves itself to be among the most powerful explanatory variables so far as urban service expenditures are concerned.

2. Having said this it should also be pointed out that the results in Table 6.4 are not outstandingly good. While the urban hierarchy variable does seem to be relatively powerful by comparison with the other social, economic, and political characteristics of cities, its overall explanatory power does not approach that of ecological centrality in Belgian cities, as reported in the preceding paper. We will return to this theme a little later.

3. The figures in Table 6.4 are generally consistent with the theory in

that they show high-order central places to have high expenditures on libraries, refuse, and police services, while sewage, health, welfare, and housing do not, as predicted, have any relationship with city rank.

4. Although the pattern is fairly consistent over the two years, the statistical fit is not as good in 1968/69. This may be partly because the urban hierarchy is measured in terms of shopping activity in 1961, which may have changed to some extent by 1968/69.

5. There are also some anomalies. Contrary to the theory, public health, planning, and total expenditure are not dependent upon city rank, and highways is only weakly and negatively related in 1960/61. Fire expenditure is strongly and negatively related to the urban hierarchy, while childrens' expenditure is quite strongly related in 1960/61, although the theory does not predict this. In sum, while some of the figures fit well with the theory, not all do so.

Further examination of the regression results suggests possible explanations for some of the anomalies. Among the most powerful variables in the equations (see Table 6.5) are overcrowding, rateable value per capita, percentage domestic property, and retail trade turnover per capita, and all of these are fairly closely associated with centrality; the higher the rank of the city the more likely it is to have high densities, high rateable values, a small proportion of domestic property, and a high per capita retail sales (see Table 6.3). While city size and the proportion of office property were excluded from the regressions on the grounds that they were, (a) so closely related to the urban hierarchy as to produce severe problems of collinearity, and (b) largely surrogates for centrality, these other variables were included because they do not produce severe collinearity problems. Nevertheless, they are all features of the urban hierarchy, and to this extent are associated with its explanatory power. Take, for example, the first figure in Table 6.5, that of 0.31 between overcrowding and library expenditure. There is no good reason to believe that people in overcrowded accommodation use libraries, museums, and art galleries to any great extent. On the contrary, the kinds of people who are usually overcrowded are less likely to use these facilities than the undercrowded residents of the spacious suburbs. On the other hand, there is an extremely strong and *negative* coefficient between library spending and domestic property, and yet it is precisely the people in residential areas who are likely to make the most use of libraries, museums and art galleries. The most convincing explanation for the figures related to library spending is that the higher the city ranks in the urban hierarchy, the more it spends on large libraries, museums, and art galleries, which are used not only by the residents of the city but also people who visit it from outside.

Combining the theory advanced in the earlier part of the chapter with the results produced in Tables 6.1–6.5, it is possible to go beyond a

Table 6.5   *Multiple Regression of Urban Hierarchy Related Variables on Service Expenditures of County Boroughs in England and Wales, 1968/69*

	Over-crowding	Retail trade	Rateable value	Domestic property
Per capita expenditures				
Education				−0.28**
Libraries	0.31*	−0.49*		−0.71***
Sewage	−0.33*			−0.45**
Refuse				
Public health			0.42**	
Personal health				
Children		−0.54**	0.32*	−0.48**
Welfare				−0.50**
Housing	0.29*			
Planning			0.27*	
Highways	0.37**			−0.64***
Fire				−0.50**
Police		−0.31*	0.37*	
Total	0.35**			−0.82***
Education per child				−0.33**
Children per child		−0.61**	0.49***	−0.43**

This table reports standardised regression coefficients.
*   = Significant at 0.05 using a one-tailed test.
**   = Significant at 0.01 using a one-tailed test.
***   = Significant at 0.001 using a one-tailed test.
N   = 73.
For reasons of space this table gives the results for only one year, but the figures for 1960/61 are much the same.

general statement about the probable relevance of the urban hierarchy to patterns of city expenditure, and to construct a more detailed model which helps to explain this relevance. First, central places either acquire large populations because of their centrality, or else large populations acquire central place services because they are large enough to do so. Either way, centrality and population size are closely connected as Table 6.3 shows. Population size is also related to levels of expenditure in so far as the largest administrative units may tend to suffer to some extent from diseconomies of scale. Thus:

Centrality→large population size→diseconomies of scale→high service costs.

Central places also have a high proportion of office, shops, and other commercial property, and this type of property generally has a high rateable value.[16] The wealth of the general population of the city may also be enhanced by the importance of central places in the national economy, and by the amount of business they do for surrounding areas. These relationships may be expressed diagrammatically in the following way:

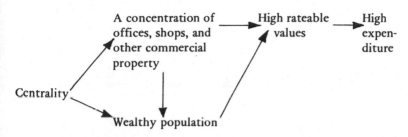

In addition, local government, no less than the private sector, provides various central place services, particularly libraries, museums, art galleries, some sports facilities, parks, botanical gardens, zoos, and special educational facilities. The need for parks and sports facilities is further increased by the fact that the open countryside is relatively inaccessible in those central places which are at the centre of large urban agglomerations.

Centrality ──────▶ high expenditure on public central place services, namely
  libraries, museums, art galleries
  sports facilities
  parks, etc.
  special education

Lastly, central places attract large numbers of commuters and visitors who use them for business and pleasure. The more important the central place, the heavier the demands placed upon some of its services, including police, planning and highways.

Centrality ──────▶ large population flows ──────▶ high expenditure on
  police
  planning
  highways

Combining this set of small diagrams into one large one produces Fig. 6.1. Though somewhat large and complex, the unified diagram serves some useful functions. It specifies the relationships between a set of dependent and independent variables and thus helps to create theoretical coherence in a research area where there is, at present, little more than a few, isolated empirical findings. Moreover, it specifies a set of causal

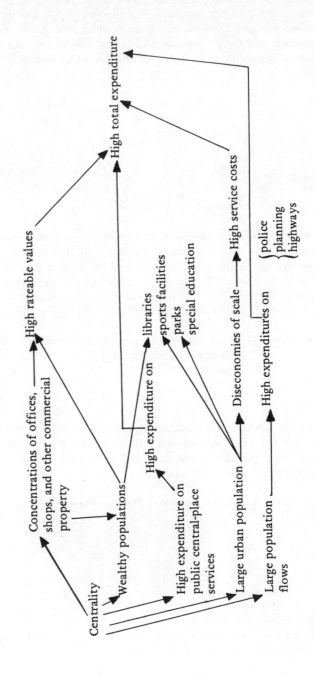

Fig. 6.1   *A causal model relating centrality and local public expenditure*

relationships between variables in a way which permits empirical tests, given adequate and appropriate data. To this extent, it also contains suggestions for future research. For example, to what extent are the higher per capita expenditures of large cities due to diseconomies of scale, and to what extent are they due to the heavy service burdens placed upon central places? Or again, what exactly is the relationship between centrality, population wealth, tax base, and their resulting expenditure patterns? Finally, the relationships suggested in the diagram have practical implications for the way in which central government distributes its grants to local government. At the moment, the needs element of the Rate Support Grant takes no account of the needs generated by a city's place in the urban hierarchy. Perhaps, as in Germany, some allowances for the extra financial burdens of central place should be built in the grant distribution formula?

Summary and Conclusions

Studies of local expenditures have not been particularly successful either in building a general theory or in producing good empirical results. This tentative and exploratory chapter has argued that central place theory, and the attendant research on the urban hierarchy, as developed by geographers, or the theory of ecological centrality, as developed by sociologists, can serve as a useful starting point for a theory explaining variations in city expenditure. Central place theory, it is argued, is relevant to public spending on two kinds of urban services. first, city governments will themselves produce central place services and facilities which, in Britain, are likely to include libraries, museums, and art galleries, parks and sports facilities, and special educational services; secondly, the large number of people who visit central place cities for business and pleasure purposes are likely to make demands upon local services such as police, planning, and highways. Consequently, the higher a city's place in the urban hierarchy, the greater its per capita expenditures on these services is likely to be, and the higher its total per capita expenditure is likely to be.

The evidence about county borough expenditures in England and Wales in the financial year 1960/61 suggests that this theory has a good deal of potential. The social and economic variables which combine to make up the complex of characteristics which form a central place are related in a statistically significant manner to a range of service expenditures, even after controlling for other social and economic variables. To this extent, the initial explorations may be counted as a success. The success is qualified in one important way, however. Centrality and the urban hierarchy does not appear to be as important a determinant of urban expenditures in Britain as in the United States or Belgium. To some extent this may simply be due to the fact that the Belgian study uses a more complicated and precise measure of centrality, but it may also be due to the fact that local government boundaries in Britain have been expanded so that the most important central places include a good deal of their hinterland within their jurisdiction. In other words, since central places are not clearly segregated from non-central places in Britain, central place expenditures are not so very different from those of non-central places.

It should also be noted that central place theory and the urban hierarchy does not offer an explanation for all local spending, much less all public expenditure. It helps toward an understanding of urban service expenditures only (as opposed to more rural authorities), and, more specifically, is concerned with some urban services, rather than the full range. Things like housing, sewage, personal health, and welfare, are not directly related to the urban hierarchy, and cannot be explained in terms of it. These important caveats accepted, there is ample evidence in this chapter about England and Wales, and in the preceding chapter by Aiken and Depre about Belgium to suggest that what is variously termed central place theory, the theory of the urban hierarchy, the theory of ecological centrality, and the urban system approach, offers a powerful theoretical and empirical tool in the analysis of urban spending patterns, and, incidentally, to many other aspects of urban life as well.

Notes

The research reported in this paper is part of a larger study of local government outputs in England and Wales which is being carried out with Jim Sharpe of Nuffield College, Oxford and which was financed by the Centre for Environmental Studies, London. I am most grateful to Clive Payne of Nuffield College and Terence Karran of the University of Dundee for computing help and advice. Paul Knox, also of the University of Dundee, offered helpful comments on an earlier draft of the paper. This chapter is a heavily revised version of a paper presented to the Congress of the International Political Science Association, Moscow, August 1979, and to the Workshop on Urban Spending and Services of the European Consortium for Political Research, Florence, April, 1980.

1. For a critical overview and an extensive bibliography of conventional expenditure studies see L. J. Sharpe Chapter 1, this volume.
2. James N. Danziger, *Making Budgets* (Beverly Hills, Sage Publications inc., 1978), 113.
3. Robert C. Fried, 'Comparative Urban Performance', in Fred I. Greenstein and Nelson W. Polsby (eds.), *Handbook of Political Science*, (Reading, Mass., Addison-Wesley, 1975), Vol. 6, 320.
4. Brian J. L. Berry, 'Cities as Systems within Systems of Cities', *Papers of the Regional Science Association*, 13 (1964) 147–63.
5. Emerys Jones, *Towns and Cities* (Oxford, Oxford University Press, 1966), 87.
6. 'towns with more complex sets of activities will possess all the central activities of lower orders plus a group of central activities that will distinguish them from the central places of immediately lower orders'. K. S. O. Beavon, *Central Place Theory: A Reinterpretation* (London, Longman, 1977), 6.
7. See, for example, Ian Carruthers, 'A Classification of Service Centres in England

and Wales', *Geographical Journal*, 123 (1957) 371.

8. For example, the GLC's grants to the arts in London are nearly as large as those of Arts Council. Evidence by the Greater London Council, *Report of the Committee of Inquiry into Local Government Finance*, Appendix 2 (London, HMSO, 1967), 278.

9. See Brian J. L. Berry and William L. Garrison, 'Recent Developments of Central Place Theory', reprinted in William H. Leahy, *et al.*, *Urban Economics* (New York, Free Press, 1970), 124.

10. John D. Kasarda, 'The impact of the suburban population growth on central city service functions', *American Journal of Sociology*, 77 (1972), 1111–24; Brian J. L. Berry and John D. Kasarda, *Contemporary Urban Ecology* (New York, Macmillan, 1977), 210–27.

11. Unfortunately one of the best empirical studies of British cities which classifies them according to their range of central services and facilities neither ranks them hierarchically nor gives them central place scores. See Garbis Armen, 'A Classification of Cities and City Regions in England and Wales, 1966', *Regional Studies*, 6 (1972) 149–82.

12. W. I. Carruthers, 'Major Shopping Centres in England and Wales, 1961', *Regional Studies*, 1 (1967) 56–81. See also Carruthers, op. cit. (1957).

13. R. D. P. Smith, 'The Changing Urban Hierarchy', *Regional Studies*, 12 (1968) 1–19.

14. British research is summarized in K. Newton, 'Comparative Community Performance', *Current Sociology*, 26 (1976) 50–55, and American work is summarized in W. F. Fox, J. M. Stam, W. M. Godsey, and S. D. Brown, *Economies of Size in Local Government: An Annotated Bibliography* (Washington, D.C., United States Department of Agriculture, Rural Development Research Report No. 9),

15. Details of the argument are spelled out in K. Newton, *et al.*, *Balancing the Books: The Financial Problems of Local Government in Western Europe* (London, Sage Ltd., 1980) 161–83.

16. For evidence on this point see Newton, op. cit. (1976) 75–6

SECTION 3

DEBTS. CUTS, AND CRISES

7 FISCAL STRAIN AND AMERICAN CITIES: SIX BASIC PROCESSES

TERRY NICHOLS CLARK and LORNA CROWLEY FERGUSON

The fiscal difficulties of New York City since the spring of 1975 have stimulated considerable commentary and public debate. Much discussion remains cloudy, with ideology and special pleading often mingled with efforts to unravel the issues. And despite the billions involved, remarkably little scholarly analysis has been undertaken of New York City or more general urban fiscal difficulties. Passage of Proposition 13 by California voters in 1978 made explicit another dimension of the problem. Urban fiscal strain provides a strategic research site for analyses of community power, urban politics, and municipal finance.

This paper seeks to clarify the causes of urban fiscal difficulty in American cities by outlining the dynamics of six distinct processes. These operate differentially in many American cities; together they converged to produce the acute difficulties in New York City. They are nevertheless distinct enough to consider separately both for analytical coherence and for policy intervention; the causes and solutions to each are distinguishable . enough to warrant separate attention. The six processes are, 1. national trends, 2. attracting and keeping jobs, 3. the politicization of municipal employees, 4. the poor-redistribution cycle, 5. maintaining a non-poor population, and 6. maturing fiscal obligations.

What is Fiscal Strain?

Our conception of fiscal strain is an imbalance between city government spending or debt and private sector resources in the city. Fiscal strain can thus be measured using a ratio of city government spending or debt to local resources such as median family income, taxable property value, and population size. Such measures can be in the form of *levels* for comparisons at one time across several cities, or *changes* over time in one or numerous cities. Twenty nine fiscal strain indicators have been computed and analyzed elsewhere for the Permanent Community Sample of the National Opinion Research Center.[1]

One important finding from this empirical work is that fiscal strain differs considerably across cities at one point in time, as well as in change rates from 1960 to the late 1970s. New York City has much higher levels of debt and spending than most other cities, and increased spending rapidly in the 1960s, but has been cutting back in some areas since 1975.

Other cities exhibit altogether different patterns. The magnitude of differences among cities leads us to focus in this paper on primarily local factors generating fiscal strain, rather than national trends which affect all cities.[2] We nevertheless begin with certain basic propositions about national trends.

National Trends

Here we include broad national changes affecting virtually all cities. The most important for urban fiscal questions are economic growth and federal assistance. Economic growth is nationally uneven in most countries, whether the economy is largely operated by the central government, privately, or mixed. In a dynamic economy, some cities and regions prosper, and others suffer, in so far as consumer demands and technologies change and these differentially 'fit' with the resources available in different urban locations. Such spatial differentiations will be discussed shortly. Here it is enough to note that national recession generally hurts municipal governments.

P1. *The greater the downturn in the national economy, the greater the fiscal difficulties for cities.*[3] The apparent simplicity of this idea can still be misleading. Although recession may decrease city revenues, it may also decrease certain expenditures such as police services for tourists. What matters is the marginal change in revenues compared to the change in expenditures due to recession. The same is true for the effects of inflation on city governments. High inflation rates were widely blamed by urban leaders as causing fiscal problems in the late 1960s. Many products that cities had to purchase (capital facilities, fuels, etc.) increased in cost faster than did municipal revenues. The situation is complicated by the high labour-intensiveness of most municipal services, and hence minimal changes in productivity compared to more technologically dependent sectors of the economy. Growth in municipal expenditures thus translates, more than anything else, into growth in municipal employee salaries. This expenditure side of the fiscal strain equation is elaborated below. In terms of revenue, the fundamental variable mediating national economic trends and local fiscal health is the municipal revenue structure.[4]

P2. *The more elastic the revenue structure of a municipal government, the more its revenues contract in time of recession.* This simple economic tautology remains an important proposition for distinguishing among American cities. Boston obtains over 80 per cent of its local revenues from property taxes; New York about 50 per cent; many cities in the South, like Birmingham, under 20 per cent. The property tax was attacked in earlier years precisely because it was inelastic, and did not increase as rapidly as the rest of the economy.[5] New York City moved away from reliance on the property tax in the 1960s, and thereby captured revenues and income taxes and charges on local businesses. These increased with economic prosperity. This changed revenue structure left New York more exposed in the early 1970s recession, however, compared for example to Boston or other cities with less elastic revenue structures.

The economic base of the city also affects reactions to economic difficulties.

P3. *The more diversified a city's economic base, and the less it is composed of cyclically-sensitive industries, the less extreme are fluctuations in revenue for the municipal government in time of national recession or rapid growth.* Economic diversification dampens fluctuations in so far as the different sectors of the local economy differentially lead and lag through the trough of a recession. Detroit's lack of diversification, by contrast, makes it particularly dependent on expansion or recession as experienced uniquely by the automobile industry. Still, even national economic growth remains unevenly distributed, and often involves movements of individual firms or industries (such as shoe and textile manufacturers leaving New England towns). Cities that succeed in diversifying their local economies have some degree of protection against such developments.

Similarly, some industries like steel fluctuate considerably with business cycles, while others are far more stable.[6] Cities with more cyclically-sensitive industries are more open to fluctuations in municipal government revenues (unless their revenue structures avoid dependence on such industries).

Federal government grants also affect cities importantly, and although 'more is better' is argued by most urban leaders when in Washington, the proposition is not altogether convincing. Simply the New York City case questions the assertion, as in 1974–75, 48 per cent of total expenditures for New York City were reimbursed by intergovernmental revenues, while the figure for all US cities was 40 per cent.[7] More generally, in cross-sectional correlations and regressions for fifty-one cities, we found almost no significant relationships between the percentage of municipal revenues from intergovernmental transfers and the level of fiscal strain.[8] Much of the econometric work on intergovernmental assistance concludes that, if anything, intergovernmental transfers stimulate more, rather than substitute for, locally raised revenues.[9] In a study of six European countries, Newton *et al.* found no relationship between urban fiscal strain and the degree to which the central government had assumed responsibility for local services.[10] Perhaps more important for the local official than the quantity is the form of the intergovernmental assistance.

P4. *The more clearly defined the amount, the longer the term, and the fewer restrictions in intergovernmental assistance to cities, the less the urban fiscal strain.* From proposition 4, cities should suffer less fiscal strain if established formulae are used continually, as approximated by General Revenue Sharing. By contrast, fiscal strain is more likely associated with the uncertainties of categorical grants, especially those allocated via competitive bidding. New York, Boston, New Haven, and other cities that did particularly well in submitting proposals, suffered declines in federal assistance in the early 1970s.[11] These examples illustrate both the uncertainties of competitive bidding and the effects of changing to formula grants.

Complex interactions among variables should also not lead us to omit simple verities.

P5. *The weaker the fiscal condition of the municipal government, and the more extended it is in terms of debt, the greater the fiscal problems which are likely to emerge with national recession.* Just as a critically ill patient risks more than a healthy person when both catch colds, so New York was more exposed than many cities in the early 1970s. A 'weak fiscal condition' as in P5 is often associated with declines in jobs and population. We turn to these in the next sections.

Attracting and Keeping Jobs: Maintaining the Economic Base

A sound economic base is the most commonly cited source of fiscal health, the goal of many local officials, the key criterion for many municipal credit analysts. It is simpler to document its association with fiscal strain than to explain causally in turn, but documenting this association is at least a first step.

P6. *The more stable the economic base, in terms of jobs per resident, the less the fiscal strain.* In times of rapid inflation, 'stable' in proposition 6 should be read as 'after adjusting for inflation'. This still remains imprecise, for economic growth may signal better long-term prospects than stability. Growth in jobs per resident, however, brings changes in the tax-base mix and the services the local government will be requested to deliver. It implies expansion in terms of roads, sewerage, gas, electricity and similar facilities, often funded by long-term municipal debt. The few cases of municipal default since the Second World War have usually occurred in small communities that became overextended in planning such growth.[12]

What in turn are the sources of such a strong economic base? Certain private sector characteristics seem of considerable importance.

a. Low density and low land value — permitting construction of single-story assembly plants and warehouses.
b. Low cost of labour in the local private market.
c. No unions, or at least unions ready to co-operate with new firms.
d. Access to major rail and road transit lines — for industry if not all local service activities.

To such a basic list may be added some quasi-social and governmental variables.

e. Reasonable crime rates.
f. Stable social and economic characteristics of the city.
g. Low tax burden.
h. Stable and co-operative local government — for re-zoning, assembling land packages, help in negotiating union contracts, etc.
i. Co-operative local institutions — for credit, land, labour negotiations, etc.

Still, despite the frequency of such variables as these in repeated studies,[13] there are also considerable differences and interactions with type of job. The above list applies most to reasonably modern industry and many service activities; it is less adequate for specialized services like finance, advertising, publishing, law, merchandizing, and entertainment which also depend on other characteristics such as higher density and physical access to specialized clients. Cities like New York have more of a comparative advantage for such specialized services than for most heavy or light industry, or more routinized services.

It is primarily the logic of variables a to i which has generated the growth of suburbs and many Sunbelt cities. In the face of such forces, many cities have simply declined dramatically — many older industrial towns of New England have lost jobs since the turn of the century. City government officials can seek to encourage the growth of local jobs and population, but the evidence to date suggests that their efforts have limited effects compared to the broader national forces. By contrast, public officials have considerable control over city government. Most adaptation of local officials to shifts in jobs and population has been through changing the activities of the local government. For example, Pittsburgh, which has lost jobs and population like many other cities, has cut back its municipal labour force and held the line on municipal debt and expenditures so that it has remained much more competitive in its tax burden than Boston or New York. New York, since 1975, has been moving in the same direction,[14]

Such adaptation is not easy. In older cities, the costs of maintaining an aging physical plant (roads, sewers, public transportation) are usually high. When supported by a declining population, per capita costs escalate. But adaptation is largely a problem of leadership, not of the economic base. Leadership is also central to the next section.

Organized Groups, Political Leadership, and Policy Outputs

The Politicization of Municipal Employees
The Poor-Redistribution Cycle
Maintaining a Non-Poor Population

As the next three processes share several elements, they are partially dealt with together. Each is summarized in a separate figure, however, to indicate its basic elements (see Figures 7.1, 7.2 and 7.3).[15]

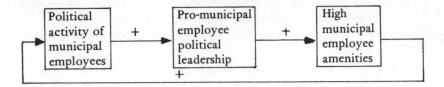

Fig. 7.1. *The politicization of municipal employees*

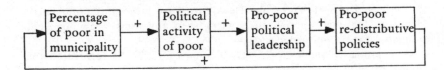

Fig. 7.2. *The poor-redistribution cycle*

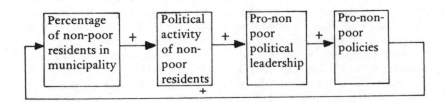

Fig. 7.3. *Maintaining a non-poor population*

It is primarily on the basis of surveys of individual citizens that we distinguish three basic sectors with distinct interests in urban public policy.[16] The poor favour redistributive policies oriented toward themselves. Municipal employees favour higher salaries, pensions, and other amenities for themselves. The non-poor favour maintenance of basic municipal services at a level that keeps the city liveable — something hard to assess meaningfully with only fiscal output data. They favour a low tax burden. They oppose redistributive policies. This need not imply a total absence of concern for general social welfare; without some broad-based public support for income redistribution, little would be accomplished. But if the preference for redistribution to the poor is stochastically distributed across the non-poor, and lower than among the poor themselves, our basic results should follow. More formally we may specify a policy congruence function as follows:

$$PO_{ij_c} = -(PO_{ij_a} - PO_{ij_d})^2 \tag{1}$$

where

i = sector =   1 if municipal employees
i = sector =   2 if poor
                 3 if non-poor
j = policy issue in question
a =   actual level of policy outputs for issue j
d =   desired level of policy outputs by sector i for issue j
c =   congruence of the desired level sector i with a, the actual level of policy outputs for issue j

As PO_{ij_a} comes closer to PO_{ij_d}, that is, the desired level of policy output sector i moves closer to the actual level, PO_{ij_c} increases. Conversely, as the disparity between PO_{ij_d} grows, the congruence term PO_{ij_c} decreases; the policy may thus be said to be less congruent with the preferences of sector i.[17]

The basic issues desired by each sector are as follows:

$$PO_{1j_d} = \max(A)$$

$$PO_{2j_d} = \max(R)$$

$$PO_{3j_d} = \max(MS, 1/TB)$$

where

A = amenities for municipal employees
R = redistributive policies oriented toward the poor
MS= basic municipal services
TB= tax burden in the municipality

If we define PR_i as the proportion of the community population included in sector i, then a basic proposition is

$$PO_{ij_c} = f(PR_i) \tag{2}$$

That is, P7 *the larger the proportion of the community population included in sector* i, *the more congruent will policy outputs be with preferences of sector* i. (Here and in equations below, coefficients such as f in equation 2 indicate a positive hypothesized relationship.)

The relative size of each sector is doubtless important in explaining policy outputs. But converting the number of sector members into policy outputs is facilitated by resources such as organization. If we define O_i as the degree of organization of sector i (such a membership per capita in a leading sector-related organization), and O_o as the degree of organization of other sectors in the community, then

$$PO_{ij_c} = f(O_i/O_o) \tag{3}$$

That is, P8 *policies should be more congruent with the preferences of a sector if it is more highly organized than other sectors of the community.*

Proposition 8 is weakened if there are conflicts among different organizations within a sector. Such potential intra-sector differentiation is considered in proposition 9, perhaps best introduced verbally, and then more formally. P9. *The fewer the lines of cleavage within a sector, relative to other sectors, the more policy outputs are consistent with the sector's preferences.* For example, if all poor persons are black, and all blacks are poor, they should be easier to organize. Let C_k be a social characteristic k of a community population of significance for its mobilization (e.g. black racial identity). Let P_k be those members of the community population that share k (i.e. black residents). Then

$$PS_{ik} = S_i \cap P_k = \text{persons in } S_i \text{ with characteristic } k \tag{4}$$

$$M_1 = \frac{PS_{ik}}{S_i} = \text{proportion of sector } i \text{ with } k \tag{5}$$

$$Q_k = P_k \cap \overline{S}_i = \text{persons with } k \text{ not in } S_i \tag{6}$$

$$T_k = \frac{Q_k}{P_k} = \text{proportion of persons with } k \text{ not in } S_i \tag{7}$$

The idea of cross-cutting cleavages for S_i on characteristic k may then be expressed as

$$XC_{S_{ik}} = f(M_i) + g(T_k) \tag{8}$$

Such cleavages should be greater if k is shared by a smaller proportion of the sector (M_i) and a larger proportion of the rest of the population (T_k). When $XC_{S_{ik}} = 0$, k is found only in S_i. If $XC_{S_{ok}}$ is defined as the cross-cutting cleavages for sectors other than S_i, we may restate P9 as

$$PO_{ij_c} = f(XC_{S_{ok}} / XC_{S_{ik}}) \tag{9}$$

Consider now empirical patterns of organization for our three sectors. The poor are a sector which decades of social organizers and theorists have sought to activate in US cities with remarkably little success. Efforts which have succeeded have generally coalesced around some specific characteristic shared by the poor. The most important example since the 1960s is race.[18] Building on the momentum of national civil rights organizations, several black urban political groups succeeded in organizing blacks to register, vote, demonstrate, and boycott – in Cleveland, Gary, Atlanta, and Birmingham with notable political impact.[19] Although survey evidence indicates that the poor generally share preferences for more redistributive public spending, it has been poor blacks who have been most successful in organizing as a sector and making an impact on the local political process.

Municipal employees illustrate a much higher level of organization. Although they have had professional associations for decades, municipal employees unionized in large numbers only in the late 1960s, inspired in part by the success of blacks and the ability of unions in cities like New York to win major wage increases.[20] The shared characteristic k in this example is dependence on a common employer whose leaders in turn visibly depend on groups who have brought them to office. And indeed, in cities where municipal employees have succeeded in reaching higher levels of organization, they have also obtained more amenities.[21]

By contrast, efforts to organize the non-poor have been minimally successful. Obviously subsectors of the non-poor are highly organized – in special interest groups like neighbourhood associations, environmental groups, etc. The critical point for urban fiscal questions, however, is that such organizations are primarily concerned with affecting specific policies which usually increase expenditures. It is the normally 'silent majority' of the vast non-poor sector which prefers lower taxes, even while its individual members prefer more spending on matters of special interest to them. Although the fiscal conservatism of this sector has been clear in survey data for years (in the sources cited above), it was generally ignored until 1978 when proposition 13 gave expression to these concerns. In principle such concerns could be translated into fiscal policy through organization as in the above propositions. Given the large number of votes but the ephemeral character of most broad-based organizations, however, political leaders often play an especially important role in capturing such fiscally conservative preferences.

Given the opposition between policies favoured by the non-poor and the two other sectors, we could also include arrows connecting the non-poor process in Fig. 3.7 to the two others. Such 'oppositional feedback' clearly limits the potential of the poor and municipal employee processes to find an 'equilibrium' of spending at positive infinity, as do the anticipatory calculations of political leaders and organized group representatives concerning the degree to which the non-poor will remain quiescent. It is only when such calculations fail that 'taxpayers' revolts' emerge.

Figs. 7.1 and 7.3 indicate that policies are effected only if the political leadership is persuaded to act. Although changes in the socio-economic base (e.g. percentage black) provide the underlying dynamic for many such changes, socio-economic changes are not automatically translated into policy changes. Typically policy changes are the result of a new sector or coalition bringing pressure to bear on the political leadership, or similarly a new mayor or city-council member seizing the opportunity to forge a new base of popular support. In such instances, the sectors that previously benefited from government are likely to resist actively the new leadership initiatives. Such confrontations between blacks and Irish, Italian, and related white ethnic groups have been common in American cities since the early 1960s. In many suburban areas, by contrast, conflicts often arise between older residents with preferences for low spending patterns and newer residents who prefer more services.

A dynamic political leader can play a critical role in articulating the concerns of a new sector, or in the case of many cities in the 1970s, in helping adapt expansive citizen preferences to the austerities of available resources. Mayors Richard Daley in Chicago, Peter Flaherty in Pittsburgh, and Richard Hatcher in Gary have all played important roles in these respects.

These examples can be modelled using a notation similar to that developed above.

$$L_{pj} = \frac{L_{nj} - L_{rj}}{L_{nj}} \tag{10}$$

where

L_{nj} = number of political leaders (e.g. city-council members) acting on issue j

L_{rj} = number of leaders opposed to issue j

L_{pj} = proportion of leaders favouring issue j

Then we may state P10:

$$PO_{ij_c} = f(L_{pj}) \tag{11}$$

P10. *The larger the proportion of political leaders favouring interest on an issue in sector* i, *the more likely it is to be implemented.*

Coalitions among leaders and sectors are a complex topic that we mention only briefly.[22] We consider the major leadership configurations likely in terms of the three basic sectors in this analysis. These appear in Table 7.1; an equation predicting fiscal strain could be developed using a general linear, additive model without distorting most of the leadership effects in this table. The major exceptions are L_2 and L_3. Although the poor and non-poor are not likely partners for leadership, their relative importance is likely to interact, as shown in Table 7.2.

The second interaction term in equation 12 is for the poor-municipal employees configuration. Political involvement of these two sectors is

Table 7.1   *Likely Outputs of Basic Leadership Configurations*

Leadership	Dominant actors	R	A	MS	TB	Comment
L_1	p + mec	H	H	M-H	H	Most expensive (illustrated by New York City)
L_2	p + np	M	L	M	M	Unlikely
L_3	np + me	L	H	H	M	Example?
L_4	np	L	L	L	L	Least fiscal strain (Waco?)
L_5	me	L	H	M	M-H	Unlikely
L_6	p	II	L	M	M-H	Unlikely
L_7	p + np + mc	M	M	M	M	General compromise (approximated by Chicago)

Policy outputs likely span R A MS TB.

p = poor
np = non-poor
me = municipal employees
H, M, and L are high, medium, and low spending
R = poor-oriented redistributive activities
A = amenities for municipal employees
MS = basic municipal services
TB = tax burden.

Table 7.2

Hypothesized coefficient of d (L_p) (L_{np}) in equation 12	Dominant actor leadership score	
	Poor	Non-poor
−	L	H
0	M	M
+	H	L

likely to interact to increase spending. A partial model for fiscal strain in terms of leadership patterns involving these sectors might thus read:

$$GE = aL_p + bL_{me} - cL_{np} + d\,(L_p)\,(L_{np}) + e\,(L_p)\,(L_{me}) \qquad (12)$$

where a, b, c, and d are coefficients to be estimated, and GE is an indicator of overall general expenditures for the city.

The degree to which preferences of political leaders are translated into public policy depends in good part on resources available to them.

All are likely to interact and to effect P10 in the same direction.

P11. *The greater the resources of political leaders, the greater their ability to implement their preferences.*

$$PO_{ij_c} = L^f_{pj} \, RES^g \tag{13}$$

where

RES = resources of political leaders
g = coefficient to be estimated

Examples of leaders' resources are legal authority, informal power, networks of social contacts, and the like, empirical measures of which are analysed elsewhere,[23] where we find indeed that a mayoral power measure enhances the impact of mayor's preferences on fiscal policy.

The various determinants of PO_{ij_c} may now be brought together in a single statement summarizing proposition 7 to proposition 11.

P12. *The larger the proportion of community residents included in sector i, and the more highly organized is sector i, the fewer other lines of cleavage cross-cut the sectoral cleavages, the more leaders favour the interests of sector i, and the more resources available to the political leadership, the more the preferences of sector i will be reflected in local public policies.* Or more formally:

$$PO_{ij_c} = PR^a_i (O_i / O_o)^b \, (XC_{S_{ok}} / XC_{S_{ik}})^c \, (L_{pj} \, RES)^d \tag{14}$$

where $a–d$ are coefficients to be estimated.[24]

Thus far the propositions have addressed the basic horizontal linkages depicted in Figs. 7.1–7.3. Consider now the feedback arrows. The general idea in each case is: P13. *The higher a policy output favourable to a given sector, and the greater its increase in a given time period, the greater the expansion of that sector in the next time period.*[25] Clearly many other variables affect residential choice, but with our attention focused on the dynamics of these public-policy issues, other variables are here summarized simply as OV. Obviously there are dozens of 'other variables' which may play quite significant roles in affecting residential choice, but we make no attempt to review them here.

Three increasingly complex simultaneous equation models outline the feedback processes. The simplest is a one-time, non-lagged model

$$PR_i = PO^f_{ij_c} \, OV^g$$

$$PO_{ij_c} = PR^b_i \, OV^q \tag{15}$$

This might be estimated with a cross-sectional analysis of the level of policy outputs compared across cities. A slight refinement would be to lag the policy output for a period of time (perhaps 5 years) during which it could affect residential choices, and they in turn affect subsequent policy outputs:

$$PR_{it} = PO^f_{ij_{c\,(t-1)}}\ OV^g \tag{16}$$

$$PO_{ij_{ct}} = PR^b_{i\,(t-1)}\ OV^q$$

If one considers changes in sector size over time, however, this is likely to be affected more by changes in the policy outputs than the level of policy outputs, as in

$$PR_{it} - PR_{i\,(t-1)} = [PO_{ij_{c\,(t-1)}} - PO_{ij_{c\,(t-2)}}]^t OV^g \tag{17}$$

$$PO_{ij_{ct}} = PR^b_{i\,(t-1)}\ OV^q$$

A still more refined model of change in sector size includes both the past level and change in policy outputs:

$$PR_{it} - PR_{i\,(t-1)} = PO^f_{ij_{c\,(t-1)}}\ [PO_{ij_{c\,(t-1)}} - PO_{ij_{c(t-2)}}]^g\ OV^b \tag{18}$$

$$PO_{ij_{ct}} = PR^q_{i\,(t-1)}\ OV^r$$

Maturing Fiscal Obligations

Maturing fiscal obligations are contracted by past local officials, but their burdens fall on present and future officials and citizens. The most obvious examples are debt payments and pension liabilities. Indeed, some observers have suggested that it is simply good politics for municipal leaders to deliver immediate benefits to their constituents, and to postpone as many costs as legally possible. The basic idea here may be quite simply stated.

P14. *The larger the maturing fiscal obligations as a proportion of municipal revenues, the greater the fiscal strain.* That is,

$$FS = f\,(MFO/GR) \tag{19}$$

where

FS = fiscal strain
MFO = maturing fiscal obligations
GR = general revenue

This implies a cross-sectional, or at least one-time perspective. A refocus on marginal changes into the future involving the same basic process suggests: P15. *The greater the increase in maturing fiscal obligations as a proportion of municipal revenues, the greater the fiscal strain.* Or restated:

$$FS_t = f(MFO_t - MFO_{t-n} / GR_t - GR_{t-n}) \tag{20}$$

where n = number of years before obligations mature.

Consider capital construction projects such as schools, roads, and parks, which cities finance in different ways, varying in the degree to which they will constitute 'maturing fiscal obligations'. The fewest obligations are passed on to the future if the project is financed from current revenues. Numerous capital projects are funded in this manner by American cities, although the exact proportion is difficult to compare across cities given the reporting formats of different cities and the US Census (in the *City Government Finances* series).[26]

Payment for a facility at the same approximate time that it is constructed is consistent with the public finance principle of 'pay-as-you-acquire'.[27] The second basic alternative principle is 'pay-as-you-use'. Here the facility is paid for over the period of its approximate useful life, such as 20 years. One can reasonably argue that some portion of the costs of a facility should be shared by future citizens if they are to benefit from capital facilities. Our concern is not to assess the appropriateness of such funding vehicles, but simply to consider them in terms of the degree to which they constitute obligations which in turn can create fiscal strain in future years. One useful indicator would be the proportion of capital projects funded from current revenues. Another is the schedule of debt payments (including interest and repayment of principal) which the city must meet in future years. These indicators could be used to measure the *MFO* terms in propositions 14 and 15. There may be some interaction effects involving the size and type of project; debt is more likely for projects which are large and for purposes generally acceptable to the debt market.

Under continual pressure from political leaders, municipal finance directors have developed numerous procedures to speed up revenue collection and postpone expenditures. A recently debated case is that of Philadelphia, where in 1975 Mayor Rizzo, up for re-election, pressed his finance director for more expenditure without alienating voters through a tax increase.[28] Lennox Moak, Philadelphia's highly respected finance director, was concerned that a deficit would raise the already high interest costs for the city. They decided to change several accounting procedures (from cash to accrual basis, estimating questionable revenues, etc.) which generated a substantial (one-time) surplus of cash for the 1975 fiscal year. The surplus was announced in 'tombstone' advertisements in the

New York Times and *Wall Street Journal*, which did not mention the accounting procedure changes. Apparently the advertisements initially helped lower the cost of borrowing for the city. Before long, however, the accounting procedure changes became known as the source of the surplus. Philadelphia was widely criticized by the investment community and the next year was forced to impose a 30 per cent property tax increase, and met increasing difficulties in selling bonds.

This example illustrates the enormous pressures on some local finance officials to generate immediate cash flows and to postpone tax burdens, even to the extent of pursuing policies that hurt the city in the very near future. And it was not only the city finances that suffered. Mayor Rizzo suffered politically with the voters, and Finance Director Moak became the subject of a highly publicized SEC investigation for fraud, which in turn generated numerous lawsuits and a movement by many finance directors to vote out Moak from his position as president of the Municipal Finance Officers Association.

New York and Philadelphia illustrate the same basic point in their pension funding arrangements. Mayor Rizzo was elected mayor as former police chief, and some observers felt that his questionable fiscal efforts were in good part due to his concern to improve the amenities of Philadelphia police officers. Although John Lindsay was by no means elected to represent municipal workers, he too ended by granting benefits to municipal employees that were apparently designed to be hidden from local citizens. In New York, salaries per se for most municipal employees (i.e. police, fire fighters and teachers) were broadly similar to those in many other cities in the late 1960s and early 1970s. The big increases were granted in hard-to-see benefits, particularly pension benefits.[29] One should recall that, until the mid-1970s, in most cities pensions remained a highly esoteric area relegated to a few specialists. Only since revelations about New York — and increasingly about other cities — have the press and general citizenry begun to become aroused sufficiently to make pension settlements a more visible part of the municipal fiscal agenda.

But if the concern has increased, the data remain woefully inadequate. Very few cities have released precise data concerning specific benefit packages for fringes and pensions, levels of funding of pension plans, numbers of workers in various benefit categories, and actuarial estimates of worker retirement patterns.[30] Only one-quarter of forty-six cities recently studied published actuarial tables with their bond prospectuses, and very few of these reported the specific actuarial assumptions on which the tables were based,[31] although this is gradually improving.[32]

Conclusion and Policy Implications

The basic conclusion of this analysis is that local officials and others concerned with urban fiscal strain should not look for a single cause, or waste undue effort debating 'the Sunbelt' versus 'fiscal mismanagement' as general sources of urban difficulty. Six important and distinct sources of urban fiscal difficulty are isolated above, each with its own set of sources and solutions. If a city like New York suffers from most of these, this is by no means the case elsewhere. And even if a single city suffers from all six problems, isolating the dynamics of each process points to the specificity of each in terms of solutions as well. Different aspects of these issues can serve as important research sites for continuing work on public opinion, voluntary associations, political mobilization, coalition theory, and other traditions.

Notes

Terry Clark and Lorna Crowley Ferguson share equal co-authorship of this paper, which is a conceptual statement we prepared as part of the Project on Urban Fiscal Strain. The Project, nearing completion, has led to several papers and a major volume, Terry Nichols Clark and Lorna Crowley Ferguson, *Political Processes and Urban Fiscal Strain* (tentative title). The volume elaborates and tests empirically many propositions stated in this paper. This is a revision of a paper presented at the annual meeting of the American Sociological Association, Chicago, 6 September 1977. For comments we thank Ronald Burt, Reid Charles, Irene Rubin, Arthur Stinchcombe, and Erwin Zimmermann. Support was generously provided by the Twentieth Century Fund and USPHS, NICHD, HDO8916-3.

1. T. Clark, I. Rubin, L. Pettler, and E. Zimmermann, *How Many New Yorks? — The New York Fiscal Crisis in Comparative Perspective*, Comparative Study of Community Decision-Making, Research Report No. 72 (Chicago, University of Chicago, 1976); T. Clark, 'Fiscal Management of American Cities: Funds Flow Indicators', *Journal of Accounting Research*, 15 (1977) 54-106.
2. In this respect our approach obviously complements those of others who have focused primarily on national phenomena, e.g. D. Bell, 'The Public Household: on 'Fiscal Sociology' and the Liberal Society', *The Public Interest*, 37 (Fall 1974) 29-68; J. O'Connor, *The Fiscal Crisis of the State* (New York, St. Martin's Press, 1973); R. Friedland, F. Piven, and R. Alford, 'Political Conflict, Urban Structure, and the Fiscal Crisis', presented to annual meeting of American Sociological Association, 5-9 September 1977, Chicago.
3. P1 designates proposition 1.
4. Empirical work on the effects of recession and inflation on city government is very limited as almost no studies have compared the marginal effects on both revenues and expenditures. One of the few that has suggests that net revenue losses from these national trends are small (about 5 per cent each for the 1975 recession). Advisory Commission in Intergovernmental Relations, *State-Local Finances in Recession and Inflation* (Washington DC, ACIR, 1979) Report A-70.
5. D. Netzer, *The Economics of the Property Tax* (Washington, DC, Brookings, 1966), presents the basic argument about inelasticity of the property tax. Although Metropolitan Studies Program of the Maxwell School, Syracuse University, *The Fiscal Implications of Inflation: A Study of Six Local Governments* (New York, Syracuse University, 1975), and G. Peterson, 'Finance', in William Gorham and Nathan Glazer (eds.), *The Urban Predicament* (Washing-

ton, DC, The Urban Institute, 1976), 53, point out that housing values often increased as rapidly as sales about 1970, property taxes are more politically difficult to increase than others, and they are less likely to decline in recession than sales taxes and many charges.

6. Cf. G. Vernez, R. Vaughan, B. Burright, and S. Coleman, *Regional Cycles and Employment Effects of Public Works Investments* (Santa Monica, RAND, 1977), Report R-2052-EDA.

7. Cf. US Bureau of the Census, *City Government Finances in 1974-75*, (Washington, DC, USGPO, 1976), Series GF75 No. 4.

8. T. Clark and L. Ferguson, 'Local Autonomy and Fiscal Performance', background paper for conference of Section on the Community, American Sociological Association, University of Chicago, 18-19 March 1977.

9. E.g. W. Oates, *Financing the New Federalism* (Baltimore and London, Johns Hopkins University Press, 1975); Advisory Commission in Intergovernmental Relations, *Federal Grants: Their Effects on State-Local Expenditures, Employment Levels, Wage Rates* (Washington, DC, USGPO, 1977), ACIR Report A-61.

10. K. Newton, et al., *Balancing the Books* (London, Sage Publications, 1980).

11. The pre- and post-1973 rates of average annual increases due to non-local sources is striking:

New York City percentage of revenue growth from:

Period	Local revenue	State and Federal aid	Net annual borrowing
1965-73	37%	55%	8%
1973-75	22%	8%	70%

Source:Peterson, 'Finance', in Gorham and Glaaer op. cit., 64.

12. Advisory Commission on Intergovernmental Relations, *City Financial Emergencies* (Washington, DC, USGPO, 1973).

13. J. Meyer, J. Kain, and M. Wohl, *The Urban Transportation Problem* (Cambridge, Mass., Harvard University Press, 1965); H. Perloff and L. Wingo (eds.), *Issues in Urban Economics* (Baltimore, Johns Hopkins Press, 1968); R Berry and F. Horton (eds.), *Geographic Perspectives on Urban Systems* (Englewood Cliffs, N. J., Prentice-Hall, 1973); R. Vaughan, *The Urban Impacts of Federal Policies*, Vol. 2, *Economic Development* (Santa Monica, RAND, 1977), Report R-2052-EDA.

14. T. Clark and E. Fuchs, 'New York City in Comparative Perspective', in Temporary Commission on City Finances, *The City in Transition: Prospects and Policies for New York — The Final Report of the Temporary Commission on City Finances* (New York, Praeger, 1977), 295-311.

15. Our formulations in this section bring together ideas from four normally separate traditions: citizen preference models (e.g. W. Ricker and P. Ordeshook, *An Introduction to Positive Political Theory* (Englewood Cliffs, N.J., Prentice-Hall, 1973)); group theory and work on voluntary associations (e.g. R. Dahl, *Who Governs?* (New Haven, Yale University Press, 1961); J. Coleman, *Community Conflict* (Glencoe, Illinois, Free Press, 1957); W. Gamson, *The Strategy of Social Protest* (Homewood, Illinois, Dorsey, 1975); studies of political leadership (e.g. Dahl, *Who Governs?* chapter 17); and residential choice analyses (e.g. C. Tiebout, 'A Pure Theory of Local Public Expenditure', *Journal of Political Economy* 64 (October) 416-24; A. Hirschman, *Exit, Voice, and Loyalty* (Cambridge, Mass., Harvard University Press, 1970); W. Frey, 'Central City White Flight: Racial and Nonracial Causes', *American Sociological Review* 44 (June) 425-448.

16. W. Hoffman and T. Clark, 'Citizen Preferences and Urban Policy Types', in *Urban Affairs Annual Review* (Beverly Hills and London, Sage Publications, 1979); Advisory Commission in Intergovernmental Relations, *Changing Public Attitudes on Governments and Taxes* (Washington, DC, ACIR, 1979); and *Public Opinion* 1978–79 issues.

17. The policy congruence function is very similar to the sort of loss function analysed by Ricker and Ordeshook, op. cit. 307 ff. and others in the public choice tradition. It is given a negative sign in equation 1 so that a larger value implies greater policy congruence, to facilitate subsequent exposition.

18. Cf. S. Greenberg, *Politics and Poverty* (New York, Wiley-Interscience, 1975); J. Coleman, *Resources for Social Change: Race in the United States* (New York, Wiley-Interscience, 1971).

19. C. Levine, *Racial Conflict and the American Mayor* (Lexington, Mass., Heath-Lexington Books, 1974); W. Nelson and P. Meranto, *Electing Black Mayors* (Colombus, Ohio State University Press, 1977).

20. Cf. H. Wellington and R. Winter, *The Unions and the Cities* (Washington, DC, Brookings Institution, 1971); A. Chickering (ed.), *Public Employee Unions* (San Francisco, Institute for Contemporary Studies, 1976).

21. Cf. R. Ehrenberg and G. Goldstein, 'A Model of Public Sector Wage Determination', *Journal of Urban Economics* 2, 223–245; R. Bahl, R. Gustely, and M. Wasylenko, 'The Determinants of Local Government Police Expenditures: A Public Employment Approach', *National Tax Journal* 31 (1979) 67–80; Clark and Ferguson, 'Local Autonomy and Fiscal Performance'.

22. Leadership configuration is a term we prefer to coalitions as it does not imply binding commitments concerning present and future policy outputs among leadership members. Measures of leaders' policy preferences are available from NORC–PCS surveys based on such items as would you prefer more, less, or the same amount of spending in eleven different policy areas, and do you favour or oppose a series of public policies (e.g. municipal employee unions).

23. T. Clark and L. Ferguson, *Political Processes and Urban Fiscal Strain*, book ms., 1979; Clark and Ferguson, 'Local Autonomy and Fiscal Peformance' (see note 8).

24. This sort of multiplicative equation, which can be estimated using a log-log functional form, seems most consistent with the substantive relationships among the variables. That is, they all depend considerably on the relative size of the sector, and then in turn reinforce each other.

25. In equations 15, 16, and 17 where i = municipal employees, the PR_i should be interpreted as the organization or politicization of municipal employees, rather than their number. This is because for poor or non-poor residents sector size is determined by migration decisions of sector members. By contrast the number of municipal employees is mainly a decision of the city administration, while their political organization is mainly their decision. If such political organization succeeds in increasing amenities above those for comparable levels found in other cities or in the private sector in the same city, politicization of municipal employees is likely to increase further; 1. to prevent their benefits from being lost, 2. to restrict the entry of new workers into the municipal labour force (unnecessary if amenities remain at market levels), 3. to help influence the political leadership to maintain more general policies that will keep municipal employees an important element of the leadership configuration. Clearly policies 1, 2, and 3 feed back on each other and on municipal employee amenities in a continuing manner. In terms of the logic of the process, policies 1, 2, and 3 will become increasingly important as the distance of municipal amenities from comparable market alternatives increases. And as amenities fall back toward market levels, politicization should decrease.

26. This is because monies received from borrowing are normally placed in a separ-

ate fund and may be paid out only over several years because of delays in construction (E. Lynn and R. Freeman, *Fund Accounting* (Englewood Cliffs, HJ, Prentice-Hall, 1974); National Committee on Governmental Accounting, *Governmental Accounting, Auditing, and Financial Reporting* (Chicago, Municipal Finance Officers Association, 1968)). Especially as debt issuings are often for several combined projects, it is difficult to match issuings with specific capital construction expenditures.

27. Cf. L. Moak, *Administration of Local Government Debt* (Chicago, Municipal Finance Officers Association, 1970), 192–95.

28. J. Livingston, 'The Lennox Moak Solution', *The (Philadelphia) Sunday Inquirer*, 9 May 1976.

29. Clark and Fuchs, 'New York City in Comparative Perspective' in Temporary Commission on City Finances, op. cit.

30. Cf. R. Bahl and B. Jump, 'The Budgetary Implications of Rising Employee Retirement System Costs', *National Tax Journal* 27 (September) 479–90; S. Davidson *et al. Financial Reporting by State and Local Government Units* (Chicago, Center for Management of Public and Nonprofit Enterprise, Graduate School of Business, University of Chicago, 1977).

31. Coopers and Lybrand and the University of Michigan, *Financial Disclosure Practices of the American Cities* (Ann Arbor, Michigan, 1976).

32. Ernst and Whinney, *How Cities Can Improve Their Financial Reporting* (New York, Ernst and Whinney, 1979).

8 FISCAL STRAIN IN AMERICAN CITIES: SOME LIMITATIONS TO POPULAR EXPLANATIONS

LORNA CROWLEY FERGUSON

Introduction

New York City's quasi-default in 1975 made urban fiscal strain a prominent issue throughout the United States. Visible difficulties in Buffalo, Yonkers, and Cleveland led observers to project the worst. How many other cities would confront similar problems? Fiscal strain was also an issue in the passage of Proposition 13 by California voters in 1978 — a taxpayers' revolt that continues to receive national attention.

Discussions stimulated by these events have made it clear that the future role of American government is very much at stake. The prosperity and optimism of the 1960s seem distant. What to preserve in the face of austerity has become the more common concern. Certainly, the financial sums involved are huge: in 1980 some 200 billion dollars was spent by American local governments, about 8 per cent of the gross national product (GNP), an amount roughly equal to the total GNP of Italy or the United Kingdom.

The causes of urban fiscal problems are neither simple nor clear. Indeed the range of explanations, and hence suggested policy responses, covers a wide spectrum from national economic conditions to local political decisions. This paper examines those explanations which can be labelled 'national trends'. Such trends include population movement, inflation, and recession, or more generally those pervasive demographic and economic shifts which are generated by forces external to specific local governments. To what extent can municipal fiscal policy be viewed as a response to these broad, national factors?

Obviously, national trends have an impact on local fiscal policy. But, on the whole, the effect is less dramatic than many popular accounts have suggested. Considerable room remains for local decisions to shape local fiscal policies. Cities and their elected officials are not self-sufficient, but neither are they simply cogs in the national economy. They can exercise sufficient autonomy to shape the impact of non-local forces.

The perspective behind this paper suggests that local politics play a more important role in local finances than many have realized. Both evidence and theory have grown from a larger work analysing the impact of a range of causes — demographic, economic, political, and social — on the fiscal conditions of American cities.[1] The results of the larger study indicate that local political pressures and decisions remain important in shaping municipal fiscal conditions even after demographic and economic factors have been taken into account. The current analysis examines only the demographic and economic factors, looking at those elements of most significance and suggesting the complex linkages between national phenomena and local conditions. The intent is by no means to underestimate the importance of national trends but rather, through accurate estimation, to pinpoint their strengths and weaknesses as explanations of urban fiscal strain.

The analysis draws upon original data from the Permanent Community Sample of American cities,[2] and reviews of existing data from numerous other sources. The fragmentation of sources is inevitable since no single available data set can answer the range of questions posed. A further caveat on fragmentation seems in order. Such seemingly disparate phenomena as population shifts, inflation, and recessions are treated together here because all are generated by conditions extrinsic to city governments. The specifics of each are still sufficiently distinct, however, to allow for separate discussion below.

Demographic Changes

Of all national trends influencing urban finances, none has been so consistently and directly associated with fiscal strain as changing demographic patterns. Loss of population is interpreted as indicating a declining economic base and a large concentration of low-income residents, with multiple social problems. This complex of characteristics is often linked with geographic location, in such popular referents as the 'northeast syndrome' or 'frostbelt cities'. In this perspective, population loss is seen as a root cause of urban fiscal difficulties by producing increasing demands for public services from the remaining population, and by generating declining local revenues.[3]

Some commentators have used population decline as a central element of urban 'hardship' or 'distress'.[4] Others have seen population loss as a direct cause of fiscal strain. The idea that population loss either defines or causes fiscal strain has become sufficiently accepted among leading urban policy makers to be emphasized in the background report for President Carter's national urban policy, to help justify the Urban Development Action Grants and aim them toward the 'neediest cities', and to incorporate population change in the 1978 dual formula for Community Development Block Grants.[5]

The treatment of the connection between population loss and urban fiscal strain in the present study differs from these views. Population change is considered important, but as a trend to which local fiscal policy may or may not respond rather than one which directly causes fiscal policy. Fiscal strain involves inadequate adjustment between city-government expenditures and local resources. Population shifts are treated as changes in local resources. This treatment makes an explicit distinction between public-sector policies and private-sector resources. The former — including municipal expenditure, debt, and revenue — can be directly influenced by city officials. The latter — including population change, job loss, and shifts in community income levels — are beyond the direct, short-term control of municipalities, and hence represent conditions to which the public sector must respond or eventually face fiscal problems.

Conceptually, this treatment of fiscal strain thus distinguishes between the economic, social, and fiscal aspects of cities.[6] The next two sections indicate the empirical basis for this distinction. First, the rather tenuous link between different types of demographic and social characteristics suggests that the 'northeast' or 'declining' city syndrome overstates the case. Secondly, the relatively weak associations between aspects of the 'declining' city and municipal fiscal policy indicate that population change and similar variables are not axiomatic determinants of local fiscal decisions.

The 'Declining' City Syndrome

Population loss is sometimes treated as an indirect cause of fiscal difficulties through its association with other economic, demographic, and social problems. Such loss is frequently linked to the presence of a large, poor population, predominantly concentrated in large, old, northeastern cities. Similarly, older cities may have older physical plants which may be more expensive to maintain. Density is sometimes added to this syndrome as encouraging urban maladies or adding to costs of service provision.[7]

To ascertain just how much these characteristics comprise a 'declining' city syndrome eight indicators often identified with the syndrome are isolated; population change, region, age of city, age of housing stock, population size, population density, percentage of poor families, and percentage of non-whites. Using the Permanent Community Sample cities, the connections among the eight demographic and social indicators are examined to see how much they overlap.

The correlations in Table 8.1 indicate some limited clustering. Population loss is only moderately associated with northeastern region, proportions in poverty, or non-whites, and not at all associated with population size. On the other hand, population loss is strongly associated with older housing stock. Except for older housing stock none of the remaining seven indicators explain as much as 20 per cent of the variance in population loss. With evidence of relatively loose couplings between population loss and other components of the 'declining' city syndrome, a case can clearly be made for not treating population loss as a surrogate measure of overall urban 'decline'.

Characteristics of the 'declining' city are not necessarily translated into municipal fiscal policy. In Table 8.2 eight demographic and social

Table 8.1 Relationship between social and demographic indicators:* the declining city syndrome

	LPOP 6070	LPOP 7075	LPOP 75T	PC70 OLDH	CITY AGE	NE	NE and N Central	City DE70	PC70 NONW	PC70 LOCL
LPOP6070		0.5579	0.0596	−0.7724	−0.4457	−0.3173	−0.2868	−0.3698	−0.2111	−0.3343
LPOP7075			−0.0493	−0.6438	−0.3804	−0.1856	−0.3743	−0.3383	−0.3006	−0.0992

* Correlations exceeding ± 0.21 are significant at the 0.10 level; those exceeding ± 0.32 are significant at the .01 level

** *Key to acronyms:*

LPOP6070: Log of percentage change in population 1960–70
LPOP7075: Log of percentage change in population 1970–5
City age: Decade when city reached 20000 population
NE: 1 if Northeastern Region, 0 if not
NE and N Central: 1 if Northeastern or North Central Region, 0 if not
LPOP75T: Log of population in 1975
CITYDE70: Population per square mile, 1970
PC70LOCL: Percentage of families with income under $3000, 1970
PC70NONW: Percentage of families non-white, 1970
PC70OLDH: Percentage of housing constructed before 1950

Table 8.2   *Relationships between social and demographic indicators and fiscal indicators**

	LPOP 6070**	LPOP 7075	CITY AGE	NE	NE and N Central	LPOP 75T	CITY DE70	PC70 LOCL	PC70 NONW	PC70 OLDH
Tax Burden										
(FS27072)	−0.09	−0.2284	0.2279	0.2029	0.0826	0.1793	0.5629	−0.2865	−0.0837	0.2486
Long Term Debt										
(FS01Y76)	−0.006	−0.2038	0.4819	0.0326	−0.1559	0.5829	0.2017	0.3109	0.3424	0.0693
Common Functions										
(FS08Y76)	−0.3410	−0.397	0.5111	0.1691	−0.0031	0.3899	0.5283	0.2272	0.3706	0.4061

*   Correlations are Pearson r Those exceeding ± 0.21 are significant at the 0.10 level; exceeding ± 0.32 they are significant at the 0.01 level.

**   *Key to acronyms:*
FS2072: Total local tax burden per capita, 1972
FS01Y76: Long-term debt per capita, 1976
FS08Y76: Expenditures per capita on nine common functions, 1976
LPOP6070: Log of percentage change in population 1960–70
LPOP7075: Log of percentage change in population 1970–5
City age: Decade when city reached 20 000 population
NE: 1 if Northeastern Region, 0 if not
NE and N Central: 1 if Northeastern of North Central Region, 0 if not
LPOP75T: Log of population in 1975
CITYDE70: Population per square mile, 1970
PC70LOCL: Percentage of families with income under $3 000, 1970
PC70NONW: Percentage of families non-white, 1970
PC70OLDH: Percentage of housing constructed before 1950

indicators are correlated with three measures of local taxing, debt, and expenditure policy.[8] Of the total number of correlations, one-third are insignificant (at the 0.10 level). And in only one-fifth of them is more than 17 per cent of the variance explained. City age, size, and density show the strongest relationship with at least two of the fiscal indicators. Older, larger, and more densely populated cities do spend more on common functions, for example, than younger, smaller, and less densely populated cities. Differences are probably due in part to higher costs of maintaining ageing physical plants and other directly physical and demographic causes. But these are also cities where there are citizens and political leaders of different styles. Further, upon closer examination, great uniformity in spending is not found among similarly old, large, and densely populated cities (see Table 8.3). Newark, for instance, spends about 80 per cent more per capita on police than Pittsburgh; and Boston spends almost two-thirds as much on all common functions as Chicago. Given such differences in fiscal policy among cities generally similar in their demographic characteristics, it is clear that other variables must enter to explain remaining differences.

Population Change and Urban Fiscal Policy

We return to population change again since it is perhaps the single characteristic most commonly identified as distinguishing northeastern from 'sunbelt' cities. A first question is, do cities declining in population suffer greater fiscal strain because they are spending more? This can be answered in terms of three basic indicators by the first three columns of Table 8.2. Popular belief to the contrary, population change is mostly unrelated to the total tax burden or to long-term debt outstanding. Cities declining in population, however, do spend more on common functions.

These are cross-sectional relations involving fiscal commitment levels. What of changes? If population declines, and so do fiscal commitments, then the ratio of the two will not increase, and the city will not suffer fiscal strain. But the inertia of policy makers, and expectations of many citizens and organized groups, especially municipal employees, can make it hard to adjust fiscal policy in direct proportion of population change. New York City in particular has been commonly cited as an instance where there was considerable lag after the onset of population decline and before fiscal policies were adjusted.

One reading of Table 8.4 suggests the generality of this phenomenon. It shows that from 1960 to 1965 population change and change in general expenditure were unrelated. But from 1965 to 1972 the relationship was negative (also from 1970 to 1974, but the correlation is not significant); that is, cities losing population were increasing their per capita expenditures faster than cities increasing in population. Finally from 1974 to 1976, the relationship reversed itself, so that cities decreasing in population

Table 8.3   *Old, large, densely populated cities spend different amounts on the same functions*

Sixteen of the sixty-two sample cities above the median on age and population size and density	1977 expenditures per capita on		
	Total common functions ($)	Police ($)	Fire ($)
Boston	303	105	63
Buffalo	213	60	44
Milwaukee	202	70	31
Minneapolis	256	51	33
Newark	267	96	65
Pittsburgh	165	54	40
St Louis	213	82	26
St Paul	214	46	37
San Francisco	271	76	57
Seattle	290	68	47
New York	258	95	40
Chicago	209	102	35
Los Angeles	203	83	35
Philadelphia	271	94	30
Detroit	249	90	32
Baltimore	285	87	47
Median for all sixty-two sample cities	186	52	35

Source: US Bureau of the Census, *City Government Finances in 1977.*

also decreased their expenditures more than growing cities. The same pattern holds for own revenues as for general expenditures, suggesting that intergovernmental revenues did not affect these relationships dramatically. If these data were the only information available, they might suggest a lagged process of adjustment to population decline.

But this interpretation should not be applied too mechanically. Let us inquire into the processes by which population loss may generate fiscal problems. For this to occur, city government revenues would have to decrease with declines in population, and decrease more than the changes in expenditures necessary to service a smaller population. Consider the two components of this argument, expenditures first. Expenditures could well increase if the population remaining in the city were older, poorer, and in other ways more costly to local government. The results shown in Table 8.1 indicate that cities declining in population did in fact have

Table 8.4   *Only from 1965 to 1974 did municipal expenditures and revenues increase in cities losing population*

	Change in population, 1960–70 (%) (LPOP6070)	Change in population, 1970–75 (%) (LPOP7075)
Percentage change in general expenditures, 1960–65 (LGEXP605)	0.038	
Percentage change in general expenditures, 1965–72 (LGEXP6572)	−0.396	
Percentage change in general expenditures, 1970–4 (LGEXP7074)		−0.207
Percentage change in general expenditures 1974–6 (LGEXP746)		0.228
Percentage change in own revenue, 1960–70 (LONRV607)	−0.441	
Percentage change in own revenue 1970–4 (LONRV704)		−0.241
Percentage change in own revenue, 1974–6 (LONRV746)		0.258

Correlations are Pearson *r*: those exceeding ± 0.21 are significant at the 0.10 level, exceeding ± 0.32 at the 0.01 level.

slightly more poor and black residents. Nevertheless, this relationship is less than overwhelming and such changes in population composition are analytically distinct from population decline. Moreover, many federal and state grant formulae include poverty and other characteristics of target populations, such that intergovernmental revenues respond, in some manner, to changing population composition.

Population loss leads to smaller and less densely populated cities; if larger population size of high density were important to achieve economies of scale in public service delivery, changes in them could increase per capita costs. Although less than conclusive, the best research to date suggests the operation rather of diseconomies of scale for certain services like police and fire protection.[9] Problems in adjusting expenditures to a declining population seem to stem less from demands of constituents than the inflexibility of the labour force. Reducing the numbers of municipal employees is not easily accomplished even when population declines dramatically. In brief, the evidence is weak that population loss alone inherently increases service costs; there simply are too many other variables at work.[10] But existing fiscal commitments may make it difficult for a city to reduce spending in the short run.

Let us then turn to the other part of the argument: declining revenues. Certainly population decline *per se* does not spell lost revenue. It must operate through specific revenue sources. The property tax is the most important single source for city revenue. Do property values decrease with declines in population? They might if all else were equal, but one critical variable which is not constant is the size of urban households. It has been declining for several decades, enhanced in recent years by longer life spans, later marriages, fewer children, and more singles.[11] The net result is a greater demand for housing per capita than was the case in earlier years, which provides more support for taxable property values. Undoubtedly large and persistent outmigration eventually produces lowered property values, but it is not clear how much this has occurred.[12] Property values are still high and increasing in many 'declining' cities. Further, the conversion of property-value changes into city-government revenues is far from automatic, as analysed in the next section. Nor is property the only source of city revenue. Whatever the local sources, recall that Table 8.4 showed that declining cities in the Permanent Community Sample managed to increase their own source revenues in every time period from 1960 to 1974; this changed only from 1974 to 1976.

Some of the concern about population decline largely reflects a projection of what might happen if it continues too far. The newness of the phenomenon has been such that little discussion or analysis of it was undertaken before the mid-1970s. The initial reactions were often exaggerated and based on a cursory examination of actual cases. Local officials in Pittsburgh, for example, point out that the relatively large declines in population there helped eliminate some of the worst slums in crowded areas, permitted construction of more spacious parks, and generally reflect a shift in land use to one more consistent with the life style of current residents than the crowded and cramped quarters of the steelworkers a few decades ago.

In brief, population changes, and other demographic and social characteristics of a city are important in defining the problems to which local officials must adapt. Whether and how they adapt, however, is not determined by the problems, as is clear from the large differences across cities confronting similar social and demographic circumstances. Demographic and social characteristics serve as resources, they are not fiscal policies.

Inflation and Recession

Like demographic shifts, inflation and recession are major national trends. It is often implied that city governments participate in these trends like the rest of the economy. Much anecdotal evidence has cited their deleterious effects.[13] But what evidence is there of a more systematic sort? Unfortunately little. With little to build on, this section discusses briefly some major fiscal effects of inflation and recession. It pays special attention to how local officials can and do cushion such effects.

How Large Are the Effects of National Business Cycles on City Governments?

A first question is simply how large are cyclical effects for cities? Two obvious bases of comparison are the private sector and federal and state governments. Compared to the private sector, city governments seem to suffer less marked fluctuations. The long-term growth curves of city revenues from various sources are generally smooth from the Second World War until the late 1970s. Fig. 8.1 shows the 1968-77 period. There is no sign of a downturn here for the 1974-5 recession, the largest since the 1930s. Considering individual cities, a few began to cut back in 1974-5, but retrenchment grew much more after the recession. Several private-sector indicators show clearer downturns.[14]

How do cities compare to federal and state governments in these respects? Higher level governments fluctuate more in their revenues due to reliance on more elastic sources, especially income, corporate, and sales taxes.[15] Expenditure responses also vary due to differences in functional responsibility, with managing the national economy a major responsibility of the federal government, which in Keynesian manner has often increased deficit spending during a recession. State governments have primary responsibility for administering unemployment compensation and related benefits. More elastic revenue sources, combined with anti-cyclical programme responsibilities, create cyclical deficits and surpluses for state and especially federal governments to a degree unparalleled at the local level.[16] But just how large are these differences?

Funds flows indicators, such as total revenues minus total expenditures, have been used to gauge cyclical fluctuations of the federal government. Similar indicators for the 'state and local sector' have been constructed as part of the National Income Accounts, and results interpreted as 'surpluses' or 'deficits'. These are among the most widely discussed fiscal indicators of state and local governments in Washington and the national news media.[17] Their major advantage is that they are kept more current than other sorts of indicators. But they are current because they are only estimates from a sample of all states and localities. This methodology ignores differences between states, other local governments, and cities,

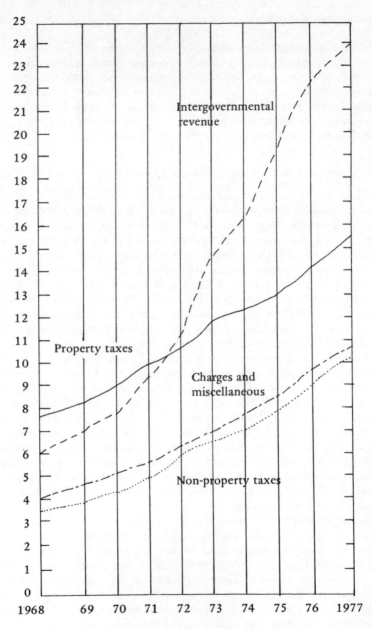

Fig. 8.1   *Trends in city general revenue from selected major sources:*
1968-77 (billions of dollars)
Source: US Bureau of the Census, *City Government Finances in 1977*, p. 2.

as well as variations among individual cities. Such indicators thus may be appropriate for certain types of macroeconomic analysis, but as indicators of urban fiscal strain, they are too aggregate.

If funds flows, despite their widespread discussion, are misleading, how should one assess effects on cities of recession and inflation? This question is best addressed in two separate parts:

1. Do city expenditures increase faster than revenues in time of inflation?
2. Do revenues decrease faster than expenditures in time of recession?

Both questions stress the importance of considering simultaneously marginal changes in revenue and expenditure. In discussing both we also inquire as to how much such changes are 'automatic' or more amenable to local policy intervention.

Inflation and Cities

Experts on inflation suggest addressing our first question by comparing individual cities using city-specific price indices. Only one study has done this carefully for six local governments.[18] The authors computed inflation indices for factors affecting revenue and expenditure. Comparison of their revenue and expenditure indices speaks to our first question.[19] The results appear in Table 8.5. For example, for Atlanta the expenditure inflation index increased from a 1971 base of 100 to 127.9 in 1977, while the local revenue index increased to 121.8. The difference of 6.1 per cent, in column three, is the amount that expenditure inflation exceeded revenue inflation for Atlanta. These differences range from a low point for Atlanta, where expenditure inflation outstrips local revenue inflation, to a high point for Snohomish County where local revenue inflation was greater than expenditure inflation by over 36 per cent. Still, local governments can choose whether or not to increase revenues and expenditures at the same rates as such inflation indices. These six governments varied considerably in their policies, both from one another and by type of revenue. Consider property and sales taxes, the two major types of local revenues.

Property taxes have been frequently criticized for increasing less than the rate of inflation for expenditures. This was true in four of the six cases studied by Greytak and Jump; in the other two the inflation index for property taxes (column 4 of Table 8.6) increased at a rate equal to or faster than the expenditure inflation index (column 1 of Table 8.5).[20] To explain rates of change in actual property tax revenues collected, however, the points of possible change must be distinguished. A city can experience an increase in property tax revenues for three reasons: growth in the value of existing property, addition of new taxable property, and increase in the property tax rate or assessment ratio.[21] Only the first is due to inflation (at least in part). The other two are determined by local

Table 8.5   *Comparison of local revenue and expenditure inflation indices for six locations*

Location	Total current expenditure inflation index	Total local revenue inflation index	Difference between (1) and (2)
Atlanta, Georgia	127.9	121.8	−6.1
Lexington, Virginia	121.0	123.5	+ 2.5
New York City, New York	121.4	133.1	+ 11.7
Erie County, New York	124.1	121.1	−3.0
Orange County, California	117.3	133.9	+ 16.6
Snohomish County, Washington	123.9	160.0	+ 36.1

Source: Greytak and Jump, *The impact of Inflation on the Expenditures and Revenues of Six Local Governments, 1971–1979,* Tables II-B and III-B.

Table 8.6   *Comparison of total local revenue growth due to inflation, 1971–74*[a]

	Revenue growth index[b] (1971 = 100)			Inflation index for local revenue[c] (1971 = 100)		
Location	(1) Property taxes	(2) Sales taxes	(3) Total	(4) Property taxes	(5) Sales taxes	(6) Total[d]
Atlanta, Georgia	103.9	—	121.8	121.9	—	114.1
Lexington, Virginia	99.0	128.6	123.5	116.5	123.4	115.8
New York, New York	124.2	116.6	133.1	120.6	114.4	116.7
Erie County, New York	101.2	267.9	121.1	123.6	118.6	120.4
Orange County, Cal	126.0	165.6	133.9	121.0	115.9	117.0
Snohomish County Washington	115.7	161.7	160.0	124.7	121.6	119.5

a   *Source:* Greytak and Jump, *The Impact of Inflation on the Expenditures and Revenues of Six Local Governments, 1971–1979,* Tables III-A and III-B.
b. Revenue Growth   = Percentage increase in actual amounts of revenue
c   Inflation Index   = Potential increase in revenue for property taxes due to increase in value of existing property in 1971. Assumes amount of taxable property and tax rate remains constant. Inflation indices calculated separately for different types of property and different types of sales taxes in each city and county. Total calculated by summing each type of tax and weighting by proportion contributed to total local revenue.
d   The Total Indices include all types of revenues. Only property and sales taxes are listed separately here.

political and administrative decisions, such as annexation, taxing previously tax-exempt property, increasing the assessment ratio, or increasing the actual tax rate. To increase tax revenues commensurate with increases in market value of property, however, necessitates reassessments, and the property tax as a visible, lump-sum payment is one of the most disliked taxes.[22] Thus even if property values increase rapidly, many city officials are understandably reluctant to capture this potential revenue due to taxpayer resistance. New York City still increased its revenues from property taxes (column (1) of Table 8.6) more than its inflation indices (column (4) of Table 8.6); Atlanta and Lexington followed the opposite policy.

What of sales taxes? For four of the governments studied by Greytak and Jump, the sales tax inflation indices (column (5) of Table 8.6) increased less than the property tax indices (column (4) of Table 8.6). This contradicts most discussions of these matters, which have suggested that property-tax revenues are less responsive to inflation than sales taxes.[23] The early 1970s may have differed from earlier periods in this regard, but a related argument for sales over property taxes is that they increase automatically with inflation, so that the government need not increase the tax rate to capture increased revenues; but for all of these governments, increases in actual collections (column (3) of Table 8.6) equalled or exceeded the inflation index increases (column (6) of Table 8.6).

These results show that while these six local governments did experience inflation, in only two instances did inflation clearly outdistance actual revenue growth. Inflationary effects vary considerably across cities. Moreover, the six governments analysed here, seldom let their revenues or expenditures increase or decrease simply with inflationary forces; they often shifted them considerably, by implementing local decisions.

Recession and Cities

Consider now the second question: how do these patterns shift in time of recession? The property tax then becomes a blessing; it normally does not decline even if property values do, since assessments and tax rates are usually not altered in recessions.[24] By contrast, sales-tax revenues are likely to drop if local sales receipts do.

No study like that of Greytak and Jump has been done for recession. Still, Elizabeth Dickson finds that of thirty-one cities studied in the 1974–5 recession, only four showed absolute declines in tax receipts (from property, sales, and income). But she did not determine the degree to which revenue flows were maintained by changes in tax rates.[25]

What policies can city officials pursue to prepare for future recessions? A decade or so ago two recommendations were common: avoid the property tax and diversify revenue sources. Many cities followed these policies, primarily by expanding non-property tax revenue sources. The major arguments against the property tax were that it was regressive and inelastic. Both arguments have been undermined by more recent work.[26] The argument for diversification in revenue structure was based on the above criticisms of the property tax plus the view that downturn in one source could be offset by strength in others. This argument in turn depended on differences in timing of cyclical fluctuations by industry. These do exist, but more important than diversification *per se* seems to be the type of industry, because some industries are far more cyclically sensitive than others.[27] Thus to the degree that local officials can seek to encourage location of different types of firms, they might seek less cyclically sensitive industries to avoid recessionary downturns.[28]

Summary of Inflation and Recession Effects

Inflation and recession are fiscally troublesome for cities, but cities generally suffer less than most private firms and the federal government. Although many fiscal problems are blamed on these national trends, they are so bound up with local processes (involving municipal employees, taxpayers, and others) that cities differ in their responses to the same national trends. Some cities suffer from inflation in that their revenues increase less rapidly than many expenditures. Such patterns vary considerably across cities, however, and the single largest expenditure item, personnel, is locally determined. Property values in the early 1970s generally increased as fast as most expenditure indices, questioning the traditional view that they are inelastic. Cities varied considerably in the degree to which they captured such property value increases in tax revenues. Local sales often increased proportionately less than property values, but many cities chose to increase their sales-tax revenues faster than property-tax revenues.

In recession, property taxes have the advantage of seldom decreasing, but sales and other revenues often do. The extent of such decreases, however, is not clear from research to date. Two traditional arguments against the property tax, regressiveness and inelasticity, have been largely undermined by recent research. Diversification of revenue source seems less effective as a defence against downturn than cyclically insensitive local industries.

Conclusion. Is There Room for Local Politics?

Returning now to the original question: do economic and demographic effects leave room for local political decisions to shape local fiscal policy? Yes, but economic and demographic factors do provide constraints. Cities experience net revenue losses from combined effects of inflation and recession, but these are relatively small. Cities do adjust to population losses, but the adjustment takes time. Older, larger, more densely populated cities spend more than their younger, smaller, less dense counterparts, but the older cities also vary considerably among themselves. The extent to which local officials can shape local policy within the prevailing constraints, however, is perhaps best illustrated by the case of Pittsburgh.[29]

By the late 1960s, Pittsburgh experienced many of the same problems of other old, northeastern cities, but in some respects earlier or more acutely than did Boston, New York, or Philadelphia. Pittsburgh lost more jobs and residents in the 1960s than most other cities, and increased its percentage of poor, non-white, and welfare-supported residents. Nevertheless, through new and innovative local leadership Pittsburgh reduced municipal expenditures.

Peter Flaherty ran for mayor in 1960. Although a Democrat, he grew increasingly ciritical of the Democratic Party 'machine', less on ideological issues than because it had simply grown rusty and inefficient. His views were popular with voters, and his campaign slogan was 'Nobody's Boy'. He ran as an unendorsed independent Democrat against traditional Democratic and Republican endorsed candidates and won in most wards of the city.

Once in office, Flaherty discontinued several of the dramatic projects involving civic and business leaders that had defined the Pittsburgh 'Renaissance'. He openly scorned the Democratic party and the city council which it still controlled. He fired leading party officials from patronage jobs. He gradually appointed new, young, aggressive department heads to the city agencies who began to look for efficient procedures. Municipal workers and union leaders, however, initially ignored or tried to subvert such efforts toward efficiency. Tension mounted with the new administration. A leading opponent was Thomas Fagan, head of the Teamster's Union, the leading spokesman for the municipal employee unions, and an active city-council member. Pittsburgh had numerous highly paid drivers and chauffeurs in part due to Fagan. As an austerity measure, the new mayor and department heads gave up the chauffeurs and limousines they had inheritied. Then, near the end of his first year in office, Flaherty asked the water meter installers to give up their chauffeurs too. The Teamster's Union refused to comply and called a strike which was joined by about half of all city employees. The issue was made to order and Flaherty made the most of it, denouncing the excesses of municipal employees. The newspapers were on strike but the television stations publicized the issue, and many observers felt that a common citizen reaction was outrage at the workers. After a few weeks of the strike, court battles, and negotiations, the clear victor was Peter Flaherty. From the 1971 strike, until he left office in 1977, Mayor Flaherty had his way in all significant disagreements with non-uniformed municipal employees — and usually the council as well. From 1970 to 1974, the municipal work force was cut by 18 per cent, more than any of the other Permanent Community Sample cities; the average city expanded in this period. These reductions were mainly achieved through attrition; few workers were actually fired.

There was a good deal of room for improving productivity in Pittsburgh, even though a leading Flaherty administrator claimed that 'we could do the same thing in most big cities east of the Mississippi'. The mayor and his department heads would arrive unannounced at work sites and police stations, asking questions, and subsequently redefining tasks and reassigning hundreds of municipal employees.

Crew sizes were reduced, many unnecessary jobs such as cuspidor cleaner were eliminated, a fire boat manned by disabled fire fighters was sold, many management jobs titled 'Assistant to' or 'Deputy to' were cut out. Policemen sleeping on the job were given citations, complete divisions were merged or assigned new tasks. Over time, middle-level administrators adapted to the more efficient style. The highly dissatisfied left. The overall reductions in workforce size should also be seen in the context of Pittsburgh's population decline, 13 per cent from 1970 to 1975. Many other cities lost population in this period; Pittsburgh was unusual only in adapting its work force size to its population earlier than most other cities. In the absence of systematic performance data, it is impossible to know if there were changes in service quality in Pittsburgh in the Flaherty years. Certainly, municipal employees claimed that their reduced staffing levels impaired services. If there were service declines, however, they seem to have been insignificant enough not to have been missed. The press and political opponents were looking hard for such failures, and seem to have found few. Over time, most citizens and even opposing political leaders became convinced that the Flaherty approach made sense.

Flaherty stands out as an example mainly because his policies came early in the history of municipal fiscal retrenchment. With mounting taxpayer opposition to government spending in the late 1970s, many other examples can be found of local leaders searching out and implementing policies to curtail municipal debt and expenditures within the constraints imposed by larger economic and demographic factors.

Notes

1. The larger work, co-authored by Lorna Crowley Ferguson and Terry Clark, has been supported by The Twentieth Century Fund and their permission to publish this article is gratefully recognized.
2. The Permanent Community Sample is a stratified, random sample of cities over 50 000 in population. It includes sixty-two American cities.
3. See, for example, Charles L. Schultze, Edward R. Fried, Alice M. Rivlin, Nancy H. Teeters, and Robert D. Reischauer, 'Fiscal Problems of Cities', in Roger E. Alcaly and David Mermelstein (eds.), *The Fiscal Crisis of American*

Cities (New York, Vintage, 1977).

4. See, Richard P. Nathan and Paul R. Dommel, 'The Cities', in Joseph A. Pechman (ed.), *Setting National Priorities: The 1978 Budget* (Washington, DC, Brookings, 1977), 283–316.

5. See, Urban and Regional Policy Group, *A New Partnership to Conserve America's Communities: A National Urban Policy*, HUD-S-297 (Washington, DC, Department of Housing and Urban Development, 1978; Richard P. Nathan, *et al.*, *Block Grants for Community Development* (Washington, DC, US Department of Housing and Urban Development, 1977); Harold L. Bunce, 'The Community Development Block Grant Formula', *Urban Affairs Quarterly*, 14 (June 1979), 443–464.

The politics of the National Urban Policy, and the three 'distress standards' (pre-1939 housing, poverty, and below-average population growth), did not escape one Texas observer: this 'discriminatory urban package . . . [is] clear evidence that the Administration has associated itself with Massachusetts speaker Tip O'Neill, New York Senator Jacob Javits and other members of the Frostbelt coalition [which] has been hard at work pushing through discriminatory legislation deliberately designed to let the Northeast raid the federal treasury at our expense'. See R. J. Hoyer, 'President Carter's Urban Policy: Some Second Thoughts', *Texas Town and City*, 65 (October 1978), 5-12.

6. Some recent analyses use a similar distinction, indicating more general awareness of the need for distinguishing separate dimensions of urban problems. See Peggy L. Cuciti, *City Need and the Responsiveness of Federal Grant Programs*, (Washington, DC, Congressional Budget Office, 1978).

7. See, for example, Schultze, *et al.*, 'Fiscal Problems of Cities' in Alcaly and Memelstein (eds.), op. cit.; George E. Peterson, 'Finance', in William Gorham and Nathan Glazer (eds.), *The Urban Predicament* (Washington, DC, The Urban Institute, 1976).

8. These three fiscal indicators are used to capture basic aspects of urban fiscal policy. The total local tax burden includes revenues generated by all overlapping local and state governments. Common functions expenditures are expenditures on those services commonly provided by all cities. Long-term debt outstanding by the city government is not adjusted here for the problem of different functions performed by different city governments, the correlations between the range of functions and the amount of long-term debt is $r = 0.40$ for the PCS cities. The correlations between the range of functions and 1960 to 1975 population change is $r = 0.13$.

9. See, Elinor Ostrom, 'Metropolitan Reform: Propositions Derived From Two Traditions', *Social Science Quarterly*, 53 (December 1972), 474–493, and Ostrom *et al.*, *Community Organizations and the Provision of Police Services* (Beverly Hills and London, Sage, Sage Papers in Administrative and Policy Studies, 1973).

Some costs such as fixed equipment maintenance are, of course, less susceptible to short-term reductions when population declines.

10. Another factor which mitigates the apparent effects of population decline is the large number of illegal aliens in many cities. Data are especially rough on this matter as illegal aliens avoid public officials.

11. William Alonso, 'The Current Halt in the Metropolitan Phenomenon', in Charles Leven (ed.), *The Mature Metropolis* (Lexington, Mass., Heath-Lexington Books, 1978).

12. The less acute decline in households than in total population, and the persistent growth of the market value of property in many cities declining in population, appear in a table from George Riegeluth, 'The Economic Base', in George Peterson *et al.*, *Urban Economic and Fiscal Indicators*, (Washington, DC, The Urban Institute, 1978).

	Population change		Household change		Market value of property change
	1960–70 (%)	1970–5 (%)	1960–70 (%)	1970–5 (%)	1971–6 (%)
San Diego	22	11	30	N.A.	67
Denver	4	−6	11	N.A.	79
Los Angeles	14	−3	17	N.A.	19
Baltimore	−4	−6	5	−2	36
Boston	−8	−1	−3	−8	80
Buffalo	−13	−12	−7	N.A.	27
Detroit	−10	−12	−3	−7	−12
San Francisco	−3	−7	0	N.A.	33
Minneapolis	−10	−13	−3	1	31
St Paul	−1	−10	5	2	16
New York	1	−5	7	N.A.	43

For example, although Boston lost more households than other cities from 1970 to 1975, its property value increased more than that of San Diego. Data are from the Census, unadjusted for inflation.

13. In the early stages of the New York fiscal crisis, it was often interpreted, especially in arguments used in Washington, as due to recession. See the news media and *Congressional Record* for this period.

14. One study of cyclical employment trends found that during the four post Second World War contractions (1957–8, 1960–1, 1969–70, 1973–5), private-sector jobs decreased respectively −4.0, −1.0, −0.9, and −1.4 per cent, while state and local-government jobs increased 5.1, 4.7, 4.3 and 3.1 per cent. This rate of state and local job increase was almost identical to that in periods of expansion. Advisory Commission on Intergovernmental Relations, *Countercyclical Aid and Economic Stabilization* (Washington, DC, ACIR Report A-69, 1978), Table 2.

15. Revenues raised from own sources by level of government in 1973 were as follows:

	Local	*State*	*Federal*
User charges	26.1	12.4	5.8
Property tax	54.1	1.4	–
Income tax	3.0	16.1	41.7
Corporation tax	–	5.6	14.6
Sales, gross receipts	6.4	40.3	8.0
Death, gift, other	1.8	5.4	2.6
Miscellaneous	6.4	3.9	3.1
Insurance	2.2	15.1	24.3
Total (%)	99.9	100.0	100.0
Total ($)	81,216	97,108	247,849

Source: **Paul Peterson**, *City Limits*, forthcoming

16. Certain cyclical federal programmes have been temporarily administered by local governments — most especially the Economic Stimulus Package (ARFA, LPW, CETA) in the mid-1970s.

17. An example of such results follows:

	Federal government surplus or deficit (−)	State and local governments operating surplus or deficit (−)[a]
1970	−12.1	−4.0
1971	−22.0	−3.8
1972	−17.3	5.6
1973	− 6.7	4.1
1974	−11.5	−2.8
1975	−71.2	−5.1
1976[b]	−58.3	0.8

[a] Operating surplus or deficit excludes social insurance funds
[b] Preliminary

Adapted from Council of Economic Advisors, *Economic Report of the President*, transmitted to Congress January 1977 (Washington, DC, USPGO, 1977), 76, cited in Advisory Commission on Intergovernmental Relations, *State-Local Finances in Recession and Inflation* (Washington, DC, ACIR Report A-70, 1979), Table 14. See also, David Ott, Attiat Ott, James Maxwell, and Richard Aronson, *State-Local Finances in the Last Half of the 1970s* (Washington, DC, American Enterprise Institute for Public Policy Research, 1975).

18. David Greytak and Bernard Jump, *The Impact of Inflation on the Expenditures and Revenues of Six Local Governments, 1971–1970* (Syracuse, NY, Maxwell School of Citizenship and Public Affairs, Metropolitan Studies Program, 1975).

19. Their procedures are difficult to summarzie briefly. In general they disaggregated expenditures and revenues into several components, and assigned each component to a (usually) national price index (mainly the Consumer Price Index, Wholesale Price Index, and Boeck Construction Index). Where available city specific indices were used. Then they created inflation indices for each city.

For a detailed example let us look at inflation for the non-labour expenditures in Atlanta from 1971 to 1974. Expenditures for all non-labour items (material, supplies, equipment, and contractual services) were disaggregated into over eighty separate categories. To each category a specific inflation index was applied, e.g. the Consumer Price Index–Postal Charges was applied to Postage or the Wholesale Price Index (0132)–Hogs was applied to Purchase of Hogs. Index changes were examined from 1971 to 1974. For example if the WPI for hogs increased 25 per cent between 1971 and 1974, the Greytak and Jump hog inflation index would be 125 for 1974. Eighty such indices were generated. Each was then added into the total inflation index for non-labour expenditures according to its proportion of total non-labour expenditures. As shown in the following equation:

$$I_{\text{non-labour}} = \sum_{i=1}^{n} (I_i W_i)$$

where:

$I_{\text{non-labour}}$ = inflation index for all non-labour expenditures
I_i = inflation index for each of n components
(n = 80+ for Atlanta)

$$W_i \quad = \quad \frac{E_i}{E_t}$$

E_i =   expenditure for each component i

E_t =   total non-labour expenditures

Analogous procedures were followed for labour expenditures, and different types of revenue sources. The inflation index for each separate type of expenditure or revenue was then weighted according to the proportion of the total expenditure or revenue it represented.

Roy Bahl, Bernard Jump, and Larry Schroeder estimated revenue and expenditure inflation indices for more cities, but with less precise methods than Greytak and Jump. See R. Bahl, B. Jump, and L. Schroeder, 'The Outlook for City Fiscal Performance in Declining Regions', in R. Bahl (ed.), *The Fiscal Outlok for Cities* (Syracuse, Syracuse University Press, 1978).

20.   Irene Rubin's intensive study of a middle-sized city estimated that 1972–6 inflation effects (holding constant tax rates) for expenditures were 8 per cent, for sales taxes 8.5 per cent, and for property taxes 2.6 per cent (from 1970 to 1976). This city was undergoing more rapid population decline than most of Greytak and Jump's cities, which may explain the lower increase in property value. See Irene Rubin, *Social, Economic, and Political Causes of Urban Fiscal Strain,* unpublished manuscript.

21.   This may be shown as a simple equation:

$$TR = r\,(a/m)\ (M_e + M_n)$$

where:

TR =   property tax revenues
r =   nominal tax rate
a/m =   ratio of assessed to market value
M_e =   full market value of existing property as of the last assessment
M_n =   full market value of new property since the last assessment

22.   Numerous surveys have shown this. For example:
Which do you think is the worst tax — that is, the least fair?

Federal income tax	30
State income tax	11
State sales tax	18
Local property tax	32
Don't know	10
	101%

This item was posed to a national sample of Americans in 1978 by the Opinion Research Corporation; identical items posed annually from 1973 to 1978 show consistent responses. Advisory Commission on Intergovernmental Relations, *Changing Public Attitudes on Governments and Taxes* (Washington, DC, ACIR Report S-7, 1978), 1.

23.   Dick Netzer, *Economics of the Property Tax* (Washington, DC, The Brookings Institution, 1966). See also discussion of elasticity in footnote 26.

24.   Still, property owners may withhold taxes more in recession, increasing foreclosure rates, and decreasing city revenues.

25.   Elizabeth Dickson, 'Fiscal Trends: Local Revenue Bases, Expenditures, and Tax Burdens', in George Peterson *et al., Urban Economic and Fiscal Indicators* (Washington, DC, The Urban Institute, 1978).

A quite thorough study came to my attention after completion of this article. Although it deals with all local governments, it is far more thorough than most studies to date. The authors address questions 1 and 2 just as I posed them above (the only study besides this one to do so). Using time series regression procedures, they estimate the distinct effects of recession and inflation for revenues and expenditures separately, as well as the combined effects of these national trends. For the effects of inflation, they find small net gains for local government: revenues exceed expenditures by 2.4, 3.4, and 1.6 per cent in 1974, 1975, and 1976. For recession, however, they find net losses, such that the combined effects of inflation and recession amounted to −0.2, +1.4, −2.4, and −3.7 in 1973, 1974, 1975, and 1976. The report reviews several other studies that bear on related matters and concludes that, despite widespread views to the contrary, 'the overall estimated losses are not excessively severe'. Advisory Commission on Intergovernmental Relations, *State-Local Finances in Recession and Inflation* (Washington, DC, ACIR Report A-70, 1979), Tables 20, 21, and p. 34.

26.   Estimates of the elasticity of the property tax, based on national data prior to the 1970s, indicate a considerable range, from 0.80 to 1.30 (see following table). In contrast to the personal income tax the property tax does appear relatively inelastic. Compared, however, to forms of taxation, such as sales and motor fuels taxes it does not appear as inelastic. When elasticities for specific states and cities are included with the national data the range of elasticities for all taxes widens considerably (see Advisory Commission on Intergovernmental Relations, *State-Local Finances in Recession and Inflation*, Table 11). As the Greytak and Jump results suggest, the inflation index for property taxes often rises as fast as the inflation index for sales taxes. Moreover, property values fluctuate over time, such that in the 1970s housing costs increased more than other goods and services, making the property tax relatively more elastic than the sales tax for this period (Frank deLeeuw, Ann Schnare, and Raymond Struyk, 'Housing', in William Gorham and Nathan Glazer (eds.) op. cit.

Recent work suggests that the property tax is not regressive. Such current views bear little resemblance to those held even a few years ago. One traditional view of regressivity assumed that housing expenditures were a larger proportion of income for low-income families. This has been challenged on the basis that for home owners the ratio of housing expenditures to income increases with income, making the tax progressive (Henry Aaron, *Who Pays the Property Tax?* (Washington, DC, Brookings, 1975)). And for renters the landlord does not pass on the full burden of the property tax (Larry Orr, *Income, Employment, and Urban Residential Location* (New York, Academic Press, 1975)). More basic than these challenges, however, is an entirely new view that the property tax acts as a tax on all owners of capital, making the full effect of the tax progressive (see Aaron, op. cit., for a review of the new view). 'Circuit-breaker' laws, providing tax relief for the aged, poor and other special groups in most states, further counteract the regressivity of the property tax.

Tax	Investigation	Elasticity
Personal income	Harris	1.80
	Groves and Kahn	1.75
	Netzer	1.70
Corporate income	Harris	1.16
	Netzer	1.10
General property	Mushkin	1.30
	Netzer	1.00

Tax	Investigation	Elasticity
General property	Bridges	0.98
	McLoone	0.80
	Rafuse	0.80
General sales	Rafuse	1.27
	Netzer	1.00
	Harris	1.00
	Davies	1.00
Motor Fuels	Harris	0.60
	Rafuse	0.43
Total state revenue	Netzer	1.20

Source: Advisory Commission on Intergovernmental Relations, *State-Local Revenue Systems and Educational Finance*, 1971.

27. See Georges Vernez, Roger Vaughn, Burke Burright, and Sinclair Coleman, *Regional Cycles and Employment Effects of Public Works Investment* (Santa Monica, RAND, R-2052-EDA, 1977).

28. A different argument for diversification applies not to industries, but to individual firms. If a few firms dominate the local economy, they can either fail or threaten to leave the city and thus cause potential problems. These may be sound arguments for diversification of firms, but they do not depend directly on business cycles.

29. The case study of Pittsburgh is based on interviews with city officials in the Flaherty and subsequent administrations, interviews with other local informants, and monitoring of newspapers and available published sources. Thomas Panelas collected much of this information.

9 URBAN MANAGEMENT UNDER FISCAL STRINGENCY: UNITED STATES AND BRITAIN

ANDREW D. GLASSBERG

Students of American urban politics who look beyond national boundaries immediately observe certain similarities in popular descriptions of American cities, and Great Britain as a whole. Both northeast and midwestern US cities, and the entire British polity, are regularly portrayed as being in chronic 'decline', and periodically portrayed as being in 'crisis'. One major consequence of this matched pair of afflicted political units is that both British and American cities have been early settings for the 'politics of scarcity'.

Although problems of fiscal stringency have received growing attention in recent years, much of the 'classic' literature on public-sector spending omits the issue. Most literature on budgeting, for example, assumes that increasing resources will steadily be made available to public organizations. In Wildavsky's *Politics of the Budgetary Process*, for example, three successive sections are entitled, 'Defending the Base: Guarding Against Cuts in the Old Programs', 'Increasing the Base: Inching Ahead with Existing Programs', and 'Expanding the Base: Adding New Programs'. Indeed, the 'Defending the Base' section begins by arguing that, 'A major strategy in resisting cuts is to make them in such a way that they have to be put back'.[1] Recent urban experiences, both in the US and in Britain, clearly indicate that a chapter on 'Decreasing the Base' could appropriately be added to the next edition.

Because of the absence of public-sector models it is useful to turn to private organizations for examples of organizational response to substantial budget declines. While this pattern is not the norm in the private sector either, it is more often part of the visible spectrum of organizational possibilities. Although public-organization bankruptcies have been rare since the depression, and unknown in large public organizations, private bankruptcies present many opportunities for investigation. Well short of bankruptcy, a substantial number of private organizations every year go through forms of reorganization which involve substantial decreases in available resources. Technological change alone guarantees that numerous organizations, or corporate divisions, will find themselves 'stuck' with an obsolete technology and/or declining sales.

Indeed, the fact that public and private organizations increasingly turn to similar sources of aid in times of fiscal crisis makes the two sectors less different in such times than they might otherwise be. Several observers have noted the increasing tendency of public-sector managers to adopt styles closer to the private sector when faced with budgetary restraints.[2] Possibilities for acting in such a fashion are undoubtedly facilitated by a persistent set of American public attitudes supportive of the idea of economy in government. Survey data collated by Richard Fenno shows a steady 'public demand for economy, with substantial percentages of respondents supporting reductions in government expenditure'.[3] In a more recent study, Fenno argued that public attitudes such as these have influenced congressional behaviour and made many Congressmen more supportive of economizing.[4] It is reasonable to think of lower levels of the public sector as being subject to similar attitudes.

One need not adopt a rhetoric of private-sector efficiency versus public-sector profligacy to observe a tendency in public organizations to be more responsive to private-sector models in times of fiscal stringency than they were in times of relative resource abundance. Indeed, the preconditions for such attitude changes may have been present all along. A comparative study of budgeting practices in fourteen American cities reports that budgetary decision makers in these communities support the idea that, 'a city, like a business, should be on the basis of professional management techniques'.[5] Decision makers adhere to a 'management budget orientation',[6] and the newly-popular 'performance budgeting' could be exploited to cut expenditures.[7] Thus, both mass-public opinion and elite attitudes are supportive of government economy in the US.

Periods of austerity in the United States, therefore, can lead to a much more conscious adoption of the rhetoric of private business management in the public sector. Indeed, significant numbers of private managers have entered the public decision-making process in New York. Such a change can take place, however, only in a society with a strong underlying belief in the greater efficiency of private management. It is this belief which makes it possible (and sometimes inevitable) for public officials to bring in private managers as part of a 'rescue' effort.

I am not here arguing that this underlying belief is necessarily correct, rather, that it permeates American society. (I am aware that the question of the relevance of private management techniques for the public sector is a controversial one, with many analysts arguing that parallels are inappropriate).[8] Nevertheless, it is clear that one significant response to the New York crisis has been an importation of private managers, and an adoption of much of the language of private business management by public-sector decision-makers. It needs to be understood that this influx is not limited to the external organizations set up to supervise New York City affairs such as the Emergency Financial Control Board. The regularly elected city government has itself imported significant numbers of private-sector managers into its own administration. In this context, the pattern of budget reduction seen in New York, with selective cuttings of particular functions perceived as 'unnecessary' by national leaders, becomes more possible. Significant staff reductions in New York City public employment also are consistent with styles of management common in the American private sector.

In Britain, by contrast, the rhetoric of private efficiency and public profligacy is far less deeply rooted in society. It is not nearly so attractive politically in Britain to argue for the importation of private managers to direct the affairs of local government bodies. Two other factors also work against any strong British parallels with the American experience. One important difference is that public sector managers in Britain are 'nationally professionalized', with certifications and qualifications from their own independent bodies. In addition, management traditions in Britain, even those which operate in the private sector, also work against significant importation of private managers in times of budget crisis. The rationale for their importation, of course, are that they are particularly skilled in 'cutting the fat' and 're-ordering priorities'. But the literature on British management suggests that its patterns of decision making are more collegial than those which operate in the US.

Comparisons of leadership patterns in Britain and the US have suggested that peer relationships are more important to English managers than to American.[9] Examinations of British managerial styles have suggested that there is little reward for effective 'internal competition' within the same enterprise.[10] Heclo and Wildavsky report that new techniques of national government budgeting, such as the Public Expenditure Survey Commission, have reinforced a 'fair shares' approach to budgeting, with agency budget patterns coming to mirror each other.[11] As a result, I would argue, there is less scope for the importation of 'high-powered' 'efficiency experts' from national governments to administer local budget cutting as can be done in the US.[12] This American pattern can be contrasted with British experience, where introduction of new budget techniques reinforces collective responsibility. Eddison reports that with the introduction of corporate planning into British local government, 'certain chief officers accept responsiblity for the affairs of more than their own department. It is expressed through a chief officers group that concerns itself with the authority as a whole.'[13]

As a result, one is less likely to find decision-makers in either the public or private sector in Britian who have made careers as 'tough-minded budget cutters'. Such an orientation requires that the individuals involved have career patterns in which success can be built despite the unpopularity and isolation of the role. The more collective pattern of British decision making makes individuals of this type less likely to develop. The relative absence of this type of decision maker in British private life makes it far more difficult, of course, to import him into the public sector. Public managers are more able, therefore, to retain their autonomy.

Prevalent American attitudes towards management have created a climate in which it seems appropriate and possible to bring in private managers when public management has 'gone wrong'. British patterns make such an importation unlikely. Thus, the differing managerial patterns of the US and Britain serve to reinforce the possibilities of external control in the New York case, but make it less possible in London.

Local Autonomy Under Fiscal Stringency

'Cultural' variations in management, therefore, form one element of variation between American and British responses to fiscal stringency. As these variations make clear, it would be wrong to assume that fiscal stringency necessarily produces the same effects on all affected local governments. Alternative explanations are likely to be needed for different settings.

Just as alternative interpretations of the role of the private sector are needed for the US and for Britain, it is also necessary to look for different interpretations in the two societies of the impact of local fiscal stringency on local autonomy and spending patterns.

I would like to suggest three alternative hypotheses about the effect of budgetary stringency on the spending patterns of local governments in the areas I am studying. One possibility is that externally imposed budget constraint will shift decision-making power to the higher unit of authority, and that its priorities will come to be more important than heretofore in shaping the spending patterns of the local unit.

Thus, under this hypothesis, the preferences of the national government should come to play a more important part in determining allocation of resources among local government services. Using its power to restrain local spending, the national government's political preferences should be at least partially reflected in the spending patterns of even those local units which have a different political colouration.

In Britain, under this interpretation, the policy preferences of the Labour Government would be reflected in the policy decisions of local authorities through the late 1970s, even those with Conservative control, while policy preferences of the Conservative government would be observable more recently, even in Labour-run local authorities. In the American example, this hypothesis would predict that the spending preferences of the national Republican administration, in power at the time of New York's fiscal crisis, would come to be a noticeable determinant of spending within New York City, despite Republican weakness within the city politic itself.

The argument here, of course, is dependent on both the availability of power to the central government, and its willingness to use it. While there can be no *a priori* basis for predicting willingness to use power, this first hypothesis would logically predict greater ability to control local spending by the British national government than the American. The differing political structures of the two countries, legally unitary in Britain, but federal in the US, suggests that the British Government should be better equipped to impose its will on a local government than would be true in the US, where the 'sovereign power' of the state governments lies between the national and local spheres.

But the basic nature of the hypothesis suggests that it ought to be correct for both countries — local weakness should permit an assertion of national priorities. That such priorities do exist is suggested by the work of Richard Rose. Rose argues that states in situations of resource constraint first emphasize their 'defining activities', such as public order and tax collection.[14] The first hypothesis of this paper, therefore, is that national governments will seek to extend their own views on how to respond to budget constraint to their local governments as well, and that they will have some success in doing so.

A second, and rather different hypothesis would suggest that the impact of budgetary constraint ought to be to reinforce the status quo in spending patterns. Within this line of argument, primary place is given to the overload on the system which making substantial budget cuts imposes. Those who seek to impose such cuts, operating from the national level, 'use up' their store of political resources simply in the struggle to get local spending reduced. This is, after all, their primary politico-economic aim, albeit one which is bound to encounter fierce resistance. The effort to overcome this resistance leaves little time or energy for controlling the details of spending priorities as well. 'Worn out' by the effort to get local budgets reduced, national decision makers are willing to let it go at that. The simplest way to cut is by percentages across the board, and this is what happens. Theoretical arguments have been advanced suggesting that adoption of innovation by governments is dependent on the availability of additional resources.[15] The argument of this second hypothesis is that the absence of such resources may work against change and reinforce the status quo between a government's various services.

In mirror-image fashion, the local government is also exhausted by the political struggle over the very fact of the cuts themselves. Local leaders concentrate their own efforts on attempts to devise strategies to avoid, or minimize, the need to make any cuts. They are in a 'no-win' situation; there is no politically popular way to cut local services, and little inclination to try to find one. Faced with the ultimate power of the central government, local leaders are forced into budget cuts.

But how to make them? One way is to impose percentage cuts and leave the details to the bureaucrats responsible for administering the specific services involved. In contrast to the first hypothesis, this second alternative would predict that the years following a 'budget crisis' would show local government budgets essentially unchanged in their allocation of resources among their various services, albeit with a reduction in the total size of the pie.[16]

But there is yet a third possibility as well. Although it is true (virtually by definition) that the national government is more powerful than its local government constituent parts, this does not necessarily mean that national government priorities will necessarily carry the day in determining the details of spending reductions. As I indicated above in the second hypothesis, national decision-makers may be satisfied simply with their assertion of control over the total size of local government spending and may, in essence, withdraw from the inevitable controversies about how the cuts are to be made.

Again, as I indicated in the second hypothesis, budget-cutting is not likely to be a popular political activity, and national figures may be just as happy to wash their hands of its messy details. In contrast to the second hypothesis, however, this third argument differs in its assumptions about the political situation of the local governments concerned. It may not be true that all forms of spending are popular with local government decision-makers. They may perceive the existence of a variety of 'sacred cow' programmes, among their local services, which the 'budget crisis' provides a first good opportunity to challenge.

This option can seem particularly attractive, since any cuts that are made can be blamed on the national authorities, which have mandated the reductions. The shock nature of fiscal crises can also be useful to some local decision-makers. It is not only politicians who may be exhausted by the struggle over the fact of the cuts. Important local pressure groups may also be weakened by the energies they have devoted to the conflicts, and less able to resist the specifics of the spending cuts, when they come. If local decision-makers have specific targets which they have been seeking to attack for some time, the existence of a budget crisis may provide a perfect opportunity/excuse for doing so. To the degree that this is so, we should expect to see changes in post-crisis spending allocations, but ones which reflect the priorities of local decision-makers rather than of national leaders.

The existence of these three differing but plausible hypotheses indicates that there is little *a priori* basis for predicting what the impact of a fiscal crisis will be on the spending patterns of the local governments involved. As I have suggested, it is possible that national government priorities will become dominant, that the status quo will be reinforced, or even that the power of local political leaders will be enhanced as they use the crisis (and its opportunity for deflecting blame onto others) to 'think the unthinkable' and assert their own preferences by cutting entrenched local services of which they disapprove. Given the conflict between these alternatives, it becomes necessary to examine the specifics of response in differing settings, in order to gain a clearer perspective on the patterns of budget cutting which are adopted in practice.

Patterns of Response

In Tables 9.1 and 9.2 I have presented data showing the distribution of local-government spending over a variety of major public services under the control of the local authority. It will be seen that these vary between New York and the London boroughs examined, but I have limited the analysis to those functions for which there is clear local responsibility, and that responsibility is held by the unit under study.

Table 9.1 *Percentage of London borough budgets devoted to specific local services*

	1974-5 (%)	1976-7 (%)	1978-9 (%)
Islington			
Public libraries and museums	4.6	4.8	4.4
Baths and sports	3.8	5.9	4.9
Parks	6.6	6.2	6.1
Refuse collection	5.6	4.6	4.5
Environmental health*	2.3	7.4	5.6
Personal social services	34.3	37.7	36.0
Town planning	4.7	3.8	3.0
Local highways*	12.1	4.3	3.2
Housing*	25.0	24.7	31.7
Cemeteries and crematoria	0.9	0.6	0.5
Tower Hamlets			
Public libraries and museums	4.3	4.1	4.0
Baths and sports	7.3	5.7	8.4
Parks	6.0	6.1	5.3
Refuse collection	6.0	6.1	5.3
Environmental health	5.1	7.3	4.0
Personal social services	39.1	39.8	40.3
Town planning*	3.3	3.7	0
Local highways	10.7	4.2	12.1
Housing*	17.9	24.1	20.1
Cemeteries and crematoria	0	0.6	0
Bromley (including education)			
Education	64.7	67.7	67.4
Public libraries and museums	2.7	3.0	3.1
Baths and sports	0.9	1.7	1.5
Parks	3.3	2.7	2.6
Refuse collection	2.3	2.4	2.3
Environmental health	0.8	1.8	2.2
Personal social services*	8.7	11.1	11.1
Town planning	1.7	1.3	2.2

	1974–5 (%)	1976–7 (%)	1978–9 (%)
Bromley (including education) *cont.*			
Local highways	9.8	5.7	5.6
Housing*	5.0	2.6	1.8
Cemeteries and crematoria	0.2	0.2	0.2
Bromley (excluding education)			
Public libraries and museums*	7.5	9.2	9.6
Baths and sports*	2.5	5.2	4.7
Parks	9.3	8.0	7.9
Refuse collection	6.4	7.4	7.1
Environmental health*	2.2	5.6	6.6
Personal social services*	24.6	34.4	34.0
Town planning	4.8	4.0	6.7
Local highways	27.9	17.6	17.1
Housing*	14.1	8.0	5.4
Cemeteries and crematoria	0.6	0.7	0.6

* These services are those with more than a 2 per cent point change in relative share of borough budgets from 1974-5 to 1978-9.

The financial year 1976–7 is the first to include the effects of explicit national government directives to reduce local-government spending.

Unlike Islington and Tower Hamlets, Bromley is an independent education authority with responsibility for its own schools. Islington and Tower Hamlets, in Inner London, form part of the territory of the Inner London Education Authority. While I have presented Bromley data, including education, since this is a borough function, I have used the portion of the table showing Bromley spending patterns, excluding education, when making comparisons with the two other boroughs.

Because of the differing service responsibilities of the local governments involved, comparisons between them on the basis of these data are largely inappropriate. What is relevant for the purposes of this analysis are the changes (or lack of changes) *within* the units. I am not concerned here with overall budget size, but rather with the distribution of available resources between the various services the local government in question administers. I have, therefore, reported the data in terms of percentage of local government budget spent on specific services.

A quick examination of the tables will show considerable stability in spending patterns for all units. In many respects this is not surprising. Even in an environment of 'fiscal crisis', the basic functions of units of local government, and the distribution of functions between levels of government, remain little changed. We are not surprised, therefore, to see major spending categories, such as social services, forming a significant fraction of local public spending both before and after the onset of the 'crises'.

In this respect, the data reported on here conform to the second model

Table 9.2   *Percentage of New York City budgets devoted to specific local services*

| | Fiscal Year | | |
	1973 (%)	1976 (%)	1977 (%)
Police	7.6	7.3	7.7
Fire	3.6	3.2	3.3
Social services	23.5	24.8	24.7
Corrections	0.9	0.8	0.9
Health	10.6	10.4	8.9
Environmental protection	4.0	3.1	3.2
Finance	0.4	0.3	0.3
Transportation (highways)	1.1	0.9	0.9
Parks	0.9	0.8	0.7
Municipal services ('housekeeping')	1.1	1.5	1.0
Board of education	23.4	22.9	24.2
Board of higher education (City University)	4.8	5.0	4.4
Hospitals	8.3	8.7	9.1
Transit authority (mass transit)	10.0	10.1	10.5

Fiscal year 1976 is the first to have reduced budgets as a result of the city fiscal crisis. Changes made during that year are included in figures.

presented above — fiscal crisis leaves spending patterns largely unchanged, with cuts made in across the board fashion between departments. A comparison of the New York and London borough figures shows differences, however. The New York figures are remarkably stable. No spending category varies by as much as two percentage points of total spending from the period before the fiscal crisis to the most recent for which data is available. But reports by external auditors who monitor city spending report anticipation of significant future cuts. In the data presented here, the only significant spending reductions (in absolute terms, unadjusted for inflation) occurred in the reductions in public spending in the City University system.[17]

Reductions in this category are not an anomaly. The City University was a distinctive and visible public service not provided by other American cities, and was the only large university system in the United States with both open admission and no tuition charges. (It is an important political point to recognize that these conditions only applied in New York City and were unavailable to residents of the remainder of New York State.) Once the city's fiscal condition required extensive outside assistance, including Federal loans, the distinctive character of New York City spending on its City University became untenable. Long the subject of controversy, the fiscal crisis provided an occasion for external forces (including the President of the United States) to end this pattern. City University has ended its open admissions policy and instituted tuition fees identical to those charged in other public institutions in New York State.

What this spending cut demonstrates is the sort of circumstances in which the first model, of increasing national power over local spending, becomes operative. Where a community under fiscal stress has historically provided services which do not fit the national pattern, we can expect those patterns to come under heavy attack, and pressure to conform to service delivery and spending patterns prevalent elsewhere. Distinctiveness of service becomes a political liability, when the support and aid of external groups becomes essential.

An examination of the data from the three London boroughs shows a considerably more varied pattern of response.[18] All three boroughs show at least two spending categories with percentage changes of at least two per cent from pre- to post-crisis budgets (while no spending category in New York City had shown such a percentage change). Spending patterns of the London boroughs under fiscal crisis were, therefore, considerably more varied than those which obtained in New York City.

But comparisons among the boroughs show differences among them as well. The three boroughs varied in the extent of their internal spending variations. Patterns in Tower Hamlets are much more stable than those in Bromley. Only two services in Tower Hamlets show changes of over 2 per cent (one being a function which, on paper at least, was completely eliminated). In Bromley, by contrast, six services show changes of 2 per cent or greater.

We can also observe that not only is there variation between London boroughs in the *extent* to which spending patterns changed, but that there is also variation in the *direction* of the changes among the boroughs. Thus, we note that the Inner London Labour-controlled boroughs of Tower Hamlets and Islington were increasing the percentage of their resources they were devoting to housing, while Bromley, a Conservative-controlled suburban borough, was making significant reductions in its housing spending.

While these shifts in priorities conform to our sense of the political makeup of the boroughs involved, they do not fit with the priorities of the national Labour Government. Despite the unitary nature of the British governmental system, and despite repeated national government efforts to direct not only the fact of spending cuts, but also the service areas to receive greater or lesser priority, it seems clear from the data presented here that the boroughs retained considerable autonomy in deciding for themselves how to respond.

How can we account for the apparently greater independence of the local units examined in London in comparison with New York City? As I indicated above, an initial prediction based solely on the constitutional forms of the two systems would lead to a reverse expectation. I would suggest that the explanation of this apparent paradox lies in the differing perceptions of the fiscal crises on opposite sides of the Atlantic. The New York crisis was presented in American political debates as a circumstance unique to New York, whose roots were to be found in the particular political decisions taken in the city. (I would not wish to argue that this is an accurate account of the crisis and its origins, only that it was the widely held national view.)

In Britain, by contrast, 'fiscal crisis' is seen as a clearly national phenomenon. The imposition of spending curbs by the British national government affected local governments throughout the country. There was nothing particularly distinctive about their impact on London, compared to the rest of Britain. This differing perception of the extent to which local circumstances 'caused' the fiscal crisis of the two metropolises produced clear differences in national response patterns. In the US, there was a search for New York City anomalies — patterns of spending (and of other types of local decision-making) which varied from the national pattern. In Britain, with a crisis thought to be national in origin, such a search would not have been as politically important. While it is clear that efforts were made at the national level in Britain to put pressure on local units to reduce their spending, these efforts had to be spread throughout the entire country. Concentrated attention and publicity were unlikely to fall on any single unit, unless its *spending totals* continued to grow rapidly. In the absence of any belief that distinctive local government services were 'responsible' for the British fiscal difficulties, there was less national government pressure (or at least less successful national government pressure) to force local governments in Britain to change their own priorities very much.

This difference between New York and London can also be observed in their differing use of staff cutbacks as a means of budget reduction. The New York crisis has seen extensive public sector layoffs, with many agencies now staffed at levels significantly below those of pre-crisis periods. In London, however, only attrition has been used, and examination of the most recent figures available show little change in staffing levels in the three London boroughs studied in this research. The data on staffing levels in New York and the London boroughs are presented in Tables 9.3 and 9.4. Once again, I would argue that this difference can be understood in terms of the differing perceptions of the origins of the crises. New York was perceived as atypically heavily staffed (and by employees of high salary), while London was not generally presented as having significantly more public employees per capita than local authorities elsewhere in Britain. The perception of New York as 'anomalous' but London as 'normal' led to more severe pressure on the former than on the latter.

What we see then, is that the response of national and local governments to their fiscal difficulties, and the extent to which national govern-

Table 9.3   *Changes in personnel employed by London boroughs*[19]

	June 1974	May 1977	Change (%)
Bromley	11841	11512	2.8 reduction
Islington	4454	5318	19.4 increase
Tower Hamlets	4965	5161	3,9 increase

Personnel data by individual services were not available.
The higher personnel totals for Bromley reflect its role as an education authority, which Islington and Tower Hamlets are not.

Table 9.4   *Changes in personnel employed by New York City*[20]

	June 1975	May 1977	Change (%)
Education	90182	71746	20.4 reduction
Higher education	25001	17006	32.0 reduction
Police	35734	29496	17.4 reduction
Fire	13921	11613	16.6 reduction
Social services	27122	23374	13.8 reduction
Environmental protect	19072	16866	11.6 reduction
Health	7472	4593	38.5 reduction
Parks	7419	4016	45.8 reduction
Transportation	5802	4666	19.5 reduction
Housing	4230	3318	21.5 reduction
Municipal services	3719	3136	15.6 reduction
Finance	1954	1720	11.9 reduction
Correction	4415	3922	11.1 reduction
All others	20810	14490	30.4 reduction
Total	266853	209962	21.3 reduction

Data do not include Hospitals or Transit Authority

ments are able to use the occasion of such troubles to re-order local priorities, will depend on the interpretations of the causes of the crisis which come to dominate public debate. In the United States, the crisis was perceived as limited to New York, and understood to be rooted in the city's unusually extensive network of public services.

In Britain, the crisis was not perceived in this way, but was much more widely thought to be rooted in a general tendency for all levels of government to increase their spending. In this latter circumstance, the search for local anomalies would not have made much sense, and the local units of government were able to retain more autonomy and greater local control of their priorities than New York City has been able to do.

Lacking these national pressures for conformity, the distinctive political configurations of the London boroughs themselves become more important in explaining changes in spending patterns than the pressures of the national government. As I indicated earlier, the three London boroughs reported in this research were chosen for their political distinctiveness, and I have elsewhere reported on their varying political styles.

In that earlier work I characterized Tower Hamlets as a 'traditional working-class' Labour Party-controlled inner-city borough, and Bromley as a 'traditional middle-class' Conservative Party-controlled suburban borough. Islington I saw as an 'untraditional' local authority, with political control in the hands of middle-class professionals who have moved into the borough, are Labour Party adherents, and have captured control of significant parts of the borough's Labour Party organizations, and of the borough council.[21]

If we look at the spending patterns for the three boroughs reported earlier, however, it is Bromley which looks the most unusual. It shows the greatest variation in its spending pattern, and a willingness to vary its spending in ways which were unlikely to meet with national government approval. I would argue, however, this does not constitute 'untraditional' behaviour. Rather, it represents the expected response of a Conservative-controlled local government to the political directives of a national Labour Government. It is not unusual to find such a suburban authority resisting pressure from above and, as Bromley's data shows, holding down its spending on public housing and reducing its relative position in borough spending. (While an examination of the data will show a perhaps unexpected increase in Bromley's social service spending, this category is less under the control of the borough than is its allocation for housing. While local governments can do little to affect the number of disabled people within their boundaries, or the number of children who must be taken into public care, they are very well able to control the number of council housing units they construct. Spending on housing, therefore, is a more sensitive indicator of local government political priorities, and we see Bromley's response to budgetary stringency is to cut its spending in this category more severely than other public services it controls.)

But examination of spending patterns involves only one side of the governmental fiscal equation. Taxes, of course, are the other. Here we observe substantial variation between the two metropolises, New York and London, and among the local units within London. As I indicated above, perceptions of the origins of the fiscal crises varied considerably between Britain and the United States. This variation had its impact on tax policy as well as on spending controls.

The widespread British perception that increases in public spending (and in taxation) rates were a major factor in British economic problems produced a national government response in which attempts were made to hold down local taxes as well as local spending.[22] In the US, perception that New York was providing unusual service levels, and that these were responsible for its problems, led to the opposite result. If New York had more extensive service systems, then part of the response to the gap between spending and revenue should be a local tax increase. While New York leaders might have had different views (and have interpreted their problems in ways closer to the British understanding), they lacked power. Thus, the American national government was willing and able to require that a part of New York's response to its 'local' fiscal crisis would be an increase in local taxes. In Britain, the national government, responding to a 'national' fiscal crisis, sought to have its local governments not only bring down their spending, but their local taxes as well.

If we examine the response of the three London boroughs, we find very different results. In Bromley, the Council kept its 'rates' ('real estate taxes' would be the American equivalent) constant for three years.[23] In this particular circumstance, the policy preferences of the Conservative-controlled borough government, and the Labour-controlled national government fitted together. Of more interest, perhaps, is the differing pattern of response between the two Labour-controlled local authorities studied in this research.

Boroughs which held down the level of increases in the rates (and therefore also held down growth in local spending) were conforming to national policy. Boroughs with higher increases were deviating from national policy.[24] The Tower Hamlets Council reported that, for the 1978/79 financial year, it was holding its increase in the rates to 7 per cent;[25] the Council reported to Tower Hamlets residents, the borough no longer had the highest rates in London.[26] While this pattern of increase does not match Bromley's recent history of no increases at all, the dramatically different political and social patterns of the two boroughs needs to be borne in mind.

A more significant comparison can be found by looking at the pattern of taxation between Tower Hamlets and Islington. In Islington, in contrast to Tower Hamlets, only last-minute action by the borough council in the period immediately preceding new borough elections held 1978/79 financial year rate increases to 10 per cent.[27] Previous planning expenditures would have resulted in increases of even greater proportion, but even its 10 per cent increases were higher than those of its neighbouring working-class boroughs in Inner London. It seems clear that national government attempts to constrain local tax increases were operating in Tower Hamlets, where the borough council not only moderated its increases, but also adopted the rhetoric of low taxation. In Islington, however, national government constraints do not seem to have been particularly effective. Only the immediate political pressure of coming elections seems to have made the difference, and even this pressure still left Islington with atypically high local tax increases.[28]

While it is often assumed that there is little support for increased tax rates, the Islington experience shows that this is not necessarily so. Members of Islington Council, at least, faced with national pressure to restrain tax increases and hold down local expenditure, showed clear preference for higher local taxes in order to continue to finance local expenditures. That they were ultimately forced to moderate this policy somewhat only underlines the ability of the borough council to act autonomously. It was not pressure from the national government which ultimately acted as a significant restraint, but rather the process of local political calculation.

As with spending policy, an examination of tax policy in London and New York shows greater autonomy for the London boroughs than New York City enjoyed. Among the London borough studies, Islington had the most extensive history of non-traditional politics, and the British fiscal crisis did not force it to end this pattern.

Difference in Public Management Styles

In comparing top-level national administrators in the US and Great Britain, Richard Neustadt argued that the British civil service was distinguished by a career structure which promoted the development of 'generalists' with broad experience in administration, but also with detailed background work in the political sector as well.[29] The career structures of the civil service provided opportunities to be confidential aides to government ministers without relinquishing civil service status. No such opportunity structures existed in American politics, Neustadt argued.

Thus, one fundamental facet of British public administration is, in this view, leadership by a group of people who have worked with each other for long periods of time, share common values and experiences, but are not likely to be 'technical experts'. As such, the leadership of national British administration appears to fit with our understanding of the operation of British leadership patterns more generally. One of the 'causes' of the British crisis, it is frequently argued, is societal undervaluing of technical expertise as opposed to more prestigious 'generalist' training.[30]

By contrast, British local government is reported to have been considerably more interested than central government in encouraging its employees to obtain specific training in their own specialized fields.[31] This pattern in British local government can hardly be explained by reference to the national 'political culture'. Indeed, British descriptions of British management patterns often emphasize the distinction between the national civil service and its traditions, and the very different recruitment patterns and traditions of local government service.[32]

The separateness of these traditions in Britain can be noted in the very language used to describe the respective institutions. In the US the term 'civil service' covers all bureaucratic systems, from federal to local. In Britain, however, 'civil servants' work only for the national government.

Comparable figures at subnational levels are 'local government officers'. One recent study of the 'British philosophy of administration' explicitly excludes the operations of British local government from its purview.[33]

Any discussion of urban management in Britain, therefore, and any attempt to compare this system with American counterparts, must begin with two cautions. Administration in British local government cannot be inferred from observations drawn from national British experience, and variations within the patterns must be anticipated, even when only the local level is being considered. (In a very different context, Graham Allison has warned us of our tendency to accept without question the existence of varied bureaucratic systems acting within our own country, but to begin our analyses of other societies with implicit assumptions of homogeneous national styles and purposes throughout that society's bureaucracy.)[34] Within the US the very complexity and variation in administrative procedures has been noted by one classic study of comparative administration to be the 'focal point of American administrative dysfunctions'.[35]

Despite these caveats, there are certain regularities to British and American urban administration, and contrasts which can be drawn between them. I suggested earlier that differing perceptions of the 'causes' of urban fiscal crises was one such variation. A second major variation between the two countries can be found in the differing ways in which urban public services are funded in the US and Britain. I suggest that particular attention needs to be paid to the much greater reliance on central government 'revenue sharing' in Britain than in the US.[36] While the overall percentage of local expenditure which comes from central government sources is less in the US than in Britain,[37] this is probably not true for 'fiscal crisis' central cities in the US, which have come to rely upon federal aid for disproportionately large shares of their revenues, in comparison with other American local governments.[38]

In fact, a mere comparison of the available data on these points understates the difference. It is necessary to understand not only the extent to which unrestricted (as opposed to earmarked) national funds are available to local governments, but also the extent to which the provision of such funds has become routinized.[39] The use of the Rate Support Grant has now become an accepted part of the British political process. This does not mean that no debate about it takes place, but rather that controversy centres around the funding formula, not the existence of the aid programme itself. While central governments can and do alter the RSG formula for their own programmatic purposes, they really cannot control what local authorities do with the funds they receive, nor can central government credibly threaten to eliminate the payments.

Even the new Thatcher government proposals for changes in the Rate Support Grant do not fundamentally challenge this point. Proposals for a new block grant system for 1981/82 will enhance central power by providing a weapon against those local authorities which engage in what central government regards as overspending, yet the mix of local spending will not be directly affected. Indeed, the fact that central government sees a need for additional powers to limit aggregate local government spending demonstrates the relative freedom that local authorities in England have enjoyed up to now. In Scotland, by contrast, the Scottish Office has been more advanced than central government for England in controlling local spending by suggesting appropriate total current spending levels.[40]

Despite proposed increases in constraint on total spending by British local governments, the relationship between central and local government in Britain continues to follow the pattern which Bulpitt characterized as a 'dual polity',[41] in which local government is permitted considerable autonomy on the details of policy, and central government only involves itself when local government actions have the potential for disrupting central government policies. The recent proposals for Rate Support Grant alteration fit this pattern. A new government, having a reduction in total public expenditure as a central theme, takes action to more stringently limit aggregate local government spending as one item in this catalogue of government spending reductions, but leaves untouched local discretion regarding the mix of this expenditure.[42]

In the US, by contrast, revenue sharing remains a new and uncertain programme. As experiences with the Anti Recession Fiscal Assistance Program demonstrate, local governments in the US cannot be assured of comparable sums of federal assistance from one year to the next.[43] Thus, not only is a greater proportion of central government aid in the US in the form of programme-specific grants, but even that portion of federal funding which is unrestricted in nature comes under political circumstances which must make American urban administrators wary of relying too heavily on its continuation. This second variation in American and British patterns also suggests greater relative freedom for British urban administrators than would be true in the American situation.

A third variation can be found in the formal constitutional arrangements of the two societies. The amount of external control to which American urban managers are subject is enhanced by the American system. While it is of course true that Britain is a unitary system in which central government has sovereign powers over its municipalities while the American federal government does not, the role of state governments in the US provides another setting for constraint to be imposed on American urban managers. State assertion of authority is by no means a purely theoretical matter. Longstanding political traditions in many American states (reinforced by cultural attitudes and the historical legacy of anti-urban apportionment patterns in state legislatures) lead to recurring state control of American local governments which are far more detailed than those exercised by British central government over British local authorities.

In addition to emphasizing the role of direct central government constraints, many British analysts have directed their attention to the perceived growth of 'corporatism', and have argued that this too constitutes a growing limit of the freedom of decision of local governments, and those who manage them. The concept of 'corporatism', usually used in a pejorative context, suggests that tripartite arrangements of government, big business, and large labour unions in fact take collective decisions on major points in the national economy.[44] Since local government expenditure is such a point, it too is subject to the influence of corporatism.

Whatever the merits of this view, there is no inherent reason why the growth of collective decision-making across a variety of governmental and industrial sectors necessarily reduces the autonomy of local government *vis a vis* central government. If such patterns do indeed grow, and this itself is by no means certain, the relative power of all levels of government as independent 'sovereign' powers might be reduced, however.

The growth of concern about corporatism, and its possible risks for democratic decision making, fit a more widespread pattern of critical analyses of British political systems. This changing trend can be observed in American analyses of Britain as well. Long-standing trends in American political discussion have presented British experiences as models to be emulated.[45] Samuel Huntington has suggested that this pattern of emulation can be traced back to the origins of the American republic.[46]

More recently, however, the British experience has been presented as a model to be avoided. One early sign of this changing fashion can be found in the generally cool analyses of British urban reorganizations as possible models for American cities.[47] More recent commentary has centred on British difficulties in maintaining a wide range of urban public services.[48]

The argument of this paper has been somewhat different. I have suggested that local government elites in Britain have been better able to retain freedom of choice in setting local government priorities than have been some comparable American actors, but I have attributed these differences to variations in both the structural setting of British local government, and more broadly cultural attitudes about business and government in Great Britain.

Whether this is a good thing or a bad thing depends on one's perspective about the policy outputs of the local governments involved. It does suggest, however, that the formal centralism of British government has not resulted in the elimination of local government autonomy, even under circumstances of severe fiscal stringency, nor does the American federal structure necessarily provide a secure defence for local governments against external control.

Notes

This essay is part of a larger study of the politics of budgetary stringency in British and American cities. This work has been supported by research grants from the City University of New York Research Foundation, the Center for International Studies, University of Missouri–St Louis, and by Faculty Research Fellowship support from the University of Missouri–St Louis. Portions of this article have also appeared in 'Organizational Responses to Municipal Budget Declines', *Public Administration Review*, 38 (1978), 325–32; and in 'Response to Fiscal Crisis: Big City Governments in Britain and America', *Studies in Public Policy Series*, No. 55, Centre for the Study of Public Policy, University of Strathclyde, Glasgow, Scotland, April 1980.

Further reports will be found in 'The Urban Fiscal Crisis Becomes Routine', *Public Administration Review*, Fall, 1980, and in *Managing the Urban Fiscal Crisis: A Comparative Perspective* (London, Macmillan, forthcoming).

1. Aaron Wildavsky, *Politics of the Budgetary Process* (Boston, Little Brown, 1964), 102.
2. R. Dworak, 'Economizing in Public Organizations', *Public Administration Review*, XXXV (1975) 158; J. B. Ukeles, 'Towards a Strategy for Urban Management', *New York Affairs*, 4 (1977) 4.
3. Richard Fenno, *Power of the Purse* (Boston, Little Brown, 1966), 11.
4. Richard Fenno, *Congressmen in Committees* (Boston, Little Brown, 1975), 47.
5. Lewis Friedman, *Budgeting Municipal Expenditures* (New York, Praeger, 1975), 176.
6. Ibid., 176.
7. Ibid., 180.
8. For expressions of this view, see H. H. Rainey, R. W. Backoff, and C. Levine, 'Comparing Public and Private Organizations', *Public Administration Review*, 36 (1976) 233–44, and Blanche Blank, 'Myth of Management Magic', *New York Affairs*, 4 (1977) 24–32.
9. II. Landsberger, 'The Horizontal Dimension in Bureaucracy', *Administrative Sciences Quarterly*, VI (1961) 299–332.
10. D. Channon, *The Strategy and Structure of British Enterprise* (Cambridge, Harvard University School of Busniess Administration, 1973), 213–14.
11. H. Heclo and A. Wildavsky, *The Private Government of Public Money* (Berkeley, University of California Press, 1974), 351–2.
12. For an example of such an effort in New York, see Frederick O'R. Hayes, *Productivity in Local Government* (Lexington, Mass., Lexington Books, 1977).
13. Tony Eddison, *Local Government Management and Corporate Planning* (Leighton Buzzard, England, Leonard Hill Books, 1975), 160.
14. Richard Rose, 'On the Priorities of Government: A Developmental Analysis of Public Policies', *European Journal of Political Research*, 4 (1976), 247–89.
15. Richard Bingham, *Adoption of Innovation by Local Government* (Lexington, Mass., Lexington Books, 1976), 212–13.
16. For evidence that this was at least the initial pattern of response in New York City see *New York Times*, 11 June, 1975.
17. Data for New York is drawn from Office of the State Comptroller, Office of the Special Deputy Comptroller for New York City, *Fact Sheets for Fourteen Major Agencies in New York City* (New York, Office of the Comptroller, 20 October 1977).
18. Data for London is drawn from Chartered Institute of Public Finance and Accountancy, *Financial, General and Rating Statistics 1978–79* (London, CIPFA, 1978) and its predecessor series, *Return of Rates*.
19. Data for London is drawn from Greater London Council, *Annual Abstract*

of Greater London Statistics, 1976 (London, Greater London Council, 1978) and earlier volumes in this series.

20. Data for New York is drawn from Office of the New York City Comptroller, *Comptroller's Report*, 2 (1977).

21. Andrew Glassberg, *Representation and Urban Community* (London, Macmillan. 1981).

22. See the argument by Peter Else that in the European context (but not the American) it is useful to treat national macro-economic policy as a separate and important element in government control of local public expenditure. Peter Else, 'New Developments in Budgetary Decision-Making', in David Coombes, *et al.* (eds.), *The Power of the Purse* (London, George Allen and Unwin, 1976), 339–63.

23. Bromley Times, 2 March, 1978.

24. Among the many reports on this view see, 'Turning Off the Town Hall Tap', *Sunday Times*, 6 June 1976, 62.

25. *Tower Hamlets News*, April 1978.

26. Ibid.

27. London Borough of Islington, Council Agendas, *Report of Policy and Resources Committee Working Party*, 16 March 1978.

28. Political controversy over spending in Islington has centred on a £2 million gap in the borough's 1976/77 accounts. See *London Evening Standard*, 14 and 16 November 1977. Outside auditors hired by the borough ultimately recommended that a 22 per cent rates increase would be necessary if the gap were to be closed and current spending patterns maintained. See *Islington Gazette*, 14 July 1978.

29. Richard Neustadt, 'White House and Whitehall', in Richard Rose (ed.), *Policy-Making in Britain* (New York, Free Press, 1969), 291–306.

30. Ghita Ionescu, *Centripetal Politics* (London, Hart-Davis MacGibbon, 1975), 85.

31. Brian Smith and Jeffrey Stanyer, *Administering Britain* (Oxford, Martin Robertson, 1976), 188.

32. Smith and Stanyer, *Administering Britain,* 178. Simon Caulkin, 'The Other Civil Service', *Management Today* (February 1978), 49. Neville Abraham, *Big Business and Government* (London, Macmillan, 1974), 300.

33. Rosamund Thomas, *The British Philosophy of Administration* (London, Longman, 1978), 4.

34. Graham Allison, *Essence of Decision* (Boston, Little Brown, 1971).

35. Michel Crozier, *The Bureaucratic Phenomenon* (Chicago, University of Chicago Press, 1964), 236. Smith and Stanyer op. cit., 176.

36. Douglas Ashford, 'Territorial Politics and Resource Allocation', *European Studies Newsletter*, 8 (1978) 2.

37. Ibid. 2.

38. Stephen Barro, *The Urban Impacts of Federal Policies'* Vol. 3, *Fiscal Conditions* (Santa Monica, Rand Corporation, 1978).

39. Richard Jackman and Mary Sellars, 'The Distribution of RSG', *CES Review* 1 (1977) 19–30. *Sunday Telegraph,* 6 February 1977, 6. Edward Page, 'Why Should Central-Local Relations in Scotland Be Any Different from those in England?', *Studies in Public Policy*, No. 21, Centre for the Study of Public Policy, University of Strathclyde, 31.

40. Page, op. cit. 31.

41. Jim Bulpitt, 'The Making of the United Kingdom', *Parliamentary Affairs*, XXXI (1978) 180.

42. For descriptions of proposed changes in the Rate Support grant see *The Government's Expenditure Plans 1980-81*, Cmnd. 7746 (London, HMSO, November 1979) and Department of the Environment and Department of

Transport, *Rate Support Grant Orders for England and Wales*, Press Notice 543, 28 November 1979.

43.   Extension of the Anti-Recession Fiscal Assistance programme failed on the final day of the 1978 Congressional session, after many large cities had already budgeted on an assumption of its extension.

44.   G. Wootton, *Pressure, Politics in Contemporary Britain* (Lexington, Mass., Lexington Books, 1975), 194; Richard Rose and Guy Peters, *Can Governments Go Bankrupt?* (New York, Basic Books, 1978), 190; C. Cawson, 'Pluralism, Corporatism, and the Role of the State', *Government and Opposition*, 13 (1978), 181.

45.   For a classic example, see American Political Science Association, Committee on Political Parties, 'Toward a More Responsible Two-Party System', *American Political Science Review*, XLIV (1950).

46.   Samuel Huntington, *Political Order in Changing Societies* (New Haven, Yale University Press, 1968).

47.   Wallace Sayre, 'The Relevance of the Greater London Governmental Experience to New York City Government', in State Study Commission for New York City, *The Neighborhoods, the City, and the Region* (New York, State Study Commission, 1971).

48.   Richard Rose, op. cit., 247–89.

10 CITIES, CAPITAL, AND BANKS: THE POLITICS OF DEBT IN THE UNITED STATES, UNITED KINGDOM, AND FRANCE

ALBERTA SBRAGIA

Central monetary policy, capital markets, interest rates, and bonds are not often discussed in either single-country or comparative studies of urban politics. While scholars have recently begun to analyse the visibly important role played by financial institutions such as banks in the economic development of a wide variety of nations, the involvement of such institutions in urban development is rarely mentioned. Yet urban governments, through their borrowing activities, are as involved with a nation's investment community as national governments are with the international financial system. In the US, for example, the amount borrowed by local governments in the long-term bond market in 1978 was roughly one and a half times as great as the amount borrowed by the entire corporate sector.[1] The links between the world of capital and the world of urban government, urban services, and urban policy-making are so strong that they often set the parameters within which local officials work. These links become important when urban governments borrow the funds they need to pay for capital facilities such as harbours, airports, mass transit, school buildings, public housing, libraries, and recreational facilities. As a borrower, local government becomes involved in a complex network of relationships with the lender(s) as well as with the central government which, in turn, has its own macro-economic and sectorial policy interests to protect.

The investment banker, as the representative of the world of finance, the city treasurer or controller as that of local government, and the Treasury, acting for central government, therefore, play a role as important for a city's well-being and financial status as it is obscure and unrecognized. The relationships which tie these worlds together are always complex, often subtle, and certainly little studied. There is, however, no doubt that analysing them is crucial for understanding the constraints and relationships which bound local policymakers' options and define the position of local government with respect to both the state and the investment sector.

This paper examines these links in a preliminary attempt to analyse the relationships in which local government as borrower is involved. I shall here, in an exploratory fashion, analyse the triangular relationship formed by leading financial institutions, central government, and local governments, and shall do so by examining three large industrial democracies. I shall then compare the borrowing strategies employed by local officials in France, the UK, and the US to maximize their own position *vis a vis* the investment community and the central government. Two propositions are used as the basis for discussion. The first is that, as compared with the private market, public lending institutions will both lend funds more cheaply and are more likely to implement the public investment priorities established by economic planning. The second is that, in the arena of capital finance, the political tactics and concerns of local officials in each country are directed toward the institution(s) or markets which lend local governments their capital funds. Where the private market is dominant, we would expect to find local policymakers' strategies directed toward that market; where public lenders are important, we would expect local officials to direct their attention to them.

I suggest, as the basis for discussion, that there are; 1. significant cross-national differences in the institutional structures within which borrowing takes place, and 2. links between those structures and the strategies which local officials use to implement their capital programming objectives. These strategies, of course, both form and are formed by the political culture of each country. In addition, they reveal those structural constraints which local officials feel to be most important. Thus, whether an authority borrows its capital from public or private sources may have a real impact on how its officials work and what they are concerned about.

Local Authority Borrowing

Local governments are key actors in the overall formation of national capital wealth. For example in the US, estimated public capital requirements for 1965–75 were 499 billion; an estimated 328 billion was destined for state and local public spending.[2] In the UK in 1967, local government accounted for 22 per cent of total gross investment; 80 per cent of total public investment excluding the public corporation, and 44 per cent of total public investment including public corporations.[3] In France, local governments account for 66 per cent of all public investments,[4] partially in their role as general contractors for national ministries.[5]

While local governments are in fact responsible for sponsoring a great deal of public capital formation, they do not generally finance it primarily from their own tax revenues. They borrow either from public lending institutions or from the private financial market. Approximately 50–75 per cent of local capital investments in the US have been financed by borrowing;[6] the equivalent figure for Britain has ranged from 60–90 per cent, while in France between 45 and 60 per cent of capital outlay has been borrowed.[8]

In aggregate terms, local governments in all three countries have borrowed enormous sums. In the US, outstanding local government debt in 1979 amounted to roughly 300 billion dollars.[9] Local government borrowing is so heavy that it overshadows the borrowing of the corporate sector. In

1978, for instance, local government borrowed between 46 and 48 billion dollars in long-term funds, while the corporate sector borrowed less than 30 billion.[10] In 1977, British local authorities owed roughly 29.5 billion pounds.[11] French local government debt has increased so dramatically that for every 100 francs borrowed in 1972, 59 francs went to repay the debt charges on previous loans while only 41 francs were spent for new capital investment.[12]

In addition to repaying borrowed funds, the interest charged on those borrowed funds must also be paid. Interest rates are highly significant for local governments, since they affect both the local budget (the higher the interest rate, the more money must be set aside in the budget to pay for such costs) and the cost, as well as the availability, of many 'public' services. For example, in the case of British public housing, the annual rent for a typical council house would be £218 at 6.75 per cent interest in contrast to £159 at 4 per cent.[13] The question of whether public lending institutions provide cities with capital at lower costs than private institutions is thus a critical one.[14]

Borrowing Context: Public vs Private Lenders

While central monetary policy serves as a general constraint on local borrowing in all systems, each of the three political systems discussed here softens the effects of such monetary policy on local capital expenditures, either by a public institution lending funds on terms not strictly defined by central monetary policy, or by tax policy which in effect shelters borrowers from the full impact of monetary policy. The importance of public lending institutions in the three countries differs, however, as we shall now see.

United States

Of the three countries, the US relies most heavily on privately-controlled investment decisions to handle the capital requirements of subnational units. The private municipal bond market is the major lender to municipal borrowers. Thus municipal borrowing interacts with, and is influenced by, the private market in a variety of ways. Further, the American political system subjects its capital investment decisions to much more citizen participation — by means such as election of finance officers and, in particular, by bond referenda — than either Great Britain or France.

Market Influences
One of the most visible and controversial private market methods of influence/control over local borrowing has been the strong influence which the two major (private) bond-rating services (Moody's Investor

Service and Standard and Poor's Corporation) exercise through their 'rating' of municipal bonds. The more risk the rating agencies assign to a bond, the higher its interest rate. Since a very slight hike in the interest rate can involve many thousands of dollars, local authorities are directly affected by their rating.[15]

But even aside from the question of ratings, local governments must accept the private money market as it exists at the time of the borrowing effort, for an alternative public loan source does not exist. That is, if private investors do not find municipal bonds an attractive long-term investment, local governments have no choice but to borrow short-term funds — in the private market. Fortunately local governments have usually been able to attract long-term funds, although at times they have had to offer unusually high yields to do so. The reason for the usual attractiveness of municipals lies in their tax-exempt status.

For investors in certain tax brackets, such as wealthy individuals, commercial banks, and casualty insurance companies, the after-tax yield on corporate and Treasury bonds is lower than is the tax-free yield on municipals. Thus, local governments are able to borrow more cheaply than are other borrowers; the beneficiaries of the tax-exemption, however, are investors as well as the local authorities. The US Treasury loses in that it is able to collect less tax revenue.[16]

Although tax policy reduces the cost of borrowing for local governments, it does not change the basic balance of power which exists between local borrowers and the private market. The private investment sector tends to dominate the public–private investment transaction involved in local borrowing. Private investors decide which local governments should be successful in their attempts to borrow, private rating agencies significantly affect the interest rates those local governments must pay, and private lenders ultimately decide important issues such as the length of the repayment period of each loan and the conditions under which each loan can be recalled. Federal proposals to reduce this imbalance have come to nothing.[17]

Citizen Participation
American localities (unlike British and French ones) are subject to a bewildering array of state-imposed constitutional and statutory constraints on borrowing, including interest rates on bonds, maximum-debt ceilings, and the life of the bonds. Further, municipalities also often require direct citizen participation in a bond referendum.[18]

American municipalities are generally required to submit general obligation bonds (backed by the full faith and credit of the issuing authority, and thus subject to state-imposed debt limits) to the voters for their approval. Many cities have failed to achieve the two-thirds majority necessary for passage, however. In San Francisco, for example, only 56 per cent received the necessary two-thirds majority vote between

1944 and 1973[19], and even statutes requiring no more than simple majority in other cities present a major obstacle. This distinguishes American municipal government from its counterparts in France and the United Kingdom, and makes it much more dependent on local political needs and voter agreement.

Conclusion

Municipal borrowing in America is dominated by the private market, on the one hand, and fairly often by voters on the other. Municipal government officials are often in the middle. The national government is conspicuous by its absence in directly funding or constraining local capital expenditure. Tax policy encourages private market investment generally in municipal bonds and there is no attempt to encourage private investment in certain policy sectors rather than others, the credit worthiness of the borrower rather than the nature of the policy sector being the criteria for investment. Since the private capital market is well developed in the US and tax policy encourages investment in municipal bonds, officials worry less about the market's operations than they do about voters' desires and statutory restraints on their borrowing activities.

United Kingdom

Unlike the American pattern, there is no direct citizen participation in investment decisions in the UK. Although the general hostility of ratepayers to tax hikes (which may be necessary to repay loans) is well known to Council members, citizens cannot intervene directly in the borrowing process. The post-war pattern in the UK has, however, fluctuated rather strongly between a reliance on public and private capital market operations.

Between 1945 and 1953, local authorities were allowed to borrow only from the Public Works Loan Board (PWLB),[20] the public body which lends to local authorities. Local authorities had no access to the private market. This gave central government complete control over local borrowing and capital expenditures. For various reasons, the 1953–5 period saw a change in policy; local authorities were allowed to choose between the private market and the PWLB. After 1955, the authorities were not allowed to apply to the Board unless they were unable to find funds on the private market.[21] This principle was later eased, but the dependence of local governments on the private market continued to be heavy. In 1973/74, for example, 62 per cent of loans came from non-public sources.[22] These loans do not enjoy the tax-exempt status of American municipals, and British local authorities, to the extent they borrow in the private market, are forced both to compete for loans with all borrowers, and to pay the same interest rates.

British, in contrast to American authorities, however, do have an alternative source of capital. The PWLB is a publicly-controlled lending body the activities of which complement those of the private market in supplying local authorities with capital. The PWLB is meant to serve primarily as a *source* of funds for capital outlays to ease local borrowing. While it usually adjusts its rates in line with the private market,[23] it tends to offer more favourable rates and access, particularly to the poorer and smaller authorities.[24] Thus British local authorities are somewhat protected from market conditions to the extent they borrow from the PWLB.[25]

The operations of the PWLB, however, constitute only one component of the centre's structure of control over local capital expenditures. In addition, the majority of loan applications have to be approved by the Department of the Environment (formerly the Ministry of Housing and Local Government). The Radcliffe Committee confidently stated that 'the capital investment programmes of the local authorities are subject to close control by the Central Government in that an authority is required to obtain a loan sanction for every project which it proposes to finance from borrowed money'.[26] Despite the use of such loan sanctions, however, the activities of local authorities have 'at times . . . embarrassed the monetary authorities, who found that their efforts to reduce liquidity in the economy were being nullified by the increase in short-term borrowing by the local authorities'.[27] This increase, of course, was due to local authorities' ever-constant search in the private market for lower debt charges. Thus, the effectiveness of such controls as loan sanctions is far from total, a matter which will be discussed more fully in the next section.[28]

France

The French system of municipal capital financing is much more concerned with central-local relationships, and the implementation of the central economic plan, than with the private market, which is relatively little used.[29] In fact, central authorities use public lending institutions, in conjunction with the awarding of capital grants, to increase their control of the pattern and type of local capital expenditure. Economic plans made in Paris directly affect local public services which are capital intensive.[30] The central government rather than the private market regulates the conditions of access and the cost of investment funds. This process subordinates the local provision of public services to central government economic policy objectives, particularly to its consistent attempt to control inflation[31] and to its policy priorities, such as its emphasis on aid to 'large, growing, middle-class communities'.[32]

The chief institution exercising central control is the *Caisse de Depots et Consignations*.[33] The CDC is the principal single lender to local units; it is also the 'auxiliaire du Tresor'.[34] The links between the Finance Ministry and the CDC are quite strong: the Ministry's suggestions about loans are generally followed faithfully. The CDC has also concentrated on loans for urban development, because these are given priority in the national economic plan. Even though the CDC may at times encourage local over-investment *vis-a-vis* the Finance Ministry's and the limits of the Plan, the Caisse is in fact the investment bank of the Plan.[35]

In general, not only have local units had to obtain approval for loan applications from the Finance Ministry (as well as the spending ministry concerned), but they also have to submit to the lending priorities established by the same ministry and implemented by the CDC.[36] The CDC also generally offers more favourable interest rates and maturity conditions than does the private market. Further, local governments are legally limited in the interest they can pay to private lenders, and these rates, while being usually higher than CDC rates, are generally too low to attract lenders.[37] The CDC thus provides and controls the bulk of local capital.[38]

Because French local government has access to long-term debts at lower than market rates, it does not engage in the short-term borrowing of British local authorities. In general, this is much less of a threat to French monetary policy and economic planning. On the other hand, the costs of such an arrangement are that capital improvements at the local level are decided not primarily by local 'need', but rather by national economic objectives.

The French system of financing municipal investments serves to increase the penetration of the centre into local policy activity. For example, in accordance with central policy for growing communities, the CDC has concentrated on loans for urban development.[39] This is not to say the policy priorities chosen at the local level are meaningless, but that they must be compatible with national policy priorities in order to become viable.[40]

French local officials are not, however, totally dominated by the policy choices made at the centre; further, nationally-determined policies offer a range of choice within which local officials may manoeuvre. The existence of central policy priorities which are implemented by the CDC does, nonetheless, have strong implications for the bargaining position of local officials, their success varying according to whether their commune is favoured by the national plan. We shall elaborate upon this in the following section.

In general, then, having investment decisions made by public lending institutions does seem to lead to more effective implementation of economic planning, as well as to the assignment of priorities among policy sectors. Public lending bodies, however, do not necessarily protect local governments from market interest rates. Although British local authorities have an alternative to the private market whereas American authorities do not, British authorities are not subsidized by the PWLB as much as are American authorities by their tax-exempt securities. Thus, our first proposition has to be modified. The cost of borrowing can be lowered by tax policy as well as by public control of lending institutions; the central government therefore has several alternative mechanisms by which it can soften the impact of monetary policy if it wishes to do so.

Strategies

Local officials do not remain passive in the face of constraints; they react in ways designed to minimize their impact, and to maximize their borrowing capacity. *Prima facie*, it seems likely that the target of their strategies would be the lending institutions which provide them with capital, and whose decisions so directly affect local policy.

United States

American local officials, while being dependent on the private market, have tried to avoid the various constraints imposed by their state governments. In particular, they have tried to circumvent state requirements for electoral participation and various state restrictions on the level of debt.

The local electorate is an important concern for municipal finance officials, for popular approval of bond proposals is often critical. This concern with the electorate may over-ride purely financial considerations such as how to 'play the market' to obtain the most favourable interest rates. As one interviewed finance official put it: 'We think of bonds as election campaigns, as political campaigns. We don't worry about interest rates that much.' In some, if not most cities, the opinions of major corporations and banks are taken seriously,[41] for they are likely to be the major contributors to bond referendum campaigns. As the same official said, 'you always need a little money for a campaign, someone to put an ad in the newspaper'. It would seem, therefore, that 'the politics of bond approval' involves a two-stage process in many American cities: the financial/corporate elite must first be mobilized to support a bond issue, and that support is then used as a springboard from which to mobilize citizen support.

The voting public and the financial/corporate elite, however, are not the only constraint municipal officials must face. Legal requirements, often written into the state constitutions, set limits on such things as debt levels and interest rates. In response to such restrictions, local officials have often used a double-barrelled strategy — one that circumvents both electoral and legal restraints.

First, municipal (as well as federal) officials have encouraged the proliferation of the special districts and public authorities in order to evade debt ceilings imposed on general-purpose municipal governments.[42] The loans of such single-purpose authorities are not included in municipal debt totals or limits. In a sense, therefore, the special district and the public authority can be thought of as a legal fiction developed by municipal officials to circumvent restraints on municipal borrowing. Municipal government officials, however, have not retained effective control over the governmental units they so zealously promoted.[43] Further, since the district officials are appointed, rather than elected, voters do not control them as they control elected officials.

Secondly, special districts and authorities typically issue bonds which differ significantly from general obligation bonds. These new types of bonds, generally called 'revenue bonds', are self-financing. That is, the funds for their retirement come from user charges, such as sewer and water charges. Although they have slightly higher interest rates than general obligation bonds, revenue bonds do not involve taxing powers, and therefore they are not usually subject to the referendum. Again, voters are excluded from special district government. Thus, by choosing revenue bonds, local officials manage to circumvent the limits imposed by state government on local borrowing.

American local officials seem to have two major reference points in the process of borrowing funds for capital investments: the electorate and the avoidance of legal barriers to local borrowing. Lending institutions and the financial mechanisms involved in borrowing seem to be taken for granted, to form simply the background for other, more pressing, concerns. The investment strategy which seems to be relevant for local officials is an essentially *political* one — political in respect of mobilizing the electorate to favour proposed borrowing, and in the establishment of local units which can borrow while the municipal government cannot.

United Kingdom

The system of capital finance within the United Kingdom illustrates the impact of international economic monetary trends on local capital investment. The UK international balance of payment problem has frequently forced central monetary policy to attempt to reduce public capital investments. This, of course, has struck directly at local authorities' capital outlays. Local investment levels therefore represent a conflict between the central government's concern with inflation and the balance of payments, and the local authorities' priority concern for public services.

Generally, the Treasury, through the Public Expenditure Surveys and negotiations carried on with the various spending ministries, assigns priorities to various broad policy sectors (such as Health and the Social Services).[44] Its primary concern is to achieve a certain *level* of capital expenditure regardless of which specific capital projects are thus financed. The Treasury also attempts to control the type of financing which local authorities use, for certain financial operations threaten the success of the government's monetary policy.

Such attempts are not met with passive compliance by local authorities;

on the contrary, they are met with financial entrepreneurship. In fact, the local authorities constantly attempt to outwit the Treasury. As access to the PWLB has been restricted, the methods have become more ingenious.[45] The arena of short-term borrowing provides a good example. Because long-term financing operations involve higher interest rates, the local authorities have increasingly substituted short-term for long-term financing.[46] The debt management concerns of local governments clash, in this instance, with central government's concern about the impact of short-term borrowing on central monetary policy. Nonetheless, the local governments continue to use the technique as a component of their financial entrepreneurship.

In attempts to make local borrowing consistent with its policy, the Treasury has used access to the PWLB in order to bargain with local authorities. This strategy, however, has often had rather unfortunate results. For example, the Treasury fashioned a compromise (the White Paper of October 1963 on Local Authority Borrowing) establishing a quota for local temporary borrowing from the private market in return for greater access to and better conditions from the PWLB. The result was predictable:

> Treasurers and the money-brokers soon realised that by borrowing for periods slightly in excess of one year, local authorities could evade the control on temporary money. The net result therefore of all this was a little sign of re-adjustment in temporary borrowing and a sharp increase in the demands on the PWLB[47]

Local authorities are thus faced with conflicts between their need for loans, increasingly high interest rates, and the Treasury's (as well as the Bank of England's) desire for an integrated monetary policy:

> Government policy and their own inclination urge them to expand, while the Treasury grows increasingly alarmed at local authority invasion of the capital market. In an attempt to meet this critical situation the local authorities have invented a series of devices which have come up against Treasury and Bank Restrictions[48]

Local authorities press for PWLB loans, but the central response to such pressure, influenced by macro-economic planning considerations, has been to encourage dependence on the private market, while using access to the PWLB as a carrot to induce overall local compliance with central monetary objectives. Consequently, local authorities have devised a basic strategy of 'playing the market' in attempts to minimize interest while bringing pressure on the Treasury to increase access to the PWLB.

The private market thus influences local policy, but its effects are much more indirect and complex than in the American case. For in the

UK the market itself, is at times, a pawn in central-local bargaining – that is, the uses local governments can make of the market are the subject of complex central–local negotiations.

In brief, local officials employ a financial strategy in their central–local bargaining, a strategy which is shaped more by international monetary conditions than by specific policy priorities adopted by the centre.

France

While the American case emphasizes the policy constraints imposed by statutory limits and citizen participation, and the UK highlights the limits of a mixed public-private lending system, the French case indicates the constraints imposed upon local governments by central economic planning. While the French plan is, of course, indicative in its overall outline, it is somewhat more than indicative *vis-a-vis* local policy activity.

The relative unimportance of the private market seems to prevent French communes from bargaining in the same manner as local authorities in the UK. Nonetheless, the lack of the private market does not mean that no bargaining takes place; it means that we have to look for it elsewhere. The state administration is the obvious place: the state administrative elite is continually bargaining with local elites.[49]

In the politics of borrowing, we would expect to find the French mayor bargaining for his commune with central government in his role as a policy broker. As Tarrow points out, there has been a

'change in the needs of local communities from the individual benefits and legal exemptions of the past to the collective programmes of the welfare state. For the mayors, this change too leads away from the politics of personal favours to developing strategies of policy brokerage.'[50]

Tarrow concludes, on the basis of his sample of mayors of villages, small towns, and small cities, that the strategy of French local officials is 'to try to expand their communities' share of the state allocations to local government through activism *within* the administration'.[51] He sees French mayors as 'activist administrative entrepreneurs', for their contacts are with the agents of the state rather than with representatives of the private sector or the party system.[52]

The central government, however, does not treat all mayors equally: the size of the mayor's commune, its socio-economic characteristics, and the number of elective positions the mayor holds affect his bargaining position and largely dictate both his bargaining strategy and its likely outcomes.

This inequality is largely imposed by the policy choices embodied in the economic plan, rather than by partisan considerations. Thus, Communist mayors of growing communities seem to be in a better bargaining position than Gaullist mayors of rural, declining communes. Exceptions can be found but, in general, growing communities are favoured by the general system of allocations, regardless of their voting preferences.[53]

Therefore, in France, in contrast to the US and the UK, the lending institutions systematically favour certain types of borrowers over others relative to access to loans. Poor communities in the US and the UK may well have to pay higher interest rates than richer communities, but in general lenders do not discriminate against them in terms of access. Declining French communes, on the other hand, are much less likely to have such access: for them, the critical question is not interest rates, but access to the borrowing process itself.

Based on available research findings, which are admittedly sketchy due to the underdevelopment of the study of French local government, we would expect to find; 1. that small and large communes obtain access to the administration by using different strategies, and 2. that the probability of successful access by small communes depends both on the socio-economic character of the commune and on the number of elective positions held by the mayor.

The mayor of a small commune has one major resource in bargaining for loans: his place in the honeycomb of interdependent relationships so well described by Crozier and Thoenig. Small-town mayors may not have the technical staff to fill out the proposals, the forms, and the financial dossiers so necessary to gain funds. But the field agents of various ministries, including the Finance Ministry, as well as prefects and sub-prefects, can fill out forms and are only too happy to do so; in fact, they may have suggested the project to the mayor in the first place.

The mayor thus uses the field administration to apply for resources from the central administration. In turn, the field administrators attempt to manipulate local policy decisions according to their policy preferences.[54] French mayors are thus integrated into the administrative system in such a way that they can bargain from within it. This system, based on a network of intermediaries, in which no one makes a decision free from the influences of others, serves not only as a means for the centre to dominate the periphery, but also as a communication network in which the periphery's demands are communicated to the centre.[55] The mayor of a small commune will find his bargaining position considerably strengthened if he holds several elective positions — if he is simultaneously a mayor, president or member of the departmental council, and a parliamentarian.[56]

The economic plan, however, strongly influences bargaining success. Mayors of the communes favoured by the plan, perhaps not surprisingly, are more likely to use the honeycomb structure than are mayors of more rural or working-class communes.[57] It may well be that the latter, cognisant of the plan's preferences, view bargaining as a waste of time, while the former think it worth their time pressing for projects. In general terms, then, it would seem that communes favoured by the plan compete amongst themselves to increase their slice of the funds; disfavoured communes are less likely even to try competing.

While mayors of large communes, so-called big-city mayors, now govern over one-third of the French population, they have not been studied as much as small-town mayors. Both Thoenig and Milch, however, have examined the activities of mayors of cities with over 100 000 inhabitants. Their findings suggest that while big-city mayors can, and sometimes do, use intermediaries, they have much more direct access to central ministries, and thus their bargaining strategy with the centre is quite different.

First of all, they have fairly large technical staffs of their own: they are less dependent on field administrators and prefects.[58] Second by virtue of their position, they have direct access to Paris. Milch cites the example of the mayor of Montpellier who went to plead his case in Paris over the head of a regional geologist; he was not only heard but was given permission to carry out his project in spite of the disapproval of the field administration.[59] Of course, the big-city mayor (and, since 1974, the mayor of the middle-sized city) is also at an advantage because his urban priorities are those of the national policy elite. Thus, representing an important city, and having priorities compatible with those of the national elite, makes the big city mayor a formidable bargainer. Further, he alone can integrate the various demands of his commune and present a unified bargaining front. The central government, with its inevitable inter-agency rivalries and lack of co-ordination, finds it difficult effectively to impose its own coherent position.[60]

Thus, while the big-city mayor negotiates with the central administration, he does so in a very different way from the small-town mayor. The latter's contacts are principally at the departmental level; the big-city mayor's contacts are at the very highest levels of the administration. The small-town mayor bargains within the administration; the big-city mayor bargains with the administration. Both types pursue administrative strategies, but their particular strategies are different.

In France, because the state controls most of the capital borrowed by local authorities, and because the state formulates economic plans within which such borrowing must be integrated, we find the most complex bargaining between the centre and local governments. Of the three countries, only France has a political system in which local representatives may also be national politicians of importance. Only in France are national and local finances so closely integrated that loan sanction, interest rates, loan terms, policy priorities, and access to lending institutions are all controlled by the central government. We thus find an institutional system of borrowing, formally dominated by the centre, co-existing with a system of political representation dominated by representatives with local power bases. These two systems intersect in complex ways, and students of French policy-making will have to examine more precisely how they do so.

Thus, the US, the UK, and France differ in the types of parameters and constraints they impose upon borrowing. Local officials also differ in the strategy they use to minimize those constraints. These constraints

Table 10.1 *Local government borrowing systems*

Main source of capital finance for local governments	*Main Institutions providing/ mediating investment*	*Investment criteria applied*	*Degree of government control*	*Other constraints*	*Type of strategy employed by local officials*
USA					
Market	Moody's; Standard and Poor's; banks; large individual investors; insurance companies	Orthodox profit criteria	Little direct control; indirect control via central monetary policy and tax-exemption for municipal securities	Referendum; legal barriers	Political
UK					
State/ Market (according to area/ period	Banks/ other private investment institutions; Public Works Loan Boards	Policy goals modified by central monetary policy profit criteria	Variable, according to macroeconomic conditions and negotiating skills	International economic trends	Financial
France					
State-parastatal body	Caisse des Depots et Consignations	Requirements for national plans	High; single allocations subject to lobbying by local government concerned	Finance Ministry's restrictive interpretation of the National Plan	Administrative

and strategies constitute a 'borrowing system', the principal characteristics of which are summarised in Table 10.1.

Conclusion

One of our initial propositions was that local officials direct their strategies at the lending institutions from which they borrow. In fact, in the US, local officials focus not on the private market, but on state regulations restricting their access to that market; in Britain, they concentrate on evading Treasury restrictions on their market operations; in France they put pressure on central agencies. Our hypothesis, therefore, obviously ignores the crucial role played by government regulations — regulations which local officials try to soften or evade.

While government-bank relations and central controls certainly affect local strategies, so does the structure of political representation.[61] Throughout our previous discussion, the structure of representation has been both implicitly and explicitly touched upon for a good reason — it is inextricably interwoven with the strategies we have outlined. The borrowing system and the system of political representation ('politics' and 'finance') co-exist, and their intersections are crucial in defining the policy-making system for capital expenditure. In conclusion, we can offer some preliminary thoughts on the nature of this system.

We know that political representation is structured quite differently in each of the three countries. In the US, local council members and mayors are separate from the national political elite; further, elected officials generally do not directly control the special districts and public authorities which abound in the US. Conversely, many local policy-makers (who are neither elected nor directly accountable to voters) exercise authority through special districts. In Britain, local council members control many of the services provided by special districts in the US, but they too are distinct from the national political elite. In France, there are a fair number of quasi-governmental bodies which (in contrast to American special districts) are linked to the central administration. Since mayors, especially mayors of large urban communes, are often also part of the national political elite, it is at least theoretically possible for them to have more actual influence over such special bodies than the American mayor.

Given these differences, what can we say about the relationship between the borrowing system and the system of representation? In the US, the borrowing system is at least partially the outcome of a system of government which narrowly delimits the autonomy of elected representatives, and of the response of elected officials to that system. One element of the American strategy was the creation of special districts, but these fundamentally changed the borrowing system itself. Rather than municipal governments borrowing for all major services, borrowing became the responsibility of different, primarily non-elected, governments unaccountable to any central body. Borrowing power became decentralized, diffused and unco-ordinated. Thus local officials structurally changed the borrowing system itself.

The restructured system, in turn, changed the very nature of political representation at the local level. By insulating special district government from voters, many local policy-makers have given themselves space for autonomous action. In essence, they have 'created' the autonomy they need to provide facilities. What does this outcome tell us about the relationship between borrowing and structures of political representation?

As Sharpe points out in a justly celebrated article, Americans have tended to see the relationship between the autonomy of government and its responsiveness to the popular will as a zero-sum game. Americans, according to Sharpe, do not accept that 'the right to choose presupposes the possibility of action on the part of those chosen'. They deny that 'if government cannot act because it is too weak — because it is not functionally effective — then democracy ceases to exist'.[62] It is certainly true that the structures of government and controls that Americans initially established were meant to limit the powers of local officials, rather than promote functional effectiveness. To be effective, local officials had to escape these structures and controls, and in this sense, were forced into non-democratic institutions. The zero-sum notion was consequently shown to be accurate, an irony to say the least.

The borrowing system of the US, then, may well have permitted American local governments to achieve a degree of functional effectiveness at the price of democracy and participation. The borrowing system, I would argue, functions as a 'safety valve' for the conflict between the 'political' and the 'governmental' systems. These two systems are not easily compatible, and the borrowing system which has evolved, with its non-accountable but functionally effective borrowing units, minimizes the conflict between the two.

Compared with the US, the borrowing system in Britain seems to complement a system of representation which gives a good deal of autonomy to both elected officials and professional bureaucrats. Elected council members and various professionals, such as the directors of the various spending services and the Treasurer, formulate each city's requests for loan sanctions. Once permission is received, professionals are available to handle the technicalities of getting the 'best deal' in the market, which may involve circumventing Treasury restrictions on borrowing. Officials therefore have ample opportunities to develop their technical skills in the borrowing market. The British borrowing system, we may therefore hypothesize, reinforces the autonomy and functional effectiveness of the system of political representation.

In France, the system of political representation weaves national and urban concerns together in a distinctive way. The *Cumul du mandats* is one of the chief ways in which national and local concerns are integrated. Howard Machin has given us some idea of how widespread this is: 47 per cent of Deputies elected in the 1958 general elections were also members of their department's General Councils; in the 1959 senatorial election, 58.2 per cent of the winners were General Councillors. Furthermore, according to Machin, 'most General Councils have at least two national political figures among their membership'.[63] Many General Councillors are also mayors, and some mayors are ministers (and prime ministers) as well. Furthermore, many more have held important positions in the Civil Service.

Big-city mayors and deputy-mayors certainly have an influence much greater than constitutional arrangements would suggest. There are few studies of how they actually affect policy-making, but Machin points out that they certainly do affect prefectoral appointments. As he puts it, 'No Prefect detested by Gaston Defferre is appointed to Marseilles; the prefectoral enemies of Louis Pradel are excluded or removed from the prefecturs of Lyone . . . The Prefect in Nice has to be acceptable to the Medecin dynasty, his colleagues at Bordeaux to Chaban-Delmas and the Prefect of the Jura to Edgar Faure.'[64]

If local officials can influence the appointment of Prefects, it is likely that they can, at least under certain conditions, influence the Finance Ministry's decisions on public investments as well as the Prefect's original recommendations. Their position would be especially strong if they represented an economic growth area, for they would then be able to draw upon the priorities of the Plan in making their case.

I suggest, therefore, that the system of borrowing in France is interwoven with the system of political representation, so that it is almost impossible to separate the two, especially in urban areas and in those governed by deputy mayors. The system of borrowing, with its urban bias and its integration into the very fabric of central–local relations, would seem to be extremely compatible with a system of representation in which many mayors of urban communes are also important figures in national politics. Public investment is a concern of most local governments in France,[65] but the distinctively French system of political representation may well make the formally centralized borrowing system particularly responsive both to mayors from urban areas, and mayors who are departmental and national politicians. The relationship between actors involved in borrowing are by and large, therefore, likely to be the same as those involved in other areas of policy-making. We may, consequently, hypothesize that the borrowing system reflects the system of political representation.

In conclusion, I suggest that borrowing systems are important in policy-making not only because they regulate how easily, cheaply, and autonomously local officials can borrow, but also because their relationship to systems of political representation helps determine both policy processes and outcomes. Borrowing systems minimize the policy ineffectiveness of American cities, reinforce the autonomy of local officials in Britain, and reflect the bias of the French system of political representation.

Notes

This paper is a much shortened and revised version of a paper initially published as Paper no. 37 by the Centre for the Study of Public Policy at the University of Strathclyde in Glasgow, Scotland. I am grateful to Professors Gordon Cameron, Diane Dawson, Bert Rockman, Richard Rose, and Martin Staniland for their assistance at various stages of this project. Ken Newton has my special thanks, for only his ruthless editing pruned the paper down to an acceptable length. Research funds were provided by The University Center for Urban Research and the Faculty of Arts and Sciences of the University of Pittsburgh.

1. *Wall Street Transcript*, 13 August 1979, 55, 253.
2. *Financing Municipal Facilities*, Hearings before the Sub-Committee on Economic Progress of the Joint Economic Committee, Congress of the United States, Ninetieth Congress, First Session, 5, 6, and 7 December 1967; Vol. I, 2.
3. G. C. Hockley, *Monetary Policy and Public Finance* (London, Routledge and Kegan Paul, 1970), 260.
4. M. Kesselman, *The Ambiguous Consensus: A Study of Local Government in France*. (New York, Alfred A. Knopf, 1967), 52.
5. S. Tarrow, *Between Center and Periphery: Grassroots Politicians in Italy and France* (New Haven, Yale University Press, 1977), 93.
6. J. A. Maxwell, *Financing State and Local Governments* (Washington, DC, Brookings, 1965), 185.
7. Sir H. Brittain, *The British Budgetary System* (New York, MacMillan, 1959), Appendix E, 285; Layfield Committee, *Report of the Committee of Inquiry into Local Government Finance*, Appendix 6: *The Relationship Between Central and Local Government: Evidence and Commissioned Work* (London, HMSO, 1976), 90.
8. A. Villani, *Le Strutture Amministrative Locali: Tendenze Evolutive Nel Campo Del' Organizzazione e Della Finanza* Volume I: *Modelli Teorici Alternative-Esame della Esperienza della Francia, Germania Occidentale e Gran Bretagna* (Milan, Franco Angeli, 1968), 440; *Economic Policy in Practice: The Economic Policy of the Central Government and the Intervention of the Local Authorities and their Specialized Finance Institutions Therein*. Results of a study carried out in different countries by the International Information Centre for Local Credit (The Hague, Martinus Nijhoff, 1968), 130.
9. Data obtained at the 1979 Annual Convention of the Municipal Finance Officers' Association.
10. *Wall Street Transcript*, 55, 253.
11. Central Statistical Office, *Annual Abstract of Statistics 1979 Edition* (London, HMSO, 1979), 401, Table 16.32.
12. P. Lalumiere, *Les finances publiques* 3rd Edition (Paris, Armand Colin, 1973), 130.
13. P. A. Stone, *Urban Development in Britain: Standards, Costs and Resources, 1964-2004*, Volume I: *Population Trends and Housing* (Cambridge, Cambridge University Press, 1970), 161.
14. *Financing Municipal Facilities*, 75.

15.   Ibid. 17–18; Twentieth Century Fund Task Force on Municipal Bond Credit Ratings, *The Rating Game*, with a background paper by John E. Petersen (New York, The Twentieth Century Fund, 1974).

16.   For a general discussion of investment in the muncipal bond market, see Twentieth Century Fund Task Force on the Municipal Bond Market, *Building a Broader Market*, with a background paper by Ronald W. Forbes and John E. Petersen (New York, The Twentieth Century Fund, 1976); J. E. Petersen, 'State and Local Government Debt Policy and Management' in J. E. Petersen D. L. Spain, and M. F. Laffey (eds.), *State and Local Government Finance and Financial Management: A Compendium of Current Research* (Washington, DC, Government Finance Research Center, 1978); Advisory Commission on Intergovernmental Relations, *Understanding the Market for State and Local Debt* (Washington, DC, GPO, 1976).

17.   For example, see P. Healy, 'Further Comments on Proposed Capital Financing Alternatives', *Tax Policy*, 37 (1970) 8–9.

18.   See F. L. Starner, *General Obligation Bond Financing by Local Governments' A Survey of State Controls* (Berkeley, University of California Bureau of Public Administration, 1961); S. A. MacManus, 'The Impact of Functional Responsibility and State Legal Constraints on the "Revenue-Debt" Packages of U.S. Central Cities', *1978 World Congress of Sociology, International Sociological Association*; Advisory Commission on Inter-governmental Relations, *State Constitutional and Statutory Restrictions on Local Government Debt* (Washington, DC, ACIR, 1961), Advisory Commission on Intergovernmental Relations, *Federal–State–Local Finances: Significant Features of Fiscal Federalism, 1973–74 Edition* (Washington, DC, GPO, 1974), 143–58.

19.   R. Hayes, *Understanding San Francisco's Budget; How City Hall Spends your Money and What you Can Do About It* (San Francisco, San Francisco Study Center and the Youth Project, 1973), 86.

20.   H. Cowen, 'Local Authority Borrowing 1955-1960 – Is the Present System Failing?' *Lloyds Bank Review*, 57 (1964) 20.

21.   *Committee on the Working of the Monetary System Report (Radcliffe Report)*, Cmnd. 827 (London, HMSO), 32.

22.   N. P. Hepworth, *The Finance of Local Government* Revised 3rd Edition (London, George Allen & Unwin, 1976), 15.   ·

23.   Brittain, op. cit. 289.

24.   L. Needleman, *The Economics of Housing* (London, Staples Press, 1965), 138–9.

25.   H. R. Page, 'Local Authorities in the Capital Market', *The Three Banks Review*, 71 (1966) 36.

26.   *Radcliffe Report*, 31.

27.   Hockley, op. cit. 40.

28.   For a discussion of the extent to which central government has channelled local capital expenditure into particular service areas, see: M. Maclennan, M. Forsyth, and G. Denton, *Economic Planning and Policies in Britain, France and Germany* (New York, Praeger, 1968), 219; D. E. Ashford, 'Territory vs. Function: Toward a Policy-Based Theory of Subnational Government', *1976 Annual Meeting of the American Political Science Association*; R. Klein, M. Buxton, and Q. Outram, 'Past Indicatives and Present Tensions', in R. Klein (ed.), *Social Policy and Public Expenditure 1975* (London, Centre for Studies in Social Policy, 1975), 31.

29.   A. Laubadere, 'Les emprunts des collectivites locales en France', *International Review of Administrative Sciences*, 28 (1962) 1–8.

30.   For an interesting Marxist/French Communist Party analysis of the relationship between French economic planning and local capital investments, see. R. Monsel, 'Capitalisme monopoliste d'Etat et collectivites locales', *Economie*

et Politique, 199 (1971) 45–71.

31. *Economic Policy in Practice*, 112–21.
32. Tarrow, op. cit. 159.
33. Ibid. Chapter 3.
34. Laubadere, op. cit. 4.
35. J. Hayward, *The One and Indivisible French Republic* (London, Weidenfeld and Nicholson, 1973), 165.
36. *Economic Policy in Practice*, 131. In the 1970s, however, the process by which communes are given approval to borrow has been in flux.
37. Laubadere, op. cit. 2–5.
38. B. Fausse, 'La Caisse des Depots et Consignations', *Economie et Politique*, 215 (1972) 57.
39. P. Traimond, *Le financement public des investissements* (Paris, Editions Cujas, 1967), 212.
40. Ibid., 216.
41. J. O'Connor, *The Fiscal Crisis of the State* (New York, St. Martin's Press, 1973), 194.
42. A. M. H. Walsh, *The Public's Business: the Politics and Practices of Government Corporations — A Twentieth Century Fund Study* (Cambridge, Mass., MIT Press, 1978), 171–2; T. Dye, *Politics in States and Communities* (Englewood Cliffs, NJ, Prentice-Hall, 1969), 307; J. A. Maxwell and J. R. Aronson, *Financing State and Local Governments* 3rd Edition (Washington, DC, Brookings Institution, 1977), 208.
43. Walsh, *The Public's Business*, 171–2; K. Newton, 'American Urban Politics' Social Class, Political Structure, and Public Goods', *Urban Affairs Quarterly* ii (1975), 243–4; R. Friedland, F. F. Piven, and R. R. Alford, 'Political Conflict, Urban Structure, and the Fiscal Crisis', *Comparing Public Policy·* in D. E. Ashford (ed.), *New Approaches and Methods* (Beverly Hills, Sage 1977), 197–226.
44. K. Judge, 'Territorial Justice and Local Autonomy: Loan Sanctions in the Personal Social Services', *Policy and Politics*, 3 (1975), 43 69.
45. Page, op. cit. 33.
46. Hockley, op. cit. 40.
47. Page, op. cit. 30.
48. Ibid., 37.
49. See E. N. Suleiman, *Politics, Power, and Bureaucracy in France' The Administrative Elite* (Princeton, Princeton University Press, 1974), 365–9; Tarrow, op. cit; Hayward, op. cit. 28–34; H. Machin, *The Prefect in French Public Administration* (New York, St. Martin's, 1977); J. Milch, 'Influence as Power: French Local Government Reconsidered', *British Journal of Political Science*, 4 (1974) 130–40.
50. Tarrow, op. cit. 132.
51. Ibid. 7.
52. Ibid. 156.
53. Ibid. 98; Tarrow's findings are corroborated by J. Becquart-Leclercq who also concluded that the level of infrastructure found in small towns was highly correlated with their size and growth rate. J. Becquart-Leclercq, *Paradoxes du Pouvoir Local* (Paris, Presses de la fondation nationales des science politiques, 1976), 65–6.
54. J. C. Thoenig, 'La relation entre le centre et la peripherie en France: une analyse systemique, *Bulletin de L'Institut International d'Administration Publique*, 36 (1976) 77–123; M. Crozier and J. C. Thoenig, 'La regulation des systemes organises complexes, le cas du systeme de decision politico-administrative local en France', *Revue Francaise de Sociologie*, 16 (1975) 3–32.
55. Ibid. 100.

56.   Ibid. 90–1.
57.   Tarrow, op. cit. 196; 161.
58.   Milch, op. cit. 157; Thoenig, op. cit.
59.   Milch, op. cit. 159.
60.   Thoenig, op. cit. 94.
61.   For a more extended discussion of the significance of government–bank relations, see A. Sbragia, 'Borrowing to Build: Private Money and Public Welfare', *International Journal of Health Services*, 9 (1979), 207–18.
62.   L. Sharpe, 'American Democracy Reconsidered: Part II', *British Journal of Political Science*, 3 (1973) 131.
63.   Machin, op. cit. 160.
64.   Ibid. 176–7.
65.   Becquart-Leclercq, op. cit.

ABOUT THE AUTHORS

MICHAEL AIKEN is a Professor of Sociology and Associate Dean in the College of Letters and Science at the University of Wisconsin, Madison. His areas of interest include organizational sociology in addition to the study of comparative urban politics. He is currently involved in a comparative study of politics and public policy in European nation-states such as Italy and France in addition to his work on Belgium.

TERRY NICHOLS CLARK is Associate Professor of Sociology at the University of Chicago and has taught at Columbia, Harvard, Yale and the Sorbonne. He has worked on urban decision making in the US, France, and Yugoslavia. He founded and is President of the Committee on Community Research of the International Sociological Association, and founded the Section on the Community of the American Sociological Association. He has consulted with numerous cities, federal and state agencies, and private firms on urban fiscal policy. He is author or co-author of about ninety papers and books, including *Community Power and Policy Outputs* (1973), and *Comparative Community Politics* (1974).

LORNA CROWLEY FERGUSON is an Associate Study Director at the National Opinion Research Center affiliated with The University of Chicago. Born and educated in England, she received her BSc degree from the London School of Economics, and her PhD in Sociology from The University of Chicago. She is co-author of *Political Leadership and Urban Fiscal Strain* soon to be published, and author of several articles on related topics.

ROGER DEPRE is Professor of Sociology at the Catholic University of Leuven, Belgium. He specializes in both theoretical and applied studies of local government in Belgium.

ANDREW D. GLASSBERG is Assistant Professor of Political Science and Public Policy Administration, and Research Associate at the Center for International Studies, at the University of Missouri–St Louis. He is the author of a study of neighbourhood government in London, *Representation and Urban Community* (London, Macmillan, 1981) and of a study of American and British responses to urban fiscal crises, which will appear as *Managing the Urban Fiscal Crisis: A Comparative Perspective* (London, Macmillan, forthcoming). In addition to academic positions at the University of Missouri, the City University of New York, and the State University of New York, Dr Glassberg served as Special Assistant to the Deputy Mayor in the administration of Mayor John Lindsay in New York.

TORE HANSEN is Lecturer at the Institute of Political Science, University of Oslo. He has written several articles on local planning, budgeting and urban finances, and is currently involved in research on urban financial problems.

STEIN KUHNLE is lecturer in sociology at the University of Bergen. He has written *Patterns of Social and Political Mobilization: A Historical Analysis of the Nordic Countries* (Contemporary Political Sociology Series, Sage Publications, London/Beverly Hills, 1975), and various contributions in books and journals on early voting rights in Norway, development of the Nordic welfare state, national equality and local decision making, and trends in political research in Norway. He is editor of the *European Political Data Newsletter*, published jointly by the ECPR and the Norwegian Social Science Data Services.

KEN NEWTON is Professor of Political Science at the University of Dundee, and has taught or researched at the Universities of Oxford, Cambridge, Birmingham, and Madison, Wisconsin. He is the author of *The Sociology of British Communism* (1969), and *Second City Politics* (1976), and articles on urban and local government and politics in west Europe and the USA. Most recently, he co-authored *Balancing the Books: The Financial Problems of Local Government in Western Europe*, (London, Sage, 1980).

ALBERTA SBRAGIA is associate Professor of Political Science at the University of Pittsburgh. She received a PhD from the University of Wisconsin and has been a visiting research fellow at the Centre for the Study of Public Policy at Strathclyde University, Glasgow. The author of various articles on Italian public housing policy, cross-national land-use policy, and the comparative politics of local borrowing, she is currently editing a forthcoming book on the politics of local finance in the United States. She is now completing a research project that compares the relationships between the central government, local government, and the financial community in the US and UK.

L. J. SHARPE is a University Lecturer in Public Administration and a Fellow of Nuffield College, Oxford. He was Research Director to the Royal Commission on Local Government 1966–9, and in addition to publishing many articles, he has published *A Metropolis Votes* (1963), *Voting in Cities* (1967), and, with Renate Mayntz and Bruno Dente, *Il Governo Locale in Europa* (1977). He has recently edited *Decentralist*

Trends in Western Democracies (1979) and *The Local Fiscal Crisis in Western Europe: Myths and Realities* (1981).

CARL-JOHAN SKOVSGAARD is Associate Professor at the Institute of Political Science, University of Aarhus, Denmark. Born in 1946, he graduated from the University of Aarhus in 1975 with a degree in political science. He now teaches public administration, urban policies and administration, and the application of policy analysis. His research includes local government output studies and urban policies and administration in Denmark, regional planning and administration in Scandinavia, cross-national projects on urban policies, and municipal finance in western Europe. His publications include the first Danish local government output study, *Studier i dansk kommunalpolitik* (Aarhus, Politica, 1977) and chapters in L. J. Sharpe (ed.), *The Local Fiscal Crisis in Western Europe* (London, Sage, 1981), and in David McKay (ed.), *Planning and Politics in Western Europe* (London, Macmillan (forthcoming)).